Nena O'Neill & George O'Neill

Shifting Gears

AVON
PUBLISHERS OF BARD, CAMELOT, DISCUS, EQUINOX AND FLARE BOOKS

Thanks are due to the McGraw-Hill Book Company for permission to quote from "Heuristic Research" by Clark E. Moustakas, which appeared in *Challenges of Humanistic Psychology*, edited by James T. Bugental. Copyright © 1967 by McGraw-Hill, Inc. Used with permission of McGraw-Hill Company.

AVON BOOKS
A division of
The Hearst Corporation
959 Eighth Avenue
New York, New York 10019

First Avon Printing, March, 1975
Seventh printing

Printed in the U.S.A.

Avon Books by
Nena O'Neill and George O'Neill

Open Marriage	14084	$1.95
Shifting Gears	23192	$1.95

TO EVERYONE:

What is, was.
What was, is.
What is to be: you, molding destiny.

Acknowledgments

This book could not have been written without the conviction that each one of us has the potential and capacity for responsible self-determination, for caring, concern, and love, and for shaping and molding a personal future which provides a sense of fulfillment and the creativity that is the very essence of our humanness.

We would like to express our gratitude to two special persons who have not only contributed ideas and many hours of discussion on the topic of this book, but who have also helped us in a very personal way to shift gears: Haskell Hoffenberg and John Astrachan. To others we are especially grateful for supportive help and insights of various kinds: Michael O'Neill, Brian O'Neill, René Champion, Paul and Jackie Morofsky, Gabe Perle, Robert C. Snyder, Nancy Abel, Edwin T. Glickman, Carola Kessler and Liz Friedman. We extend our deepest thanks to all the other people who have contributed in various ways to shape this book through endless interviews, personal disclosures, thoughtful comments and ideas, and to all the readers of *Open Marriage* whose enthusiastic letters, queries and critical comments provided us with further insights into the dimensions of personal and interpersonal problems. We appreciate the teamwork, help and suggestions offered throughout the preparation of this book by our editor,

Herb Katz, and our friend and editorial assistant, John Malone, with whom it is a pleasure to work. We are especially indebted to Dr. Edward Hornick and Dr. Alexander Levay who made valuable criticisms and suggestions after reading the manuscript.

Ultimately, however, this book is an expression of our own concern for each individual caught in a world of change who desires to take the inner journey of growth.

Nena O'Neill
George O'Neill

October, 1973

Contents

Part I

Renewing the Self
in a World of Crisis

CHAPTER ONE

Change Versus Movement

Since Open Marriage

Open Marriage, our previous book, was written in the hope of helping people to better understand the elements of a good human relationship, and to apply that understanding to the institution of marriage in today's world. When we began our research for that book some six years ago, contemporary marriage seemed in obvious trouble. Divorce was on the increase, the quality of family life was changing rapidly, and many people had become disillusioned with the institution of marriage itself. In a period of rapid and sometimes almost chaotic social change, human relationships, we felt—especially a long-term and intimate one such as marriage—offered not only something of value worth hanging onto, but also one of the best means of fulfillment and growth. We still do.

But the additional social changes of the intervening five years, together with the kind of responses we have had to *Open Marriage,* have made it increasingly clear to us that the problem of relationship in our society goes far beyond marriage itself. Many people felt staggered by the rapidity of change in the society in which they lived. It seemed to most of them that the rules of the game were being changed practically every time they turned on the television set or opened the newspapers. The constant revision of moral standards and social rules in the larger world had left some of these people with a sense of paralysis; with so many choices, each in conflict with the other, being presented to them, they felt that the best they could manage was simply to hold on for dear life and not do anything at all. Others, less afraid or perhaps just more impressionable, tended to run off in three directions at once, hoping that if they tried enough different approaches to their problems they might hit on the answer out of sheer luck. It became apparent that the problems people are facing raise new and broader questions to be examined. The questions people are asking are: How do *I* deal with change? How can I develop the personal security and emotional maturity that make it possible to grow and to have a better relationship? It became clear that underlying the crisis in marriage relationships was a more fundamental problem: the relationship of each person to himself and to the world in which he lives.

This problem is brought on by our inability to grow and direct change on an individual basis. In a world of increasing options and escalating change we find ourselves often confused about how to take the first steps toward personal growth.

The problem is that we learn to grow according to arbitrary plans set up by society rather than growing as individuals according to our own internal needs. There was a time when the societal plans worked—our growth and development were synchronized with society's development. Under those conditions you can safely measure yourself by society's yardstick. But society now presents us with such a bewildering number of options that we cannot relate them to our inner selves. And when our inner selves are not synchronized with society, then our attempts to measure up to external yardsticks become exercises in self-contradiction that may lead to a sense of isolation and anxiety. On the other hand, since the plans that society offers us are the only ones we have any experience with, we may have difficulty in effecting change on a personal basis or in a way that is comfortable for our inner selves.

Nonetheless, propelled by our internal needs for growth, we forge ahead—generally in directions that have no real meaning for us. Without meaning, we lose our sense of self—and the more lost we become, the more desperately we search for a substitute. In our desire to change and grow, we rush headlong after every current societal change and movement, responding to every new external stimulus, trying to keep up with a world that doesn't know where it's going. We have become so skillful at *responding* that we have forgotten how to *initiate*. We try to adjust to the new life-styles and the current trends; we define ourselves only in terms of our jobs or how others see us; we become our roles and deny the person behind that role; we adopt new and alien behavior, yet try to hang onto old values. We slide along or are swept along, avidly following the media hucksters and copying the habits of our peers. Personal change then becomes for us a superficial conformity to the habits of others and to a perpetually changing environment.

But somehow we know that something is wrong. We are on a treadmill and want to jump off. Change becomes so confusing and uncomfortable that we begin to feel obsolete, paralyzed and powerless, caught at times in a monumental loneliness. Our relationships become unsatisfying and troublesome; we are out of touch with *ourselves* and as a result experience either panic or apathy.

We have surrendered our inner selves to external change. In the middle of a revolution of external change, society gives us no guidelines for internal change. No one has told us how to change. No one has told us what is involved in the process of inner personal change in the new world we must adapt to.

And that is what this book is about: how to shift gears in a world of constant change and to integrate this change on a personal basis. Real personal change is, after all, a transition from the old to the new in a way that makes sense to your inner self. But nothing will make sense until you know your private self and reaffirm your personal values, until you explore your inner dimensions, until you know where you want to go, and how you want to get there.

Change we must, but it should be a change we *choose to make,* in a direction we *choose to go.* Instead of being carried along powerless and without control by the constant pace of change, we can elect to take hold of our lives and design a *life strategy* to help us meet change. Instead of following someone else's life plan or getting lost in the shuffle, we can learn the skills to help us make change work for us in a creative and challenging way. And if we choose not to change in some areas, we at least know it is our own choice. If we know how to internalize our growth plan we can then not only make a selective adaptation to external change but we can also be in touch with ourselves and with our own growth. This is the only way in which change can lead to a sense of personal security.

Looking Good and Feeling Bad

In our frantic rush to adapt to external change we often look good but feel bad. We put on the facade, keep pace with the exterior, yet increasingly feel at odds with our self inside.

We go to every new lusty movie and walk out feeling sad and depressed. We put on the latest style of clothes denoting a new life-style—and feel ridiculous. We try sensitivity groups to get in touch with our feelings, yet find no one to share them with afterward. Like a shopper in a department store we try one relationship after another, skimming over intimacy, and find that none of them touches us deeply. We try to look good on the outside but feel empty inside. Unaware of our need for inner change, we make an effort to look good by adapting to every new vogue and trend created by our cultural hucksters of artificial change. To understand why we feel so bad while trying to look so good, we should understand the difference between movement and change.

No part of the contemporary scene illustrates this more succinctly than the sexual revolution. Urged on by the media we try new partners, new positions and new purchasable stimuli in an effort to find the sexual freedom and the liberated orgasms we are now heir to. But we find that sexual fulfillment does not come so easily by following someone else's external plan. The books become boring, the movies repetitive, the novels dull and the photographs silly. Trying to capture the joy of sex which we are told should be ours, we mechanically practice the new techniques. Eventually all the external stimuli pall and we end up feeling more bereft than before. Without internal change, the spontaneous feeling is lacking. That spontaneous feeling of a merging wholeness which characterizes sexual expression as our greatest medium for sharing can only come from inside ourselves. The externals just won't do the trick.

One of our problems is that we have not learned to distinguish between *real change* and *movement* in our external environment.

To illustrate this difficulty we have only to contrast the real change offered to us by the scientific breakthrough of Masters and Johnson's research in sexual behavior with the meaningless and directionless movement represented by the gaudy, artificial and emotionless erotica of current cinematic and magazine pornography. Which of these two—Masters and Johnson or pornography—can offer us something of value to internalize in the sense of personal growth and change? Which piper do *you* follow? Or, more to the point, do you *choose* which to follow at all? Are you aware that you are being propelled and swept along by movement instead of real change? It is diverting, perhaps entertaining, and, even, for some, instructive to see a pornographic movie. But the changes which are offered us by a knowledge of Masters and Johnson's research are ones we stand more to profit from and can assimilate in a personal way.

The difference between movement and change can also be seen in the architecture of our urban areas. Movement is characterized by the directionless, random and helter-skelter way buildings are torn down without planning and without consideration for the whole community: a beautiful old postage-stamp park razed to make space for a parking lot, a dignified and regal apartment house demolished to make space for a throughway, communities torn apart, the neighborhood fragmented, the residents "relocated." Contrast this with the real change brought about by the kind of innovative architectural change that integrates the old with the new. Good architectural planning retains the color, character and value of the community yet integrates into it a vital new life-force.

One can also see the difference between movement and change in personal relationships. The man who marries four times, always the same type of woman, and divorces four times, represents movement but not change. In each relationship he has the same problems because he has not planned, has not observed, has not analyzed and has not seen the need for his *own* change. Contrast this with the divorced man who in his subsequent intimate relationships invests enough of himself to learn not only more about himself and his needs, but about the needs of his partner and how they mesh with his. Each relationship is a step in his personal growth and when he finally remarries he has changed and grown in a personal sense and can now make the commitment the new marriage requires.

In each of these examples the difference between

movement and change is apparent. Change represents a real breakthrough. It is planned, it has direction and it integrates the old with the new, transforming and merging the two. Real internal change represents choice and control, it offers challenge and growth. Movement on the other hand is random, unplanned, motivated by momentary desires. Movement is without relevance, selectivity or continuity. It fragments the self or the object and produces alienation and anxiety. Real change offers us new opportunities for enrichment.

The response to *Open Marriage* illustrates the difference between movement and change even further. *Open Marriage* was conceptualized as a model for internal and personal change in a world that made a revision in our marriage format necessary. The necessity for a more equal and honest and intimate relationship between marriage partners required a new flexibility in roles. We emphasized elements such as privacy, communication, identity, equality and trust as important factors in a relationship of growth. *Open Marriage* makes a positive statement for marriage, and it was written in response to external changes in our society that call for internal change, both in the partners involved and in our attitudes toward human relationships.

Yet those who are concerned with superficial movement consistently misinterpreted *Open Marriage*. The model is not a prescription for a swinging marriage, nor is it a prescription for lack of responsibility and caring. Open marriage is a model for change and growth in a marriage, and it calls for an understanding of the relationship between external change and internal change.

As long as we try to adapt to external movement rather than finding out how we can effect internal change we will find ourselves beset by terrific anxieties, conflict and disillusionment. We look good because we are rushing into every external movement seeking for a way to be accepted, and thus to find ourselves. But, in the process, we feel bad because we have lost our center and our inner self.

The Option Glut

The world in which we now live is a veritable kaleidoscope of options, swirling past us like a speeded-up film. New life-styles, new products, new relationships and new problems proliferate daily. Change, of course, has happened throughout human history, and each society has met the crises and change of its time—some successfully, some not. But today, people in our society and throughout the world are having to meet *more* changes at a *more* rapid pace than ever before in human history, and the effect is as likely to be as disorienting and unsettling as it may be exciting. Among all the changes, there are many which are strange and uncomfortable for us. And there are, too, many others that give us a more comfortable, healthier, more interesting life. But even the best of changes seem to have side effects about which few of us can be blamed for being somewhat suspicious. The most pessimistic see doomsday around the corner: the family structure breaking down, marriage disappearing with casual and disposable relationships taking its place, education without point or effect, pornography and pollution abounding, morality and ethics out the window. The most optimistic see change as a new deity in a mechanical and behavioristically controlled future. Somewhere in between lies a way of managing these changes and options for our individual fulfillment.

Faced with forces of change that seem to have taken on a life of their own and which we have not yet learned to manage in a personal way, a feeling of disorientation is inevitable and the questions become urgent: Where do I fit in? What is happening to me? How can I fulfill my basic needs? How can I not only survive but thrive through such change? The only answer society gives us is to change some more. We are diverted by gimmick after gimmick. "Hurry! Hurry! This way to your salvation." Today astrology, tomorrow yoga, biofeedback on Tuesday, encounter groups on Thursday. From the occult solution to the touchy-feely solution and back again we wend our desperate way. Or you can take your choice among Billy Graham, the Jesus Freaks, or the latest guru from India. Would you prefer group marriage to monogamy? It's all right if you do, they showed it on the news last week. You can have your choice between individual sex and group sex, between intimate sex with love and casual sex with friendship, or anonymous sex with orgasm the only end. If your own little nuclear family, with just Mom, Dad, Sis and Sonny, seems too constricting, perhaps you'd like to opt for an expanded family or a communal family? If it's been written up in a woman's magazine or the *Wall Street Journal* then surely it's got to be OK. And if, poor thing, you were an adult long before you ever heard about the postadolescent identity crisis, you can always have a mid-life crisis.

Is it any wonder we see strange things happening around us? The option glut was bound to produce some peculiar results. Should we really be surprised that the young have become old and burned out before their time, or that their grandparents are snapping their fingers and galloping around in a desperate search for their lost youth? Eighteen-year-old Susan wears a granny dress; sixty-year-old Lucille wears a mini. Hastily we buy the latest gadget or the latest philosophy, hoping that novelty will sate our deep longing for something that has integrity and solidity, something that will substitute for love, commitment, challenge and creativity.

But, of course, there are no substitutes.

Commitment Is a Key to Security

In the crisis culture in which we live, the need for commitment takes on a special significance. We continue to hunger for love, whatever we may tell ourselves. In our hearts we know that life cannot have real meaning for human beings without challenge and creativity. But we tend to be particularly skeptical of commitment in this period of social upheaval. What are we supposed to be commited to? The things we used to be committed to seem to change daily, in all areas: priests and ministers challenge their hierarchical superiors as ritual and dogma change; public trust is betrayed by our leaders and political ideals vanish under the impact of greed and power; groups and communities we depended on disappear; divorce increases and families are separated or split, moving into strange and unfamiliar forms. Even our children, born into a world of change, question our commitment to them as the generation gap widens. Thus, not only are we confused by the myriad options of our world, but we are also cut loose from the familiar constellations of values, ideals and causes that once commanded our genuine commitment.

The deep malaise that Kenneth Keniston ascribed to our young people in *The Uncommitted* only a few years ago has now permeated all our age ranks. In a world in flux, in which divisive causes multiply by the week, in which our cherished roots in the land, in religion, in family and in shared national aspirations are disappearing faster than we can keep track, there seems less and less to believe in—and when we become disillusioned about ideals we believed in, it is harder to muster commitment. All that is left seems to be commitment to material things and short-term gains, to profit and possession, to manipulation and survival, or even to just dancing an ever-changing tune to a succession of fast-fading pipers. And so we question the nature of commitment itself. Because commitment to what we are *supposed* to have accomplished at a certain age, commitment to a life plan we didn't design for ourselves and commitment to over-specific materialistic goals has not worked, we have thrown out commitment altogether.

Yet we desperately need commitment in our lives. Commitment is the very core of *constructive* change, of growth, and it is vital both to a sense of self and to a sustaining relationship.

In *Open Marriage* we tried to help people understand what the idea of relationship was all about. But one relationship alone cannot by itself, however good it may be, completely protect us from the confusion of the outside world and the ways in which that confusion impinges upon us personally. Our intimate relationships—both the relationship itself and each individual in it—depend in many ways upon the outside world. Each person, in or out of a marriage, exists in a world that, because of the extraordinary rate of contemporary change, is bound to create some measure of internal conflict and disillusionment. Knowing that someone loves you and that growth is possible with the tender support of your partner is a tremendous asset. But it is not enough. Not in a world where change demands new decisions and choices every day, a world where your kids are visitors from Mars, your next-door neighbors are swingers, and old ties and landmarks vanish overnight. Not in a world where values fluctuate like prices in the stock market, or in a time when you have to glance furtively at every stranger on the street and feel obsolescent from one day to the next. In a world changing as rapidly as ours, each one of us must feel at times like a prisoner returning from Vietnam after eight years.

But if there is no protection from the outside world, is there no hope of achieving a sense of personal security? The small, comfortable world of our intimate relationships offers us only a partial haven. Barring total retreat from society we cannot and should not want to escape from the outside world. Each change can be an opportunity for growth, each apparent adversity can be turned to advantage if we know how to manage it, know what we want, and are willing to meet the challenge. Man cannot, in fact, live without stimulus and challenge in his life. Without stimuli from the outside world we cannot grow.

Crisis as a Key to Growth

But certainly the world of today throws too many stimuli at us too fast. When we go to an amusement park we enjoy the successive thrills of the roller coaster, the ferris wheel and the tunnel of horror; but in between each of these periods of excitement we have time to stroll around the fairgrounds, to munch a hot dog, to sit on a bench in the sun and relax. Contemporary society tends to deprive us of the quiet moments we need between the periods of excitement. We feel as though we are on a perpetual roller coaster, without respite. The problem, then, is how to make use of the stimuli that society throws at us for our personal growth without being overwhelmed by them.

When we feel overwhelmed we define our situation as a period of crisis. Too many options, too much stimulus and no guidelines on how to manage them turns change into crisis. We feel not only overwhelmed but confused. In such a state is it any wonder that the young throw up their hands in despair and succumb to cults or numb themselves with drugs? Is it any wonder when the man or woman of thirty-five asks, Is this all there is? or when the man of fifty feels a devastating insecurity, questions his virility and the meaning of his former goals? And is it surprising at all that the woman of forty-five should look back and ask, Where have I been all my life?

Nothing could be more normal than these crises in this world of ours. Nothing could be more normal than to fear what is ahead. But what is *not* normal is the way in which we meet and deal with these crises. Of course we can't find security or fulfill our basic psychological needs when we are clutching at straws and racing after each instant panacea that the media offers us. Most of us realize that crisis is a normal and inevitable part of human existence. Most of us realize that a crisis met and dealt with increases our sense of our own worth and helps us to grow. Most of us realize that the only real security in life is something that exists within ourselves, within each one of us separately, and that without that individual sense of security no wall is high enough, no luxury great enough to protect us.

But what most of us may not know is how to meet change and crisis in a positive way. What most of us may not realize, or understand thoroughly enough, is how to go about *finding* the self that is the only real security, or how to keep that self growing. Nor do we understand sufficiently the natural internal changes that take place *within* us in the course of our adult life-span. There are long library shelves of books both scholarly and popular concerned with the development of the child from birth through puberty and adolescence to the threshold of adulthood. There are, on the other hand, very few books of any kind that deal with the natural development of the adult. We do not stop developing when we reach adulthood. We do not stop growing. Ever. Some people have a natural gift, an instinct, for adult growth. But they are unusual. For the rest of us, it is a matter of understanding the process of growth and change in relation to ourselves. Once we understand how internal and psychological growth happens, once we comprehend the skills that are essential to fostering such growth and to helping us meet change, any one of us can gain a considerable measure of control over our responses to the external societal world, and can learn to deal with it on our terms instead of its terms. We can learn, in fact, how to shift gears in accordance with the changes both within and outside our essential selves.

The Guarantee Hang-up

The option glut is all the more confusing because our society leads us to expect that if we make the right choices when we are young adults, we will be "home safe" for the rest of our lives. During the first fifteen or twenty years of our adult lives, most of us, men and women alike, set about achieving for ourselves those things and conditions which our society teaches us are the guarantees of security and contentment: career advancement, family, the ownership of a home, and the accumulation of material comforts. There is nothing wrong with attempting to achieve any of these goals; for most of us they are in fact natural goals for this phase of adulthood when our energies are at a peak and our competitive drives at their strongest. What *is* wrong, however, is the assumption that any of these goals, whether individually or taken all together, will *guarantee* us fulfillment in life. Important they are; but guarantees they are not.

Stan, a studio photographer in his early forties, put it this way to us: "I always thought," he said, "that by the time I'd got my own studio, and paid off the mortgage on the house, and the kids were old enough to look after themselves, that I'd be home safe. I thought there'd be no more problems. But it hasn't worked out that way. I worked damn hard, and I got most of the things I set out to, but they don't seem to mean what I thought they would. I'm getting bored with studio photography. I even begin to envy those guys who spend their time roaming around the world taking pictures for UPI or the Associated Press instead of playing it safe. I have a nice house, but we have spent fifteen years tied to it raising our two kids, and now my wife's fed up with it. She'd like to move back into an apartment, like we had when we were first married. These days the two of us seem to spend half our time arguing about what went wrong. We feel as though maybe we wasted a lot of time. But I don't think either of us really know what we want now— except that it's something else besides what we have."

Instead of finding himself home safe at the end of the first twenty-odd years of his adulthood, Stan feels as though he'd been stranded at second base. When, back in his early twenties, Stan placed his full belief in the myth that lifelong fulfillment could be guaranteed by achieving a few specific external goals, he was ignoring the probability of change—both the changing needs of his inner self and the changing circumstances of the world around him. In fact, of course, the concept of being "home safe" runs counter to both human nature and to the element of chance that affects us all. It would be far more realistic to recognize that, in the words of the baseball cliché, the game is never over until the final out.

The disillusionment Stan expressed to us has become almost epidemic in recent years. Some commentators have unfortunately seen this phenomenon as being exclusively associated with the middle years of life. But, depending upon individual circumstances, it can happen at any age. Another man we talked with, who made his first million before he was twenty-five, feels much the same kind of letdown at the young age of twenty-nine. Many of the college dropouts we talked to have given as one of their reasons the fact that they didn't believe the guarantee myth either; they wanted to find out more about who they were before locking themselves into a career by following a particular course of study. These young people had taken a hard look at their elders' disillusionment and learned from it. A reassuringly large number were genuinely seeking a more realistic, more open approach to the planning of their adult lives.

The feeling of having been let down by the guarantee myth can also come quite late in life. It can strike the woman in her mid-fifties whose youngest child has left home to take up his own adult life. It can undermine the confidence of the man or woman who is unprepared for retirement from a life's career. But whatever age such questioning may begin at, it is a certain signal that the time has come to shift gears. Too many people simply resign themselves to what already is—"I made a mistake," they will say, "but I'll just have to live with it." Others react in panic, making drastic changes in their lives just for the sake of doing *something,* without stopping to assess their true needs.

Life Strategy as a Key to Change

Neither resignation nor panic is necessary. We can continue to grow throughout our lives, we can discover new possibilities of the self, we can find a measure of internal security in the midst of change. But to shift gears successfully in change and crisis, from one stage of life into another, we must achieve a better understanding of the normal changes that take place in our psychological growth during the course of adulthood. And we can develop certain skills that will make it possible for us to use this understanding. This book is designed to help you develop a *life strategy* that gives you the flexibility you need to deal with change on both a personal and societal level. A life strategy designed by you and for you can help you to shift gears at the important moments of your life, it can help make it possible for you to meet change in a positive way and to put the natural and inevitable crises of your passage from one life phase to another to work in a constructive and creative way. An effective life strategy can help you at any age to reevaluate and restructure your life so as to take full advantage of your potential for the continuing growth that can alone bring fulfillment and personal security.

CHAPTER TWO

The Crisis Culture

The Assumptive State

Before anyone can deal with the normal crises of human adulthood, it might be helpful to understand what crisis really means in terms of the self. Crisis is a word greatly used, indeed over-used, by journalists. We hear constantly about the dollar crisis or the energy crisis or the possibility of a Constitutional crisis, and in this context we know well enough what the word means: things are bad and are likely to get worse. But crisis in a psychological sense has a more complex and a more *positive* meaning. To begin with, we must get rid of the idea that all psychological crises are abnormal and therefore bad. They are nothing of the kind. Puberty, for instance, is a time of psychological crisis for all human beings; the beginnings of adult sexual feeling in adolescent children force them to view themselves in a new way, to change some of their assumptions about themselves in relation to the world and other people. Obviously, there is nothing abnormal about this process—it is not bad, it is not to be feared, it is simply a part of human growth. Yet it is a psychological crisis.

The normal crises of adulthood are also a part of the growth process that begins with birth and does not end until death. To ask oneself at various stages of one's life, Where am I? Who am I?, or Is this what I really

29

want to be doing?, is not abnormal and should not be
any cause for fear. That people think in such negative terms about adult crises arises from the fact that
they do not expect them. Society has conned them into
believing that if they choose the right career and the
right mate as young adults then they will be home safe.
Believing the guarantee myth and not expecting to
have to reevaluate themselves in the course of their
adult lives, people tend to become frightened when
they find themselves questioning the assumptions by
which they have lived for ten, twenty or thirty years.
They jump to the conclusion that there is something
wrong with them, that they are falling apart, when in
fact all that is happening is that they are entering a
new developmental stage, a new period of reassessment and growth. Such adult periods of reassessment
are different in kind from the adjustments that must be
made at puberty, but they are no less normal. And
they too can lead to further growth.

The key word in discussing such periods of growth,
whether at the age of thirteen or forty-five, is *assumptions*. Each of us begins the day with certain basic
assumptions: the sun will rise, the mail will arrive,
there will be food in the market, our children will return at the end of the day—the world will still be a
recognizable place when we go outside.

For anyone who was a child growing up twenty
years ago, certain assumptions could be made: the air
was safe to breathe, the water was safe to drink, the
policeman would come when you called him, you
could reach your doctor when you needed him, you
could trust the government. Today our children have
different assumptions about the world they live in.

The assumptions with which we begin each day,
whatever they may be, comprise our *assumptive state*.
When our assumptive state is challenged, we are in
crisis.

The Normal Crisis

Let's look at a concrete example. Betty has been married for seventeen years, has three children ranging in age from fifteen to five, and lives in the suburbs of a large city. Her husband, Sam, drives to work in the city. Betty has not held a job since her marriage and defines her *self* in terms of being a wife and mother. She believes herself to be successful in both these capacities and has long been content with her role in life.

But then gradually, over a period of several months, Betty begins to feel restless. Her youngest child is now in first grade, and for the first time in years Betty has a certain amount of genuine leisure during the day. She is surprised to discover that these hours of privacy seem somehow empty. She has always said that she wished she had more time to herself, but now that she has it she isn't quite sure what to do with it. Sitting alone in her kitchen in the late morning, drinking her fourth cup of coffee, she wonders what it will be like when the children are older and still less dependent upon her. A feeling of incipient uselessness creeps over her at times—and she isn't even forty yet.

What Betty is doing is questioning her assumptive state. Her inner self and her outer role as housewife and mother have always in the past seemed one and the same thing. But now, suddenly, she isn't sure about that. And the more she thinks about it, the more it disturbs her. She is, in fact, in crisis, a perfectly normal one but still a crisis.

Betty has two or three friends who are very much caught up in women's liberation. Taking her cue from them, she could decide that being a housewife is basically a demeaning role to play, and that is why she is unhappy. But if she redefines only the *situation,* telling herself that what she once found fulfilling was really a kind of slavery, she is likely simply to become bitter about the years she "wasted," without moving on to discover new kinds of fulfillment. If she is to grow as a person, she will have to reassess those years for what they were and now, in the present, re-define *herself* as well as her situation. She will have to recognize that her view of the situation has changed because she herself has changed.

Once Betty has recognized the crisis for what it is, she can proceed to evaluate it, giving herself time to explore the available alternatives and to seek out new approaches(both within herself and in the situation). When she decides on a solution, and acts on that de-cision, Betty will emerge with a *new* assumptive state about herself and her relation to the world.

The steps from the onset of the crisis to the emer-gence of the new assumptive state (and the personal growth that comes with it) outlined in the previous paragraph will be dealt with in detail in the later chapters of this book. We will be talking further about both *why* these steps are necessary and *how* to de-velop the personal skills for carrying them out suc-cessfully. For now, however, the main point we want to make clear is that to question your assumptive state at various points in the course of your adult life is perfectly normal and indeed vital to your continu-ing growth as a person.

Society and the Assumptive State

The kind of internal crisis we are talking about, in which the assumptive state is called into question, can occur because of the influence of several different in-dividual factors or a combination of them. It can de-velop out of primarily internal considerations. Or it can be brought on by what is largely an external in-fluence, as for instance when a husband suddenly in-forms his wife of twenty years that he has fallen in love with another woman and wants a divorce. If such a man's wife has believed her marriage to be a sound one, her husband's declaration will obviously come as a severe shock to her assumptive state, forcing her to redefine both the situation (her marriage) and herself. In many cases, of course, the factors that bring on the crisis will be a combination of internal and external ones.

In today's world, however, the influence of external forces on one's assumptive state is greater than it has ever been before. Social change has always had its long-range effects on the ways in which we conduct our personal relationships, but the extraordinary rate of current change means that such effects are felt in a personal way both more quickly and more profoundly.

Many standards of behavior and attitudes have shifted in the course of only the past decade. Ten years ago, Elizabeth Taylor's romance with Richard Burton during the filming of *Cleopatra* was considered a front-page scandal; today, famous actresses cheerfully bear children out of wedlock and hardly anyone bats an eye. Ten years ago an abortion was kept a secret; today the ethics of abortion are openly debated. Ten years ago the woman who insisted that she had every bit as much right to a career as her husband was an oddity; today she is a commonplace. Ten years ago few couples would have openly discussed their sexual problems; today, many couples jointly seek professional help for sexual dysfunction.

All of these changes have in turn changed the ways that men and women relate to one another. Millions of people are questioning the priorities in their lives, and even the basic values by which those priorities are determined. Such questions are being asked at every level of society in every part of the country. A group of married women whom we interviewed in a midwestern suburb, for instance, were scornful of women's liberation as a movement, but they were nevertheless concerned with many of the same issues—equal pay, equal recognition of their personhood, equal freedom to develop their own capacities—as the movement leaders on the East coast.

But there are so many questions, all at once, that personal confusion is the inevitable result. So many new ideas, so many new options, have been introduced during the past decade that they are undermining our sense of continuity and distorting the ways in which we relate to other people, to our jobs and to our social institutions. In his book, *Man and System,* Turney-High writes, "A crisis is by definition any social or personal problem situation for which there is no adequate ready-made answer." We experience more personal crises today, and have greater difficulty in defining their meaning, because we do in fact live in a crisis culture.

The new options apparently give us greater freedom of choice, but those same new options disrupt the structures that we must have in order to put the new options and the new technology to proper use for the benefit of our human needs. As the journalist Russell Baker has said, "Too often, as we know from experience, a new scientific or technological advance means only that it will become easier to exploit, manipulate or exterminate us." Technology, and the options it brings, grows too fast for structure to keep up with it. We are losing track of the values that could keep us on course, values that are universal, substantial and human. Our society as a whole is questioning its assumptive state. When we as individuals experience a personal crisis, we cannot look to our cultural mores to give us guidance because they too are in crisis. In the crisis culture, there are no ready-made answers. We have not been able to develop a value structure that takes the rate of change fully into account. Today we need to search out new methods for reinforcing our values and for establishing norms of behavior that can guide us through change.

The Meaning of Our Loss of Ritual

It may help us to more fully understand the significance of the lack of structure in our own society, if we take a look at what happens in a society in which the cultural mores *do* help the individual to find his way through the basic life crises. In most primitive or preliterate small groups and societies, the basic crises in the life cycle—birth, puberty, marriage, parenthood, old age and death—are acknowledged and dealt with in ways proper to their importance to the individual and to his integration into the culture in which he lives. And not only these basic events, but any change in status is the occasion for acknowledgment by others.

In a realistically earthy sense, such societies recognize that to move on in life from one station to another is a crisis, that new status also means taking on new roles, new duties and responsibilities, new behavior sets and new relationships. Ceremonies, tests, trials and long periods of learning and initiation, in which everyone in the society is in some way involved, serve to give the individual a sense of recognition and integration into the whole. In these primitive societies traditional mentors and guardians lead the individual through the trial into his new status. Then, fully instructed, initiated with pomp and feathers, rituals, rattles and ceremonies, the new person is launched.

In our society, of course, we are much too sophisticated, much too "civilized" to have need of such childish displays. We smile at the rattles and feathers —and yet we are fascinated, too. Perhaps, in spite of our sophistication, we realize that we are missing something. In our own world, marriage ceremonies are becoming more informal every day, baby showers are passé, the retirement banquet and gold watch presentation are disappearing along with the family-owned firm of yesteryear. Bar mitzvahs, first communions and confirmations do still exist in diluted form, but they are mere tokens in comparison with the puberty rites of preliterate groups. We dispense with one kind of ceremony after another—the only people who really seem to enjoy their ceremonies anymore are the politicians!

Yet the ritual, the rite of passage, has in the past been a powerful force, both in primitive and advanced societies, for the cohesion of the social system. It symbolically represented and reaffirmed the solidarity of the group and of the individual's integration into the group. A ritual in this sense is an act of recognition and confirmation. But it is also a protective mechanism, designed to make the transition from one status (or assumptive state) into another more *meaningful* to the *individual,* and to help him adjust to his new status. What's more, the stages in this ritual form a close parallel to the psychological stages that any individual passes through in the course of a personal life crisis.

In his classic analysis, *Rites Of Passage,* Arnold Van Gennep sets forth the three stages of such rituals: the first is separation (from the old group), followed by transition (preparation for the passage from one status to another), and concluded by incorporation (into the new status). The transition stage is conceived of by many small-scale societies and groups as a time of danger when the individual is considered ". . . to be especially vulnerable to supernatural influences . . . and, at these times, may even pose a danger to other members of society."

The following chart illustrates our comparison between the three stages of primitive rites of passage and the three stages of psychological adjustment during personal crisis. Personal crisis is a rite of passage from one level of self-development to another—or should be. Unfortunately, in today's crisis culture, deprived of traditional societal supports or cultural mores that could help us through periods of personal crisis, many of us *fail to complete the journey.* Instead of completing the passage into a new stage of self-development and a changed assumptive state, we remain for extended periods in the transitional period,

STAGES IN RITES OF PASSAGE

In Primitive Puberty Initiation Rite	*In Personal Crisis*
SEPARATION	**SEPARATION**
From former group or state.	From former assumptive state.
According to age, physical development.	Precipitated by shock from external event or internal conflict (dissonance).
Into boys' houses or menstrual hut.	Withdrawal into self.
TRANSITION	**TRANSITION**
Time spent apart from group.	Change in mood, mental content.
Learning, training, preparing for new status.	Questioning, openness to change, vulnerability, discovery and awareness of new behavior sets, new insights.
Initiation rites, trials, tests.	
INCORPORATION	**INCORPORATION**
Into new status as adult.	Integration of new behavior sets with old.
Attendant ritual and ceremony.	Reorganization on new level, richer, more generalized.
Acceptance by the group.	External changes instigated to complement self-growth.
New identity and roles.	New assumptive state.

disorganized and in turmoil, and then, instead of growing, fall back in defeat and fear.

When we are in the midst of such crisis, who or what can we reach out to? Crisis intervention centers are few and far between. Some cities now have telephone hot lines for potential suicides or for drug addicts, but the very existence of these highly impersonal "helping hands" indicates the desperate lack of normal supportive structures. Go to a doctor for a problem and he gives you a pill. Some of us don't really trust our psychotherapists; before we are willing to ask for such help we insist upon checking out the *therapist's* views on women's liberation, pot or politics. There are marriage counselors, but divorce lawyers get much more business. The man who hopes the union will solve his work problems for him, the mother who expects the young man to marry her pregnant daughter out of plain decency, the man who hopes his family will convince his wife not to divorce him, are all relying on past patterns of coping with crisis. But the past doesn't exist anymore. The help we once could rely on from our community, our family, our ministers, our doctors or our ethnic tradition cannot be counted on now. In the big cities, community does not exist; in the suburbs people move in and out like migrating birds.

Since we have few institutionalized methods for helping us through our life crises, our friends and interpersonal relationships become that much more important. But even here we run into trouble. We are the most mobile society that has ever existed. As Vance Packard points out in *A Nation of Strangers,* "The phrase 'home town' may well fade from our language in this century. Already half of all U.S. heads of families live more than a hundred miles from where they were born—and one out of five lives more than a thousand miles from his birthplace." The average American, in fact, moves fourteen times in the course of his life, and at least a fifth of all Americans move at least once a year, according to Mr. Packard's statistics. Friends, in such a society, become as disposable as clothes, and still another supportive mechanism is lost to us.

The crisis culture deprives us of the traditional supports; in their place it offers us fads. In place of ceremonial rattles and feathers we have astrology and yoga and encounter groups, and while some of these fads may help some people in some ways, there are so many alternatives to choose from that we are faced with an additional kind of crisis, the crisis of the option glut. In primitive societies, the rituals, the rattles and feathers have very specific *meaning* to both the society and the individual. They have a specific *relevance*. But how are we to judge the relevance of yoga to our individual lives? Will it help us more than an encounter session? Is it what we really need to help us through our individual crises? We know we need something. But out of so many choices, how can we choose what is right for us?

Ideas Come Cheap

In making any kind of choice, the individual needs information. But too much information, indiscriminately selected, can be just as distorting as too little. The mass media, which provide the vast bulk of the information most Americans receive, have a powerful influence on us and are a major factor in making us aware of the option glut. Taken together, the media and the quantity of the options tend to undermine the individual's ability to determine what is and what is not relevant to his personal needs. And yet this information we get from the media is absolutely essential to preserving our freedoms and our ability to choose from among these options. We need all the information we can get, but we also need to know what to do with it.

Many of us are probably most clearly aware of the

media problem in relation to the impact of television on our children. We may know that by the time the average child reaches eighteen "he or she will have spent nearly two years in front of the tube." What we may not realize is that another aspect of television is significant not only for our children but for the adult members of our society as well. This aspect concerns the conflict in values these programs present to all of us. The impact of these discrepancies in values is exaggerated since television is an intensely focused and highly selective visual medium for providing information. Most of us are familiar with the problem of violence on TV in regard to our children. Basically we believe in nonviolence and we earnestly teach our children healthy competition and respect for others and human life. And yet our children are fed a steady diet of old and new movies and programs that glorify and accentuate violence and aggression, murder and torture, and a carelessness for human life that is appalling. Which value will our children be most affected by?

Another aspect of the conflict in values is in our attitudes toward sex and family roles. Although there has been a healthy shift in our society in the last few years toward greater equality between men and women, this change is not reflected at all in the dozens of five-, ten-, and even fifteen-year-old situation comedies that are endlessly rerun on television. The children watching these old programs may have mothers who work, but they will seldom see that reality reflected on their television screen. The children's parents may share roles and responsibilities in the home, but on the programs they watch, the woman's place is always in the kitchen and father knows best. To compound the confusion, the children might be able to watch on the same night a rerun of *Father Knows Best* and an episode of a new comedy such as *Maude* which presents a franker, more contemporary attitude toward sex roles. The problem here for the child is the discrepancy between the two sets of values and the two different "realities" being presented. As one concerned father of a ten-year-old commented: "If I were my son, I'd be awfully confused about which end was up."

Since the child is still in the process of finding out who he is, is still in the process of *forming* his values, most people can recognize the possibility of confusion that exists in these situations, and many parents (though not enough) make an effort to discuss such value discrepancies with their children and to select their programs with care. The vulnerability of the child is something we all understand. But what many of us may not fully realize is that the adult who is in a state of crisis, and is questioning his assumptive state, is also very vulnerable to outside influence. The crisis itself may be perfectly normal, a sign that it is time for the adult to move on to a new stage of development, but since he is questioning himself and looking for new answers about what he should be doing with his life, the incredible variety of conflicting "solutions" that the media offer him can leave him as confused as any ten-year-old.

The forty-five-year-old man who discovers that he is not, after all, home safe, and begins to doubt the meaning of his marriage or his career, looks around for some clue as to what he should be doing next. And what does he find? On the evening news there is a story about a family that gave up the big-city rat race for life on a communal farm. The late-night talk show he watches is featuring three couples involved in a group marriage. Nor does it stop with television. The latest *Playboy* has an article on the wonders of biofeedback, while the magazine his wife subscribes to offers an article on transcendental meditation. And as for his friends and business acquaintances, well, the couple next door says that group therapy saved their marriage and he really must read the article by their group leader in *Reader's Digest;* his business partner is into yoga ("My teacher was on the *Dick Cavett*

Show two weeks ago"); and his oldest friend has taken up smoking pot ("Don't worry about the side effects, I read an article in *Newsweek* about this research group who found it was perfectly safe unless you were psychotic to begin with. And you're hardly a psychotic, are you now?"). For the moment our friend doesn't think so, but by next week, who knows?

If the crisis culture throws new questions and new problems at us every day, it also suggests new solutions. And after a while the questions and the answers, the problems and the solutions, all look like they're one and the same thing. "If you're not part of the solution, you're a part of the problem" was a popular slogan in the late sixties. But these days the so-called solutions *are,* very definitely, a part of the problem; not because any of them are necessarily wrong, but just because there are so many of them to choose from and because they seem to contradict one another at every turn. Yoga may indeed be just the thing you need. Or group therapy. Or any one of another hundred solutions. But which one? The media will tell you about all of them; today they will emphasize this one, tomorrow that one. It is a game of emotional roulette. Instead of looking to ourselves, we look to the media to tell us what the new solution is. Halfheartedly, or sometimes maniacally, we say yes, yes, that must be it. But then we take another look to make sure the trend is holding. Is it still "in"? And so, bewildered and confused, we are pushed into emotional consumerism just as surely as has been the case with product consumerism.

And we haven't yet learned to deal with emotional consumerism. We can, with foresight, unfortunate experience and hard facts of economic reality to guide us, learn to deal with hucksterism of material products, we are getting better at it all the time thanks to the consumer and ecology groups that have come to the fore in the last few years. But faddish values, changing ethics and emotional attitudes—these we have not yet learned how to deal with. New emotions are not as easy to adopt as a different length for the skirt or a different width for the trouser leg—and once adopted they are far more wrenching to change back again.

The media are insatiable when it comes to new ideas; the latest behavioral fad becomes a household word overnight. And we as members of a consumer society are insatiable in our desire for the new and for vicarious excitement. Together, these emphases tend to distort the ability of both the media and the viewers to distinguish carefully between those ideas that are valid contributions to our understanding of human behavior and those that are mere fads or even aberrations.

What we have to learn to do is to check things out with ourselves, instead of with the externals around us. If we do not, then the nature of the media tends to make every new development seem like a new norm. It lends a cloak of respectability to the *new*, whether the particular development is a real scientific breakthrough, such as the pioneering work of Masters and Johnson into the causes of sexual dysfunction, or some hairbrained "miracle diet" that is far more detrimental to health than a few extra pounds. We can't possibly adjust to a new "norm" every two weeks, but that is what the media demand of us if we are susceptible and nonselective in our evaluation of every new trend. If we don't sift out the valuable from the ridiculous, it becomes more difficult to absorb the valid changes in all areas of life and the true scientific breakthroughs that can in fact really help us.

Is It Relevant to Me?

Change is a fact of life in all cultures. In primitive societies it may come very slowly indeed, taking generation upon generation. Whether the change comes from internal innovation in response to new needs ("Necessity is the mother of invention") or through

contact with another culture, there is a normal process
of discovery or contact, followed by absorption or
rejection. If the time is right, and the culture is ready
for change, then the society borrows or invents or
adapts what it needs without great disruption. At other
times there may be upheaval, eventually to be followed by assimilation and integration. But whether the
change is peaceful or tumultuous, time is needed for
stability to be maintained or reasserted. We, as a culture, are at a point where the contact rate and the
superficial absorption rate are so rapid that we go
from one change to another without real integration,
without finding out how to live emotionally, as individual people, with the changes around us.

Yet there are no signs that the speed of change is
likely to decrease—quite the opposite, everything
points to a future in which the speed of change will
gather still greater momentum. But that fact only
makes it more imperative to learn how to find our own
personal center, learn how to discover our own true
needs, learn how to fulfill those needs in our own time
without fear that we are not into the newest thing. Instead of checking things out with ourselves, we have
been checking them out with Stan and Harriet and Lucy
and Bert. Instead of checking things out with ourselves
we have been checking them out with the media. And
we must learn to resist the emotional salesmanship of
the media and of those who are in thrall to it.

To be sure, there may be many new life-styles, new
values that we very much need and want. We may
feel it *is* the time, high time, to change from city life to
country life, or to have a new outlook on sexual fulfillment. Men and women both may want a new
equality that gives the woman a chance to make her
own career on a level equal with a man, and that takes
the full load of providing economic support off the
shoulders of the husband. Both parents may want to
share in the raising of children, rather than being

pushed into part-time fatherhood or after-school motherhood. We may want to change careers—why should we spend forty years in the same job? But we have to be sure that *we* want the change, and that we are ready for it, inside ourselves. It has to be right for us because we know we need it and want it and are ready for it and can handle it—and not "right" for us simply because everyone else is doing it. We have to learn how to *tune in on ourselves,* not on the latest fad or trend.

What Is Relevant to Me?

If we are to deal with our normal adult life crises we need to be able to determine the answer to that question.

What is relevant to me is the right and the necessary, first question. And, interestingly, the first to ask it have been the young people of our society. The word "relevance" has been used over and over again during the past several years in respect to the crisis in contemporary education, a crisis which reflects the larger confusion in our society. Unfortunately, though, the cries for relevance on the part of college students (and high school students in many areas) have been confused with political issues. Despite the fact that many prominent educators agree entirely that education is not sufficiently relevant to today's world, the political issues served to sidetrack students, educators and the general public from the real problem.

The real problem is that education has failed completely to teach, or even attempt to teach, students to deal with the world they live in. With the pace of change accelerating, our young people are the first generation to be born into the crisis culture. Their parents, having come of age in a period that was much more stable, at least in terms of values, have been trying to deal with today's changes on the basis of the traditional values they learned as children and young adults. But the young of today have grown up in a world of change; they do not have their parents' sense of traditional values to help them cope. At the same time, of course, they are not blinded to what is happening to such values.

There are many students, it is true, who have over-simplified the problem, who have felt that everything could be solved merely by giving a few courses in ecology, or by paying more attention to the poor people in the college neighborhood. But the more perceptive of the students have been calling for something that goes beyond that: a kind of education that would teach them *how to deal with* the crisis culture. The kind of education their parents received may well have been perfectly in tune with the world in which they then lived; they are not arguing about that. What they are saying is that the world has changed, and education has to change, too. And so their cry for relevance is really a cry for help.

In the past five years, vast numbers of older people have begun to take up the same cry. They may call it by a different name, they may not even recognize their fraternity with their sons and daughters, but they are asking for the same thing. How, people want to know, can I determine which of the many choices open to me are the ones that have relevance to *me*, to my *self?*

Because any healthy adult does continue to grow and to change, that question must be asked several times in the course of a life. And the answer will be different each time, exactly because the individual has grown, has changed. But there are, we believe, a number of guidelines that can help any individual to answer that question for himself or herself at any given crisis point in his life. There are specific skills which can be developed that will make it easier to deal with the crisis culture. The particular answer to the particular problem of each individual will be different, of course. But if we can learn to ask the right question, then we are halfway to finding the right answer, each of us, for ourselves. The answers may be different, but the questions that lead to those answers will be the same.

CHAPTER THREE

The Maturity Myth

Settling Down

While our culture has been throwing out one traditional supportive structure after another in recent years, it has clung tenaciously to an illusory concept that we call *the maturity myth*. The promises offered by the maturity myth may seem supportive in the short run, but in the long run they severely limit the individual's potential for growth and make it even more difficult for him to deal with the crisis culture. We have already touched on one aspect of this myth: the idea that if you make the "right" choices as a young adult, you will be home safe by the time you are in your late thirties or early forties, that the right choices will guarantee you fulfillment for the rest of your life. During the first decade or so of adulthood, the myth may seem to be functioning as promised. You choose your career, marry, raise a family, get a mortgage on a house: you have "settled down" as our society tells you you should, and you are supposedly mature.

To settle down—this phrase, which we hear so often, is a veritable minefield of booby traps. We all know from our own experience that adolescence is an unstable period of restless uncertainty; we are unsure of who we are or what we want to do with our lives, and we long for the day when we will become a part of the "grown-up" world. Society instructs us, by way of our parents and teachers, that when we settle down we will be grown-up. The mature person, we are told, is the settled person, and the settled person is the one who plans his life according to the external goals of career, family and the acquisition of material possessions. There is nothing intrinsically wrong, as we have said before, with any of the external goals, provided that you do not make them the only goals in your life or expect them to bring you lifelong fulfillment in all areas of your existence. But that, unfortunately, is just what most of us do and just what we are led to expect.

Maturity, we are told, is the *same thing* as settling down. It is defined in terms of the external goals rather than in terms of the natural phases of each individual's internal development. This societally imposed concept of maturity assumes we will want the same things for ourselves during the next fifty years that we want, or think we want, when we are in our early twenties. But what if we don't, in fact, want the same things even ten or twenty years later, never mind fifty? What happens to us then? If, like Stan the photographer in the previous chapter, we discover eventually that we are not home safe, we are likely to feel that our world is falling apart. And that feeling will be intensified by the other false promises of the maturity myth that we have been conned into believing.

For we are not only told that we will be home safe if we settle down and organize our lives around an approved set of external goals. That is merely the first of the five basic promises of the maturity myth. The second promise is that once we settle down we will become less restless and more stable. We will not make decisions impulsively, but judiciously, on the "mature" basis of whether or not a given action will help us to achieve one or another of the external goals. Unhappily, though, in our hurry to become what society tells us is mature, we often make the basic decisions about career or marriage very injudiciously. For instance, the student who still hasn't made up his mind what career he will go into by his third year of college is looked upon as some kind of misfit. "Well, he always was a restless boy," his parents will sigh. But another student who *has* made a decision about what he's going to work at for the rest of his life may in fact have made that choice too soon and too impulsively. In order to become "grown-up," in order to demonstrate that he is stable and mature, he may make one of the vital decisions of his life long before he has experienced enough to know what he really wants. Yet it is this choice that is supposed to guarantee him lifelong fulfillment.

The third promise of the maturity myth is that once we settle down into a job and marriage we will attain emotional security. According to the myth, emotional security depends to a great extent upon marriage and the raising of a family. It is certainly true, of course, that a loving mate and children will normally enhance the emotional security of any individual. But the maturity myth ignores the fact that emotional security also has a great deal to do with the individual's inner self, how *he* judges his *own* worth, and not just with his worth in the eyes of others. If your emotional security is based entirely on your mate and your family, then you are going to be devastated emotionally if either your mate or your children should ever leave you. The soaring divorce rate should be evidence enough that the mate you choose at twenty may not be around to provide you with emotional security at thirty. What's more, many of us make the same mistake in choosing a mate as in choosing a career: in our hurry to achieve emotional security, we all too often choose someone who has what might be called built-in obsolescence. Again, in order to achieve "maturity" as rapidly as possible, we make a vital decision before we know ourselves well enough to choose not just for today but for tomorrow as well.

The fourth promise of the maturity myth is that once you have grown up and settled down your sex life will be *safe*. You won't have to *worry* about sex anymore. The groping experiments of adolescence, the insecurity of the dating game and the singles bar ("Will she or won't she?"/"Should I or shouldn't I?") will be past. Your mate will be there when you want sex, but the pressure will be off. Sex will be an ordinary part of your daily life instead of something you have to seek out, negotiate over and prove yourself at. Never mind that this promise of the maturity myth tends to reduce sexuality to the simplistic level of having an available body in the bed next to you—after all, the more simplistic things are, the safer they are. On the other hand, the vast popularity of sex manuals, the estimates indicating that at least one partner suffers from sexual dysfunction in nearly fifty percent of American marriages, and the prevalence of such phenomena as exchanging partners, group sex and pornographic movies would seem to indicate quite strongly that a great number of people have failed to find the safety or satisfaction they thought marriage would bring them.

Finally, the maturity myth tells us that if we settle down and organize our lives around the proper external goals, the future will be manageable. All of the previous four assumptions contribute to this fifth element of the myth. After all, if you can expect to be home safe by your early forties, can expect to be less restless and more stable, can count on a feeling of emotional security, and can assume your sex life will be safe, then the future certainly *ought* to be manageable. But, since the other four promises of the maturity myth are based on false assumptions, this last one collapses also. What's more, even if the others were valid, this fifth promise would still be undermined by the crisis culture in which we live. In a world of constant, almost dizzying external change, a concept of maturity that is based on conforming to external societal goals becomes a contradiction in terms.

The Dark Side of the Promises

In spite of the fact that the five promises of the maturity myth are based on false assumptions, most of us originally planned or are still planning our lives almost exclusively around the external goals in the hope that the promises will indeed be fulfilled. Not every person believes all the promises, of course, but most of us either believe or once believed at least some of them. When, wiser but sadder, we stop believing them, when we find ourselves stranded at second base instead of home safe, when we begin to ask, What am I going to do with the rest of my life?, we find ourselves inevitably in crisis. Some people begin to question the myth because external events simply do not conform to what the myth has promised. A man or woman who goes through a divorce, for instance, is bound to wonder about all those promises. Some may blame themselves for not having lived up to the dictates of the myth, but others, quite rightly, may suspect that the myth itself ought to bear a lot of the responsibility for their troubles for having got them off on the wrong foot to begin with.

Other people begin to doubt the promises of the myth not because they have been proved false by external events, but simply because they themselves, as individuals, have changed. The high-pressure career that appeared so exciting at twenty may now have come to seem an obstacle to other kinds of fulfillment, preventing the individual from realizing new interests that he has since discovered or that he conveniently ignored as a young man. Many women, like Betty, the housewife in the previous chapter who started questioning her assumptions about herself as her children became less dependent on her, may feel that they have "wasted" the best years of their lives. These people, finding that they are not the same as they were when they first began planning their lives around the maturity myth, are asking questions because they have grown internally. For the maturity myth says nothing about growth, it doesn't make allowance for it. It is based, in fact, on the idea that "maturity" is an unchanging state, a static condition that can be achieved simply by following the societal rules.

When the individual begins to question the myth he finds himself in crisis. Having lived according to the myth for ten, twenty even thirty years, it is a shattering experience to discover that it is a false concept. Because, if the myth is wrong, then what is *right?* Not right for everybody, because by now these people have come to see that something that is "right" for everybody is going to end up being right for nobody; but what is right for the particular person who is asking the question? *What is right for me?*

The answer to that question can be found. You can discover what is right for *you.* But in seeking the answer, it will help you to recognize that the promises of the maturity myth are not only false, but also imply certain negative results or assumptions. The following chart shows each of the five basic promises of the maturity myth, and opposite them we have set down these negative assumptions, corollaries, attached to each of the promises. The myth presents its promises as positive and good. And there is no doubt that they are alluring. Who wouldn't like to believe that he could be home safe by following a few basic rules? Who doesn't want emotional security? Who wouldn't like to be more stable, to manage the future? And except for the confirmed Casanovas among us, who doesn't want to feel sexually "safe"?

THE MATURITY MYTH

Positive Promises	Negative Corollaries
1. You will be home safe by the time you are in your forties.	1. There will be few or no new directions in your life.
2. You will be less restless and more stable.	2. You will be less curious about the world; your living patterns will be basically repetitive.
3. You will have emotional security.	3. Change will always be threatening, both in the outside world and within yourself.
4. Your sex life will be safe.	4. Your interest in sex will be waning.
5. Your future will be manageable.	5. The future will be without real challenge.

But each of these promises, if you believe them, implies certain negative assumptions. If you accept the idea that you can be home safe, you are also accepting the idea that there will be few or no new directions in your life. If you accept the idea that you will be less restless and more stable, you are also accepting the idea that you will be less curious about the world and that the patterns of your life will be basciallly repetitive (a guarantee of boredom). If you accept the idea that following the dictates of the maturity myth will bring you emotional security, then you are guaranteeing that change will always be threatening to you, not just changes in the external world that might jeopardize your career or the value of your home, but also the natural changes in your mate and in *yourself*. If you accept the idea that your sex life will be safe, you are also, perhaps unconsciously, submitting to the idea that

your sexual desires will be waning as you grow older,
that passion is solely an attribute of youth. If you accept the idea that the future is manageable, you are
also capitulating to the idea that the future is without
real challenge. You will be accepting, in fact, the idea
that maturity is a dead end.

The Forty-Year-Old Scrap Heap

Maturity, according to the myth, is a set condition,
a state of being. It automatically implies stasis. It puts
all its emphasis on being "grown-up" and leaves no
room for *growing*. Within this view of the world, one
comes *to* maturity, as a peach or an apple comes to
maturity, to ripeness. "Ripeness is all," says Shakespeare. But those words are the end of a sentence that
begins: "Men must endure their going hence, even as
their coming hither." Shakespeare is talking about
death. What happens to the apple after it comes to
maturity, after it ripens? It becomes overripe, and begins a swift decline into decay. It falls off the tree,
begins to rot and disintegrate. The same thing is true of
a flower. It reaches a peak of blossoming beauty, a fullness of color and form—and then it wilts, turns brown
and dies. This analogy is devastating when it is applied
to human development; yet it is exactly the analogy
that the maturity myth implies. It promises that we will
be grown-up once we settle down, and that after a few
years of consolidating our material position in the
world, we will be home safe at about the age of forty.
That is the peak, that is what all our efforts are supposed to be directed toward.

But what happens after that? According to the maturity myth, which ties the peak to a certain chronological age, there is only one thing that can happen: we
decline. We can chart the way the human life-span
looks in the context of the maturity myth.

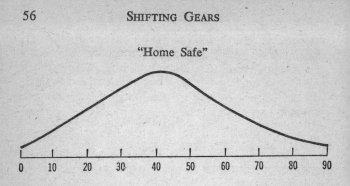

"Home Safe"

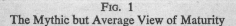

FIG. 1
The Mythic but Average View of Maturity

The base line in the above diagram represents chronological ages, while the curved line is the individual's development to the peak at which he becomes home safe and begins to decline.

A young person would tend to have a slightly different picture of maturity, distorting the chronological base line in favor of his youth, as shown in Fig. 2.

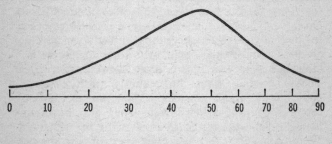

FIG. 2

To an older person, the chronological distortion might work in the opposite direction:

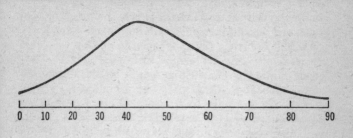

FIG. 3

What happens to you as a person when you believe that maturity is a static condition? What happens when you direct all your energies to becoming home safe by the time you reach your forties? By the time you actually reach that chronological age, you will assume that what you have achieved is all you can expect to achieve. This is it—this is the sum of what being mature means. The rewards that can be gained from the external goals can now be tallied. If your score is high, if you've met most of the standards you've set for yourself, you may for a while feel quite satisfied. On the other hand, sooner or later it is likely to occur to you that you have another thirty or forty years of life ahead of you. If this is *it,* then what about the remaining half of your life? Is it all downhill from here? That's certainly what the maturity myth suggests. Some people accept this implication just as they accepted the myth to begin with. They may be disappointed, but they resign themselves to the situation. "Well, that's life," they sigh, taking comfort in the old adage. "Asi es la vida," as they say in Spanish, with a shrug of the shoulders. Accepting what is—that's a sign of being mature, isn't it?

Other people may fight against the implication that everything is downhill from here. There are sensible and practical steps that can be taken toward a new understanding of maturity, of a creative maturity that not only permits continuing growth but is dedicated to it, and we will be detailing those steps in later chapters. Unfortunately, many people don't stop to think, to reexamine and reorganize their lives step by step; panicked by the thought that there's no place to go but down, unable to face up to the fact that they have been living according to a false myth, they dash off as fast as they can go in any direction that seems to hold out hope of salvation. One way such people often try to restore a sense of forward motion is to have an extra-marital affair; divorce and a "new life" with another partner may come next. In some cases, divorce may indeed be a sensible step to take after making a careful and rational exploration of other alternatives, but it may be far more fruitful to build that new life with the same partner. But to build a new life with the same partner requires learning how to grow again, actively, and that may take time. Those who are looking for an instant remedy aren't going to take the time. Instead of learning to grow, instead of trying to achieve a new creative maturity for themselves, they simply change the external circumstances. And that may help for a while, but it will leave them with the same problem: a false view of maturity and one's potential for growth throughout the human life cycle.

The situation is probably most disturbing to those who haven't successfully achieved the external goals dictated by the maturity myth. They are likely to despair of ever "making it." Assuming that there are no new avenues to explore, they simply stop trying. If you haven't made it by forty-five, after all, there's surely no chance of making it now! Such people accept defeat, slumping down in their chairs in front of the TV and give up on the rest of their lives.

The tendency to resignation or defeat is encouraged by false ideas about what happens to our physical, mental and sexual vitality from the forties on. Our society has begun to get away from the belief that pot bellies,

sagging jowls, flabby skin, and physical inertia naturally and inevitably come with age—and maturity. Physical fitness exercises of one sort of another have
gained a new popularity in recent years; we don't always undertake them for the right reasons, but at least
we are moving in the right direction. Even so, we
haven't got rid of the idea that a degree of mental
capacity is steadily lost as we age. The fact is, according
to recent research, that physical exercise can actually
improve our mental capacities. Doctors are now finding
that many diminishing capacities are simply caused by
disuse, rather than an inevitable and fixed biological
decline, and that these capacities, even those of our
brain, can be appreciably modified by outside means
throughout life. Although the number of neurons—
brain cells—each person has is set at birth, the quantity
of certain other cells in the brain *increases* as it
matures, and continues to increase with experience
and new skills we acquire. Stimulation, activity and increased blood flow can all help our brains to function
better. In other words, if you think your brain is too
old and slow for you to learn anything new or take on a
new career, you are simply wrong. The old dog is very
definitely capable of new tricks, if he is willing to make
the effort to learn them.

Similarly, many of us accept, consciously or unconsciously, the idea that our sexual desire and capacity
will steadily wane; this negative corollary of the maturity myth becomes in fact a self-fulfilling prophecy.
Since we believe it, it becomes true. And if we don't
find it happening, we think there must be something
wrong with us, as though there were something wrong
with having a strong sexual impulse after forty. In a
recent *New York Times Magazine* article concerning
the reaction of blue-collar wives to women's liberation,
one woman described what had happened to her sex
life since she had taken a job (over her husband's
objections). After she had been working for some
months, her husband decided that with the money she

was bringing in, he could work shorter hours as a taxi driver. And then, for the first time in many years, she and her husband began to have sexual relations again on a regular basis. Partially this was due to the fact that the husband wasn't exhausted from his work all the time. But there was another aspect as well. The woman quoted her husband as follows: "You know, Rose, we were brought up in ignorance even if we did manage to have four kids. This Masters-Johnson thing you're telling me about—I thought a wife would think her husband was a dirty old man if he kept trying to take her to bed when they were fifty years old."

Masters and Johnson have in fact concluded that, given favorable physical and emotional conditions, sexual capacity may frequently continue beyond the age of eighty. It is time for us to understand that sex does not have to diminish with age but can in fact get better as it becomes a more fully perfected response. And the more the response is used, the more it can be perfected. With age, sexual activity, so far as frequency is concerned, may not be what it was at twenty, but it should be recognized that our capacity for achieving sexual fulfillment *increases* with experience, and is closely related to our feelings about ourselves and others.

The false ideas about physical, mental and sexual vitality in the older person are not only destructive in themselves, but they contribute to the myth that maturity is a condition that does not allow further growth. Nothing can be more destructive to the human spirit and psyche than the idea that there are no more goals, that the process of growing and living is on the downswing. But it is difficult to revive a sense of adventure when for twenty years you have been systematically suppressing any impulsive response to newness, and the itch to explore other fields. After all, you were told that kind of restlessness was immature. And so you've settled down with a vengeance, smothering your creativity in order to conform to the dictates of the myth. You might as well accept it, you tell yourself, you've had it. It's too late to try anything new at your age. And so you needlessly relegate yourself to the forty-year-old scrap heap. That, all too often, is the ultimate result of a belief in the maturity myth.

Open Maturity

"Do you know what is really wrong with most middle-aged people?" a young lawyer said to us in an interview. "The trouble is that they *think* they are middle-aged, that life has passed them by, that they are not in the mainstream of life anymore." Tony went on to say, "For me, being in the mainstream means you are still growing, and that should never stop. For me, middle-aged is sixty-five or over, *if* you have to call it that. From age thirty, and I'll be there in two days, to age sixty-five is really Middle Youth."

You may feel, from your own experience, that this young man is being overly optimistic. We do not agree. He is on the right track, for he has successfully skirted the detour that we call the maturity myth. That detour inevitably leads to a dead end. Once you have accepted it, and millions of young people are still doing it, your outlook is inevitably going to be pessimistic about your potential for growth throughout your lifespan. But the myth is only myth—it is untrue. The promises of the maturity myth are at odds with reality. So are the negative corollaries that the promises imply. To believe that you can be home safe at forty is to create an inevitable crisis for yourself.

In her book, *The Sense of Self*, Louise Stringer says: "The central and unchanging goal of the mature and integrated self is to chart its own course, to choose its own direction." We would go beyond this to say that maturity itself is not a *goal* but a *process* of continuing discovery and growth. Crises come to all of us at one time or another, whether they be the normal, internally sparked crises that signal a new stage of development, or whether they are forced upon us by outside circumstances. But the person who is able to deal most successfully with crisis is the one who is capable of creative growth. The first axiom of life is growth, and when growth is thwarted, or diverted into mere replication of the past, things inevitably go wrong. We become self-destructive or succumb to despair. We die even while we still live. Or we flail about in a state of unending crisis.

One woman of forty-two whom we interviewed put it this way: "If you define maturity as being fully developed, as a peak that you reach and then drop off from, then thank God I will never be mature in that sense. Maturity for me is learning how to develop and *use* all my capacities—it's not reaching any particular goal. Lord knows, I've had plenty of them, and they change and they will continue to change. Maturity for me is process, the process of becoming more of myself and continually growing."

If we take what is a reality for an increasing number of people instead of the myth as our guideline for maturity then we can change those curves on the maturity chart (see Fig. 4) to the following:

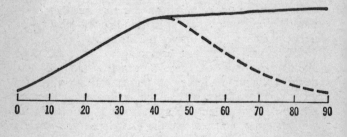

FIG. 4

Instead of following the dotted line, maturity for us can mean reaching a plateau on which we find continuing fulfillment.

Or it can, if we learn the process of shifting gears and if we look forward to psychological change and enrichment, become a time for continuing growth in many dimensions and reaching successive heightened plateaus of fulfillment, as shown in Fig. 5.

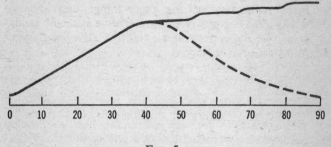

FIG. 5
Plateaus of Continuing Growth

Maturity is not a dead end or a preparation for death—it should be an open road and a preparation for living. It is learning how to live as an open self, open to life, open to others, open to new experience. We must turn our backs on the illusory promises of the maturity myth, for the garden path they lead us down ends in a "slough of despond." Instead, we must devise a *life strategy* based on our real need for continuing growth, and an understanding of how those needs change in the course of the life cycle.

If you are young, just beginning to make decisions about your adulthood, then you can start from scratch, devising your life strategy so that it will allow you to grow and to change without being distracted by false promises or imaginary peaks. If on the other hand, you are older, you can use the experience you already have to develop a life strategy that will rescue you from the illusions of the maturity myth and help you to grow in new dimensions. For it is never too late— or too early—to learn to shift gears.

CHAPTER FOUR

Shifting Gears

The Psychic Phases of Adulthood

Among all the living things of earth, human beings alone have the ability to *consciously shape* the time that lies between the biological markers of birth and death. We alone have the ability to decide not only *what* we will make of our lives, but to *change our minds* about what we will make of them. This ability is affected, of course, by the circumstances in which we find ourselves. We can't ignore the effect of the outer world on our inner selves—but neither can we afford to let the external world impose on us a life-style or life goals that violate our internal needs.

The maturity myth tells us that we should plan our lives according to externals, that the central task and the central meaning of adulthood is to define ourselves in terms of society, through career, marriage and the accumulation of possessions. Certainly, this is *one* aspect of adulthood; we all have a need to seek our niche in society, to "join the tribe" as Dr. Daniel Levinson of Yale has put it. One reason for the power of the maturity myth, in fact, is that it draws upon our natural drive to come to terms with the external world. But each of us also has an internal world that is of profound importance to our hopes for self-fulfillment. And that internal world is not a static "given" that will be with us always: it is changing constantly, usually in subtle ways, but sometimes dramatically. In the course of his or her life, each individual passes through a variety of *psychic phases*.

The existence of these psychic phases has been recognized for more than two thousand years in the religions and philosophies of the East; there they are looked upon as an expected and normal part of adulthood. But our culture does not prepare us for this normal experience of life. In our society only the psychic need to define ourselves in terms of the external world is fully recognized. The fulfillment of that need alone is supposed to bring us home safe. But in fact there are two other primary psychic needs that are of equal significance in achieving our full potential as individuals.

First, there is the need for *self-exploration*. At varying points in our lives, each of us will experience a need to develop and extend our interior selves. This need was described to us by Richard T., who had spent twenty years working in a high-pressure profession. Recently, he gave up his well-paid position with a Chicago firm to become the editor of a small-town weekly newspaper in downstate Illinois. He pointed out that although he'd had a lot of responsibility in his previous career, with more than twenty people working directly under him, he had always somehow felt anonymous. "Anybody with a certain amount of brains and experience could have done it," he said. "I was paid a lot more than the office manager of my department, for instance, but I was just as much a cog in the wheel as he was." His new life, though, gave him an entirely different feeling: "This little paper is *me*," he said. "But even more important, now I have time to read, to tune in on myself, and to discover what kind of people my wife and children are. They'd practically become strangers to me in the old job."

On the other hand, we interviewed a woman who had graduated from college with a degree in fine arts but had spent the first twenty years of her adulthood as a wife and mother. When her youngest child became

a teen-ager, she began to free-lance as an interior dec-
orator. The first jobs she got were through friends, but
within two years she had a full-fledged business, with
an office and several assistants. In her case, the means
for exploring and extending herself was to put to use
the capacities she had neglected during the first phase
of her adulthood, and to *take up* a high-pressure career.
But her reason for joining the rat race was the same as
Richard's had been for leaving it—to explore her capacities in a new way and to extend her sense of herself
as a person. There is no one way to explore oneself, no
one means to extension of the self: it all depends on
what you were doing previously, on what capacities have
already been explored by you, and on which ones have
been neglected. Richard, in order to explore himself,
shifted into low gear; this woman shifted into high
gear. The means by which the shift was accomplished
were different, but the goal was the same and was in-
spired by the same need: to explore another aspect of
the self.

Many people, at one point or another in their lives,
find that personal fulfillment comes through being involved with *something larger than themselves*. This is
the second of the psychic needs we have ignored in
our society. A former army major whom we interviewed expressed it this way: "I spent twenty years in
the army. I fought in France in World War II and I
served at command headquarters in Korea. I wasn't
romantic about what I was doing, and I don't think
I'm any more patriotic than the next guy—it was a job
I thought was valuable at the time and that I happened to be good at. But I reached a point where I
needed to do something different. I guess I felt that I
had helped to keep the world from becoming worse
than it was, but I wanted to do something actively constructive for a change. I had several opportunities to
go into business, but that just wasn't the answer for me."
The major retired from the army, returned to college
to get a master's degree in history, and has now been

teaching for ten years at a southern junior college. "Most of these kids really care," he said. "They *want* to learn, and that's exciting, it gives me something bigger than just earning a living to focus on. It makes me feel better about myself."

To define ourselves in terms of the society we live in; to explore our particular inner capabilities; to give ourselves to something larger than we are—these three separate psychic needs are always present in each of us simultaneously, but in varying degrees. During different phases of our adult experience, we may find that one or another of the three predominates and becomes the central psychic need. Which of the three will predominate during any given phase is determined not by age, but by individual needs, experience, abilities and capacity for growth. For instance, while many of the Peace Corps volunteers have been young people in their early twenties, there have also been many in their thirties and forties, and even some in their sixties; their need to be involved in something larger than themselves—just as with young people—was an expression of the psychic phase they were in, not of age or of conformity to societal rules.

Yet many people, perhaps most, fail to adjust to their changing psychic phases; they allow the pattern of their lives to be determined by age and by societal expectation. Our society, by way of the maturity myth, tells us that we will be regarded as strange or a failure if we don't get married and choose a career by our mid-twenties. If you want to be successful and happy, we are instructed, then you'd better strive to become like mommy and daddy as quickly as possible. "Shape up," we say to our children. "If you want to be treated like a grown-up, you'd better behave like one." And the implication is that only one proper psychic phase exists for a grown-up: the phase in which you define yourself in terms of externals. Our culture in fact ignores the existence of the other phases altogether.

But this denial of the other psychic phases can only

lead to a psychological crisis in the long run. What if you don't happen to be in the external phase during the first years of adulthood? If you go against your instincts and try to conform to what society says you ought to be feeling at that point, then you are all too likely to find yourself married to someone just for the sake of being married and pursuing a career that brings you little or no fulfillment. From the outside, you will appear to be grown-up, but on the inside, in your private self, you will be suffering from the fact that your psychic phase is out of sync with the life you are leading. Eventual disillusionment with your career or marriage, or with both, can easily follow. What's more, you will have short-circuited your natural psychic development, and made it much more difficult for yourself to continue growing as a person.

The Suspended Years

For the majority of people in our society, of course, the phase of external self-definition *does* coincide with the first decade or two of adulthood. That is, as we have noted before, one reason for the appeal of the maturity myth: the myth seems perfectly in accord with the reality of our psychic phase. In this situation, the denial of the other psychic phases may seem unimportant. After all, if Jim's life-style and his internal phase are synchronized with one another, he's going to feel fulfilled. The only problem is that Jim thinks this is the only phase that exists; he is totally unprepared for any changes within himself.

Most of us, at one time or another during the first fifteen or twenty years of adulthood, find ourselves saying, "I wish I had time to . . ."; we may wish we had time to paint, or time to raise roses, or time to read, or simply time to see the world. Since we make or hear such complaints so frequently, they may seem rather superficial and not really important. But they are a true reflection of our unfulfilled potentials, of our other psychic needs. If Jim concentrates exclusively on the external world, shunting aside those aspects of his personality that don't fit in with his immediate goals, he will be turning the first two decades of his adulthood into *suspended years*.

The aspects of himself that Jim represses or neglects are going to be needed at some point in the future, when he finds himself in a new psychic phase. We can illustrate what happens with a simple mechanical example. Suppose that you are going to be living in Europe for two years and don't want to take your car with you or sell it. If you simply let it sit in a garage for all that time, a good deal of rust and decay will set in and by the time you return you will have a major repair job on your hands to get it functioning properly. But if you are smart, you'll arrange with a friend to take it out and drive it a few miles every two or three weeks, to keep it in good running order. The same is true with our unused psychic potentials. It isn't necessary to give them a great deal of attention, but we should be aware that they do have future importance for us and give them occasional exercise.

If you find yourself saying, "I wish I had time to . . ."—make time; it doesn't have to be a lot of time, even a little will help. Then, later, when you find yourself entering a new phase of growth, it will be much easier to shift gears: you'll have a better idea of what your potentials are and of their relative importance to you. The less you keep in touch with your inner self, the more difficult it will be to shift into another phase. When we completely neglect those aspects of ourselves that don't relate to our immediate goals, when we leave them in suspension year after year, we are simply creating a possible future psychological crisis for ourselves.

Shifting gears from one psychic phase into another ought not to be a frightening prospect but a cause for hope. Not only is it a perfectly normal part of life, but an affirmation of what makes us unique among living creatures: the ability to shape our lives and to change our minds about how we will shape them. It only seems frightening because our culture has not prepared us for it, and because we make matters worse by allowing the early years of adulthood to become suspended years. For the individual who has swallowed the maturity myth whole, and has neglected all aspects of his personality that don't conform to the myth, the transition between one phase and another is bound to be disturbing. To get a divorce, to lose one's job—these are crises we can readily recognize. Of course we're disturbed! Who wouldn't be? But simply to feel that something is "missing," to discover that one isn't home safe after all, to suffer from an acute sense of loss when we have apparently gained all the things promised us by the maturity myth—that is a crisis which leaves most of us floundering and afraid.

And it is at this point that an understanding of the *process* of shifting gears becomes essential. The need to shift gears may also be brought on, of course, by outside events. In our crisis culture the ability to shift gears becomes doubly important: two corporations merge, a factory shuts down, a defense contract is canceled, and suddenly our lives are drastically altered. Few of us can imagine beforehand what it would be like to be told that our job of twenty years no longer exists, or that our home is to be torn down to make way for a new turnpike. Yet such things happen every day. And if we understand how the process of shifting gears works, we are at least one step ahead of the game. Whether the need to shift gears is brought on by a natural change in our psychic phase, or is imposed upon us by the random movement of the crisis culture, the *process* is the same.

Shifting Gears—The Process

The process of shifting gears can take place on two different levels. In one case, it takes place in response to the kind of crisis that challenges our assumptive state, the internal and external givens of our lives. The transition between one phase of adulthood and another can present such a crisis—so can marriage, the birth of a child, divorce, a change of job, or the death of a loved one. But, in other cases, the shifting of gears doesn't require us to move on to a new assumptive state, but simply to rearrange the components of the existing one. It is the difference between moving from one house to another and simply redecorating the one we have.

When we shift gears without changing our assumptive state, it is often possible to accomplish the change without giving it much conscious attention. An example of such a shift would be the forming of a new friendship; we meet someone, we like him, we get to know him. His friendship will undoubtedly cause us to grow and to change in a variety of subtle ways. But the process, in this case, is gradual, a slow enfolding of the new relationship into the pattern of our lives. On the other hand if we fall in love with someone, and are already married or involved in a long-standing love relationship, the process of shifting gears may not be at all easy, and is likely to present a crisis that can be resolved only by changing our assumptive state.

In order to make the process absolutely clear, we would like to detail the steps involved in terms of an actual case history. Recently, while attending a workshop at a small family-type resort in the mountains, we met Tom, a congenial and obviously happy man in his late forties. When we first met him, it was in his capacity as bartender at the resort, but it soon became clear that this was just one aspect of his life. He told us how he and his attractive blond wife, who joined in the conversation with us, had happened to get involved with the running of the lodge.

"Five or six years ago," he said, "I was buried in my business in New York City. I'd owned a construction company for fifteen years, and I'd enjoyed it up until about that time. We came up here to visit friends for a weekend. It was a totally different lifestyle—easy

pace, warm people. And it made me think about my
own situation back in the city. There was a click inside
and I began asking questions. Business was great, we
had a nice apartment in the city, everything you could
ask for, it seemed. But for a while I'd had a vague feeling of dissatisfaction, of pressure.

"I took a hard look, and I began to realize that I
wasn't working for myself. It was always a hassle with
people and time. The demands were enormous, and I
wasn't getting much fun out of it anymore. I began
asking myself how much life energy I was putting out
to make a dollar. How much was it costing out of my
gut? And the answer I came up with was that it was
costing me a dollar and a quarter worth of energy for
each buck I was making. This was a losing situation
in terms of *living,* and right then I decided to do something about it. We've all got to earn money, but if it's
costing us more than we're getting back, is it worth it?
Joan agreed and we began to search for a house up
here in this part of the country."

Tom and Joan found the house they wanted. It cost
more than they thought they really should spend, considering the change they were going to make. But Joan
said she would go back to work as a hair stylist to
help out during the transition. "So we bought the house
and moved. I continued with my business in New
York, commuting back and forth. But all the while
I was looking for a buyer for my business and planning how I could move up here full time and for good.
I thought I could work in house construction in our
new area, and we'd make it OK. So, two years later,
I sold the company and moved out of New York for
keeps. Joan did support us for a while, but gradually I
got enough business to make a go of it alone.

"Then about six months later I met Carl, who owns
this lodge. We all became good friends. One day, he
asked Joan and me to take over here for a weekend so
they could make a trip. We agreed; it was rough but we
enjoyed running the show and meeting the people who

were staying here. I got pretty good at making drinks, and I enjoyed listening to the guests' stories and telling my own. When Carl came back, he asked us to become partners—we would handle the bar and drinks, help in the kitchen, while they took care of the food and general management. Now Carl and I are building houses on some property he has—I handle the construction. We don't make much money, but we travel during the winter, and we all have great times working together—there are children in both families, and they all pitch in. Now I feel as though I'm putting out seventy-five cents for each dollar I earn." Tom paused for a moment, then added, "I'm glad I made the move. And glad I woke up soon enough to make it possible. Joan and I are really happy with the results."

Tom's story is a good example of the whole process of shifting gears. The first step in that process is *awareness*. For Tom, as for most of us, that awareness developed gradually. Many of us may feel the vague kind of discontent that Tom speaks of. But we tend to push those feelings back down, to avoid recognizing their implications for us. When our assumptive state is challenged, the first impulse is to draw our psychic wagons into a circle as quickly as possible, in order to repel the attack. This impulse is particularly strong if we have put our faith in the maturity myth: we were told that this passage through the mountains was the safest path possible, and the last thing we expect is to be ambushed, especially by our own growing needs. Many people succeed in repelling the attack, but in the process they kill their potential for growth. In the long run they will either be attacked again or will succumb to the boredom and sense of defeat that come with stagnation.

In Tom's case awareness was triggered by his trip upstate to visit friends, by his feeling that these people had a more fulfilling and wholesome life than he did. They had more time to be with their children, family and friends. The sign that awareness has been achieved is the asking of conscious questions. And the asking of these questions in a full conscious way leads to the second step in the process: *evaluation*. Tom began asking himself how much life energy he was expending to earn a dollar. He considered the small amount of time he was able to spend with his family and the kind of life his children led in the city. He began asking about his relationships with other people, relationships that were often dictated by his business. "The business world really began to get to me, the more I thought about it," he told us. "I realized that I didn't like what was going on, everybody cutting costs, cutting quality, cheating, being greedy—and I realized I might end up like that, too. There was no way around it if I was going to compete successfully."

During the evaluative stage of the process, there is a tendency for some people to get bogged down in assigning blame for the situation they are in. Regret and recriminations, whether against ourselves or others, often swamp us with an overall feeling of "if only I had. . . ." At this point it is vital to realize that nothing is wasted in your life. The feeling of waste is particularly likely to afflict those who are getting a divorce, or have spent years preparing for a profession that they now feel is unsuited to their needs. But it also affects those who have never really found a direction they liked or felt they wanted to be committed to.

The idea that we have wasted the best years of our lives is usually a false one. During the supposedly wasted years you have been gathering experience and understanding, both of yourself and the world around you. Without that experience and understanding, it is entirely possible that you would not have arrived at the point of self-awareness you have now reached. You can't change the past, anyway, but you *can* change the future. To spend time and energy lamenting the past is to waste the present and the future. Move forward, instead, to the third step, which is *exploration*.

Tom told us that in exploring what he could do to

change his life, he considered a number of alternatives. There was the possibility of getting out of the construction business and taking a different kind of job in the city. His father had been a high-school physics teacher, and Tom thought about going back to college and becoming a teacher himself. But he decided that he liked construction work in itself, he just didn't like the kind of situation he had to do business in. He didn't want to change his work, he wanted to change his life-style.

In exploring the alternatives open to you, short-term goals have to be weighed against long-term goals. Tom wanted to get out of the business situation he was in, and out of the city. That was his primary goal, it might seem. But in the long run, what he wanted was a new way of life for himself and his family. As it turned out, the achievement of this long-term goal meant that in the short term he would continue to work in the city in the same business.

The steps of evaluation and exploration are both devoted, to a large extent, to defining the priorities in one's life. And to define priorities means to discover what is essential to the individual's sense of fulfillment at that point in his life and what is less essential or nonessential. What seems essential at one point in your life may seem less essential or even nonessential at another point, during a different psychic phase. But how do you decide what is essential?

The simplest way to determine an answer to this question is to make a written list of the activities and concerns that now occupy your time in a given week or month, and add to it the alternative options that you would like to explore. The time you spend or would like to spend on each of these elements of your life can be written in the margin. Probably, the time totals will add up to more hours than there are in the week or month. Start rearranging the list you have made, putting the things you would like to spend most time on at the top, changing the time notations as you go.

It may take several days to juggle the list; you'll find that you keep changing your mind, and it is only when you've stopped changing your mind that the list can be regarded as finished—at least in regard to this point in your life.

Although this method of determining your priorities has been derived from the business management techniques of such consultants as Alan Lakein, we don't advise carrying it to the point of programming yourself like a computer. You aren't trying to become more *efficient* but rather to determine the elements of your life that are most *fulfilling*. Completing the list will make you aware of your preferences and desires. The point in making such a list is to discover which activities and concerns are less essential and can be disposed of or drastically cut back.

A modification of this technique can be used, as Tom used it, to discover how much life energy you are putting into each dollar you earn. Tom found that he was putting out $1.25 of life energy for each dollar he was earning, and he decided that was too much. He decided he would rather earn less money and have more life energy to put into other areas of his life, into his relationship with his family and into his own self-fulfillment. Having made that decision, he was ready to take another step in the process.

For Tom the next step was *experimentation* with new modes. He and his wife found a house they liked in the country, bought it and moved the family into it. However, Tom kept the apartment in the city and for two years commuted back and forth, while continuing to run his city business. This gave him, and his family, a chance to try out the new pattern. Would it really have the results they were hoping for? Would the children like it as much in the country as they thought? Would it be possible to get a new construction business going in the area of their new home? During this period, Tom also had a chance to establish contacts in the new community, including several people who were able to show him the ropes concerning the local construction situation.

Once he had satisfied himself that the move could be made with a reasonable chance of success, and had established a foothold in the business community of the new area, Tom was ready to take the step of *making the decision*. He decided to sell his business in New York and to live and work permanently in the country. The next step was to *take action*. Tom found a buyer for his New York business, and moved out of the city apartment. This action involved another step: *letting go*. Tom was letting go of the business he had owned for fifteen years; he was letting go of the income from that business. The family as a whole was letting go of the apartment that had been their home for many years, in which the children had lived from infancy; they were letting go, to a large extent, of their city friendships. There would be things and activities and people they would miss, but there was also much to be gained in terms of ongoing fulfillment. Tom had now made the final commitment to change. He had in fact completed shifting gears.

The process of shifting gears is a series of interrelated steps. Not every individual will take the steps in the same order Tom did, however. His pattern is perhaps the usual one, but that doesn't mean it is the only pattern or the best one for everyone. For example, Ellen, a widow in her forties, followed a very different pattern that was uniquely suited to her needs. When her husband died suddenly of a heart attack, she found her life without shape or meaning. She was aware of a terrible vacuum in her life and she realized that now she would have to make a new life for herself; after achieving awareness, she decided that in order to find out where she was going she would have to cut herself off completely from the associations and activities that had formed her married life. She called all her old friends, one by one, and told them that they would not be hearing from her for a while—she did not know how long. She loved these people dearly, they had been part of her life for years, but she felt that in order to create a new life for herself it was necessary to be completely on her own, with only her own *self* to fall back on. Thus she took the step of letting go before moving on to evaluation and exploration of her new situation. She didn't contact her old friends again for over a year until she had completed the process of shifting gears, by which time she had a job and had made a number of new friends, and had achieved a new sense of self and competency in her life. Ellen's case is probably an exception—but she was able to go back to her old connections as a renewed and confident self.

Tom and Ellen illustrate the way in which we can use the process of shifting gears in making a decision for some major life change. But there is another way in which we can shift gears. This occurs in the way we can use events in our everyday life and personal relationships for inner growth. Because we meet change in these areas far more often than we make major life decisions like Tom and Ellen's, this is an equally important area for examining how to shift gears. Unfortunately, many of us react to changes in our personal relationships and everyday life with a closed attitude. We resist and stand pat with a closed mind. The result is that some of us stay in first gear forever, and others spend a whole lifetime in neutral, avoiding change and blocking their own potential for growth and a full engagement with life. Yet if we are willing to be open and take the effort to shift gears, we have the opportunity every day to see life anew, and to look at it with a new attitude. It is in this encounter and meeting with change every day that we have our richest opportunities for personal growth.

Nowhere is this better exemplified than in our own families in the confrontation between the two generations, parent and child. Let us take a particular case of a father and son. The father discovers his son is smoking pot. The father yells, prohibits, stands on his authority, and in the process rejects his son along with the behavior he is incensed about. The son yells back screaming that his father drinks too much, and that alcohol is more sinister, debilitating and destructive than pot. A battle ensues, the father calling his son an addict. They are locked in combat, whether it is physical or verbal, neither able to see the situation clearly.

What has happened is that the son's behavior in smoking pot has zeroed in on something in the father's life he never solved—his own drinking problem and what impels him to do it. Consequently neither one can face the issue at hand clearly. Both the father and the son have a legitimate fear for the safety of the other, yet their emotions have blinded them to any constructive understanding of their own behavior.

This confrontation has ended destructively, neither changing, both misunderstood: the son retreating in fury and hurt, the father furious and desperately holding his ground—in part out of conviction, in part out of fear of facing the problem he never solved. His concern for his son's behavior is real, but he is blocked from dealing with it because of his unwillingness to confront himself. In this case, the father has shifted gears into reverse, losing ground and inhibiting growth. Even if the father had no drinking problem, the issue of smoking pot might become an occasion for confrontation. However, this particular father is no different from many parents who fall apart when their children start anything new that is strange and seemingly incomprehensible to them: whether it is a question of wearing long hair or dirty clothes, sexual behavior and attitudes, leaving school or making some decisions for themselves. Something in the parents' own past that they never solved blocks them from understanding the dynamics of the problem.

The occasion need not be the contemporary changes we see in our children's behavior. It need not be an issue as incendiary as addiction (either to drinking or smoking pot). *Any* developmental change in the child which occasions different behavior may touch off a parent's insecurities and feelings of deprivation. Even the *normal* maturation and development of the sexual identity of the child frequently elicits resentment in the parent and becomes an area of conflict and argument. In this case, the parent, as Dr. E. James Anthony points out, ". . . may be reacting to a deep dissatisfaction with his own sexual lot in life and envious that his child is getting something while he is being deprived." Whether it is something as simple as the length of a daughter's skirt or a son's hair or something as complicated as the child's desire for increasing autonomy, each confrontation with our children, who come into and grow up in a different world from the one we knew, forces us to face things we have ducked all our life. Yet each confrontation can become an occasion for growth for both parent and child.

We can use these opportunities in a positive rather than a destructive way for shifting gears into personal growth, facing our problems and improving our closest relationships. Let us use the father and son's case as an illustration. In this kind of personal confrontation, all the steps of shifting gears *could* be applied. With the father and son, both experienced a painful *awareness* of their differences, both in their attitudes toward each other's behavior—the father's drinking, the son's smoking pot—and of the behavior itself. If both are open, they can explore their reasons, as well as their rationalizations for smoking or drinking. They can each *evaluate* what it does for them, why they think they need it, and what makes them do it. They can be open to listening to the evaluation of the other: the father to his son's evaluation of drinking in general, and the father's drinking in particular; the son to his father's evaluation of smoking pot in general and the dangers he thinks it brings for his son in particular. Each one can *explore* the reasons for his behavior, his

beliefs, his values, his weaknesses, fears, desires and
motivations. They can explore new ways of looking at
the whole thing, new ways of understanding drinking
or smoking in general, new ways of understanding
themselves and new ways of acting. They could *experiment* with these, experiment with developing a
new attitude and openness to exploring what they are
doing and why. And then they can make a *decision*
and *take action*—even if that decision and action is
nothing more than keeping their lines of communication open so that they can continue to talk, show their
concern for each other, and explore their feelings. If
they make this effort, both of them will have shifted
gears onto a new plane of understanding of their mutual problems. And that is self-growth, that is having a
relationship. It may not provide pat answers, or easy
solutions—but it will be a big step in their lives together and in their relationship. Taking the action of
talking openly with each other is a commitment to
their relationship, to their caring and concern for each
other. It means *letting go* of old attitudes and fears for
the father, and the shaping of new attitudes and insights for the son. Even the first step of awareness of
their behavior and their need to help each other
means letting go of former assumptions and closed
attitudes in facing the problem and their inner selves in
relation to it. There are no easy solutions to any relationship problem, but the rewards more than compensate for the difficulty and impasses this process
may bring. Shifting gears onto a new plane of understanding between them, from which positive actions
and feelings can result, is a reaffirmation of self and
their relationship.

It is in this way that our personal relationships provide opportunities for personal change, deepening our
understanding of ourselves, reinforcing our competence and our belief in our relatedness to life and
others.

Shifting Gears—The Application

- Awareness
- Evaluation
- Exploration
- Experimentation
- Decision
- Commitment to Action
- Letting Go

These are the steps in the process of shifting gears. But, just as the steps can be taken in different order by different people, they also have another kind of flexibility built into them. To some people, for instance, Tom's story may sound too good to be true, or our suggestion about the father and son may seem too difficult. Does such change seem impossible for most of us to achieve? Or unrealistic? How can you be sure it will work for yourself? The answer, of course, is that you can't be sure it will work the *first time through,* nor may it work easily or perfectly at any time. The importance of moving step by step, of taking your time, is that it gives you a chance to backtrack and take a different approach. The order in which you take the steps does not matter, but taking them one at a time does.

It's possible that, at any point in the process, the new direction you're moving in may prove to be unfruitful. A plan may be based on false premises, on presumptions rather than on carefully examined facts, on goals or expectations that are unrealistic, or beyond our capacity, or insufficiently challenging. If so, it's time to start the process over again, to take these limitations into account, and to reevaluate, explore and experiment on a new plan of possible action.

The only step in the process that cannot be taken at a different point by different people is *awareness:* this is of necessity the first step, the basic catalyst that sets the entire process in motion. It is also a difficult step. Most of us know when we are unhappy—but we may not know the cause. You know things are not right, you are not finding satisfaction or fulfillment in your life situation: you are bored with your job, your husband seems endlessly the same, you know you have conquered all the challenges your present job has to offer, you have lost interest in your wife, your squabbles with the children continue nonstop from sunup to sundown. Suddenly your favorite foods taste like sawdust, you no longer have any enthusiasm for your usual leisure-time activities, you feel about as sexy as yesterday's mashed potatoes. And this feeling of lifelessness may be followed by a sense of anxiety, fear and rage at your inability to do anything about the way you are feeling.

At this point, for most of us, rationalization takes over, and we pull our psychic wagons into a defensive posture. We blame our bosses or our mates for our unhappiness and dissatisfaction; we blame society, politics, religion, we blame anything we can find including the pollution in the air. And so, carrying around our own private grudge bags—against everything and everybody—we are so weighted down we can't possibly take a step in any direction. To complicate our situation we tell ourselves that there is nothing we can do about the problem. We find a million ways to avoid taking the first step toward change. We tell ourselves we can't change things because our wives or our husbands or our children won't like it. We want a better job but explain that we can't take the time off from work even to *look* for it, that another boss would probably be just as bad, that we're too old to change. Young people today have their own kinds of rationalizations: How can I contribute anything when the world is rotten, nobody cares, and the establishment is corrupt? Why try when everything is already tainted?

So long as such rationalizations and defenses continue to rule us, we cannot achieve the kind of awareness that constitutes the first step of shifting gears. Sometimes, when we find the situation we're in completely intolerable, we do take action—but a kind of action that is based on our rationalizations rather than on the kind of self-awareness that leads to shifting gears. A classic example of this kind of self-defeating action is the man who feels unfulfilled by his wife and job and turns to a series of love affairs to renew himself. He may indeed experience a sense of newness for a time but it is usually based simply on changing the externals rather than on the shifting of gears that leads to internal change, and internal growth and development.

It is not until we have reached the level of awareness at which we recognize that internal and maybe external change are necessary to solve our problems that the process of shifting gears begins. To change only the externals will get us nowhere in the long run. To shift gears successfully, the external changes we make should be integrated with our internal development. Thus, the kind of awareness that leads to shifting gears involves four elements: (1) recognizing that we are unhappy with our current situation, (2) taking stock of the externals affecting our unhappiness, (3) facing up to our fear of change, and (4) a willingness to examine our own defenses and rationalizations.

In taking stock of how externals are affecting our situation, we should keep in mind the effects of the crisis culture. In facing up to our fear of change, both the impact of the maturity myth and the existence of the psychic phases of adulthood should be taken into consideration, and can help to put our questions into prospective. In the following chapters, we will be taking a closer look at a number of skills and techniques that can help us become aware of our own defenses and rationalizations, and skills that can help us to continue growing. But first, recognizing that most individuals will shift gears not just once but many times in the course of their adult lives, let us consider what this fact means in terms of planning for the future.

A Life Strategy

You can learn to shift gears at any age, at any point in your life. Once you understand the process, it can be applied over and over again throughout your life; the circumstances that make it necessary to shift gears are myriad and will constantly change, but the process itself remains the same. And from an understanding of the process you can develop a *life strategy*.

A life strategy is *not* a life plan. Life plans have been much discussed in recent years—ten-year plans, five-year plans, even one-year plans. But obviously, if you are talking about a period of only one year, you aren't talking about a *life* plan. Specific *goals* are vital to the psychological well-being of every individual; without them we flounder about in a kind of limbo. And to achieve our goals, we must plan. The crucial point, however, is that in the course of our adult lives we will have many different goals. Those goals will change, according to the psychic phase we happen to be in, and according to the effect upon our lives of the crisis culture. If we put all our eggs into one basket, planning our entire lives around one specific goal or set of goals, we will eventually find ourselves in trouble.

The maturity myth offers what is basically a life plan. Take this one particular route, it tells you, and you will arrive at your ultimate destination (fulfillment) without mishap. But life is not like that. In order to grow, in order to adapt to the changing needs of the self, a more flexible approach is necessary. You will want to take a certain road for a particular period of time, of course; but you should be prepared to follow the dictates of your natural curiosity, to turn off on a side road that looks interesting when you have become bored with the highway. Becoming bored with the highway is the equivalent of the first step in the process of shifting gears: awareness that the road you are following is no longer completely fulfilling. The step of experimentation is like turning off on a side road to see where it will take you. Such side roads often lead eventually into a new highway, a smooth road with more interesting scenery and new horizons. At this point you are likely to need an entirely new map, or plan, to show the way to your new goal.

We need plans to help us reach our particular goals. But as our goals change during the course of adulthood, so must our plans; occasionally the same plan can be used, with minor adjustments, to reach a different goal, but more often the plan will have to be changed. And that is why a life strategy is important. A life strategy incorporates the *change factor,* giving us an over-view that can absorb many different goals and the many different plans to reach those goals. A plan has specific ends and thus is *static;* a strategy can encompass several different possible ends and thus is *dynamic*. The chart below shows some of the differences between a life plan and a life strategy:

STATIC LIFE PLAN	DYNAMIC LIFE STRATEGY
(*Maturity Myth*)	(*Shifting Gears*)
follow	lead
external	internal
stagnation	growth
loss of self	discovery of self
anxiety	challenge

A static life plan, such as the one dictated by the maturity myth, insists that we *follow* rules set down by others in accordance with the *external* demands of society; a dynamic life strategy allows us to *lead* our own lives in accordance with our *internal* psychic needs. A static life plan creates a situation in which *stagnation* and *loss of self* become inevitable; a dynamic life strategy makes it possible for us to achieve an ongoing *growth* that will bring a continuing *discovery of self*. A static life plan means that change, whether in the external world or inside ourselves, will be a cause for *anxiety;* a dynamic life strategy makes it possible for us to accept the *challenge* created by change to further develop ourselves as individuals.

Let's look at the question in another way. Dr. Carl Edwards of Harvard University has delineated three types of adaptive social interaction—three basic ways in which the individual can deal with other people and the world around him. The first type is *cooperational*. It involves being receptive to and understanding the needs of others, with conflicts being resolved through personal sacrifice. The cooperational individual tends to give up his own needs or desires when a conflict arises; he is self-sacrificing. The second type is *instrumental*. The instrumental individual deals with situations by structuring them, relying upon lines of authority, similarity of interest and adherence to tradition. The third type is *analytic*. The analytic individual responds to people and situations by seeking to understand the underlying elements or clues, and by exploring potential courses of action aside from the usual or expected ones.

Obviously, there are times when it is necessary for us to make use of each of these responses. Personal sacrifice sometimes is the right course for us to take. At other times, the traditional answer may be the best one. But in developing a life strategy, the third kind of response takes on a special significance. When you are shifting gears, it is necessary to forget self-sacrifice and conformity for the moment, while trying to discover analytically what *new* modes of behavior and interaction are likely to be most fulfilling and growth-producing for you. Thus the strength of a life strategy lies in the fact that it recognizes the need to shift gears.

It cannot be based successfully on self-sacrifice or conformity.

Let's imagine four college friends, Bob and Susan and Joyce and Paul. Bob and Susan get married, right after graduation. Bob has accepted the maturity myth as gospel. He believes that he can work his way up in one of the big corporations and be home safe by the time he's forty-five. Basically, he's accepted a conformist approach to life. Susan had at one time thought of becoming a doctor, but she gives that idea up to marry Bob; she has adopted a basically self-sacrificing view of life, in which she defines her *self* largely in terms of Bob and their future children. Fifteen years later, Bob is bored with his job, its demands keep him from spending more than a few hours a week with his family, he is up to his neck in mortgages, and he sees no way out of his situation. His life plan, based on the maturity myth, has not brought him home safe, but he hasn't any idea how to begin to shift gears. At the same time, Susan, who has been greatly influenced by the women's liberation movement, comes to the conclusion that Bob is a male chauvinist pig and that she's wasted twenty years of her life.

Joyce and Paul also got married right after college. But they approached their future together from a very different point of view. Joyce knew exactly what she wanted in the short run. She wanted to be a lawyer, and if she couldn't be a lawyer *and* married to Paul, then she wasn't going to get married. Paul, on the other hand, wasn't sure at all about what he wanted to do with his life. He was interested in photography, in writing and in acting. Since he had more experience in photography than anything else, and had been taking pictures for both the college newspaper and on a freelance basis for several years, he was able to get a job as a photographer in the city where Joyce was attending law school. While she went to school, he supported her. They didn't have much money, but they managed. After Joyce passed her bar exams, and had been working as a lawyer for a year, Paul quit his job as a photographer and spent a year writing a novel. It was published to moderate success and led to an offer to write a film script. Between the two of them, they now had enough money so that Joyce could take the time off to have a child. What the future held, for either one of them, they weren't entirely sure: Joyce was beginning to get interested in running for political office, while Paul felt that film directing might be something that would make the greatest use of his varied talents.

The difference between these two couples is not one of ability. Bob always got better grades than Paul, and Susan could easily have made just as good a doctor as Joyce did a lawyer. The difference between them is one of outlook and attitude. Bob and Susan had a life plan, based on the maturity myth, on conformity and self-sacrifice. Joyce and Paul had instead a life strategy, based on taking things as they came, on analyzing what course would be most fulfilling for them in the short run while retaining the option of changing their minds and their lives as they went along. Bob and Susan's life plan had no built-in options; Joyce and Paul's did. This is not to say, of course, that it is *wrong* to go to work for a corporation or to have children when you are in your early twenties. That can be just the *right* thing for you. The only thing that may be wrong is to assume that you will never want anything else. The difference between a static life plan and a dynamic life strategy doesn't lie in what you *do* at any given point, but in how you *regard* what you are doing. If you think it is the *one* path to self-fulfillment, you have a life plan and not a life strategy. If you think the only possible path to self-fulfillment is to be an actor or a painter, and base everything on that, you are just as likely to run into trouble as the person who thinks that the only possible path is to work for a corporation.

There isn't *one* possible path, not for any of us. We

change, the world around us changes. We need to
have specific goals, yes; but we also need to be able to
change our minds about what those goals are. For
Joyce and Paul, their first goal was Joyce's law degree; their next goal was the completion of Paul's
novel. In achieving these two different goals, they
shifted gears, each taking a different role at a different
point. And their overall approach to life allowed this
shift, and would allow future shifts. Their life strategy
took into account the need for such shifts, it gave
them the flexibility to adapt to both internal and external change. If Joyce had failed to get her degree,
or Paul's novel had never been published, they could
have shifted gears again. Shifting gears is the process
by which we *choose change;* our life strategy is the
open-minded attitude that allows us to make that
choice.

Only you can choose change. Only you can design
a life strategy that allows you to make that choice. The
rest of this book is concerned with the skills that each
of us can use to develop a personal life strategy, the
skills that can help you to identify your own individual needs, to recognize the points of transition between one psychic phase and another, and to shift
gears in accordance with the particular pattern of
growth that is yours alone.

Part II

Formulating a Life
Strategy: The Guidelines

CHAPTER FIVE

Making Crisis Work for You

The Anatomy of Crisis

Out of every crisis comes the chance to be reborn, to reconceive ourselves as individuals, to choose the kind of change that will help us to grow and to fulfill ourselves more completely. This potential, which exists in every crisis, is nowhere better expressed than in the Chinese language. The written character for crisis in Chinese is made up of two equal symbols: one which stands for *danger* and one which stands for *opportunity*. We all know that there is danger in crisis, for it presents us with situations radically different from our ordinary ones—but too often we forget that in crisis there is also the opportunity for change and growth. Out of the insecurity, the anguish and the pain that we experience in the face of danger and the unknown, we can emerge with new vitality and courage. We can be reborn with new strength.

To come through a crisis with increased personal strength and a sense of renewal, though, we have to understand how to make crisis work for us. And we must avoid the myths and fallacies that hang us up and impede our ability to learn and grow. When you focus primarily on the danger inherent in crisis, instead of on its growth potential, you make it far more difficult to deal with—fear and despair overwhelm the opportunity for self-development. We may be only too well aware of the unknowns and the confusion (which we interpret as danger) but we should also recognize the possibilities for growth.

In Chapter Two we talked about crisis largely in negative terms, demonstrating how the crisis culture in which we live affects the individual's ability to deal with the normal, personal crises of adulthood. When a society as a whole is in crisis, we are faced with what can be called a *metacrisis*. Today we seem besieged by such crises, not only nationally but worldwide. War, economic depression, the assassination of a political leader or the loss of credibility in the ethics of our government are all examples of a metacrisis. In this chapter, we want to concentrate, however, on *personal* crisis. If we understand how to make personal crisis work for us, how to shift gears through the normal crises of our lives, then we ought to be better prepared to respond to metacrises as well, when and if we find ourselves faced by them.

Personal crisis can be brought on by the fundamental events of the human life cycle—birth, puberty, marriage, pregnancy, advanced age and death. It can be brought on by a change in the balance of our internal psychic phases. Divorce, a change in status, a career switch, moving from one community to another —these developments may also be the occasion for a personal psychological crisis, causing us to question our assumptive state. Our assumptive state is the way we view the world and ourselves in relation to it, it is what we assume or believe to be true, it is how we perceive the realities through our unique subjective perception.

For many people, these personal crises can seem like catastrophes. We tend to react to them with the same types of behavior as we would when faced by a flood or an earthquake—we panic, not knowing where to turn, shaken loose from everything we thought we could count on. In an earthquake, it is the physical bases for our lives that are pulled out from underneath us; in a personal crisis, it is the psychological bases for our lives that are shattered. And yet panic can be eased and anxiety mitigated if we know what to expect. But in either case, physical or psychological, *crisis puts us in a position from which we cannot retreat to what used to be.*

Crisis is the point of no return. It makes little difference whether your crisis is externally caused (your husband dies, you lose your job) or is the result of a gnawing internal awareness that your life is not what you want it to be (your career, though successful, has come to seem pointless, your marriage a dead end). The crises that are generated inside ourselves are often more complex and perturbing than the externally imposed crises, but in both cases you have reached a point where there is no retreat. You no longer have the choice of going back to your old position—your world is irrevocably changed.

At this crisis point you have only one option: in order to deal with the crisis, you must change. It is like being thrown into a river when you don't know how to swim—you have no choice but to learn to swim. And panic, in such a situation, is obviously the worst possible answer. If you have reached a point from which you can't retreat, then you can only go forward. Going forward into the unfamiliar, toward the as yet unknown new position that you will eventually take, is a step in growth. Inherent in being thrust forward into this new situation is the opportunity of crisis, the opportunity for renewing change and growth. Crisis can then be viewed not just as danger but as a positive force, as a situation to *utilize* for growth.

We can, of course, when faced with a crisis, try to avoid it. But by the very definition of crisis, avoidance can only make matters worse. The desire to go back or the effort to stay rooted where you are can only be self-defeating. However, if we accept it, recognize its opportunities and learn how to use it as a positive force for growth—one that can increase our capacity for dealing with life from that point onward—then we can better withstand the pain and anxiety that we may have to go through in crisis.

Our culture, unfortunately, teaches us that crisis is to be avoided at all costs, that it brings only pain and danger. No one wants to hear about pain in America—we sweep it under the rug and lock it away where it can't be seen. We want our plays and movies and books to present personal dilemmas only in ways that can be laughed at and therefore dismissed; the common objective of every situation comedy on television is to anesthetize crisis by making it unreal and laughable. And when we are confronted by pain in real life we try to get it out of sight and keep it there.

We are afraid of reality and our society panders to that fear. Living in a mechanistic culture, we have become mechanistic people. Don't do it yourself, we are told, let a machine do it for you: brush your teeth, squeeze an orange, slice a tomato, carve a roast. And just over the horizon is the possibility of producing a child outside of the womb in a glass container, without emotion and without the crisis of birth. Our inner lives have become a reflection of this mechanization, and in this anesthetized existence it is little wonder that we have lost our ability to feel and respond to life. We move like automatons from day to day, even our joys becoming as mechanical as the canned laughter on the tube.

And yet, paradoxically, these very machines that are supposed to protect us from crisis, from reality, only make us more anxious. Our culture denies crisis, pain and imperfection and provides a thousand ways to avoid them, yet deep within ourselves we know this is at odds with our humanity. Between our innate sense of ourselves as individuals and what society would make of us there is a yawning gap, a disparity between reality and fantasy, between a robot world free of crisis and our human needs for growth and change, a gap that can only produce anxiety and new kinds of problems. We are told to put on a facade that everything is just fine (looking good and feeling bad) while at the same time we are being presented with new causes for anxiety every day.

Today we hear a great deal about the mid-life crisis. This crisis is in fact a perfectly normal point of transition into a new phase of adulthood. But because our maturity myth assures us that we won't have any crises in growth if we follow the rules, the natural changes that take place at mid-life become something to fear, and are inflated into a crisis of major proportions. Since our society ignores our needs for change and growth throughout life, it *creates* an unnecessary degree of crisis out of a natural phenomenon of adulthood.

Our culture also denies time as a factor in solving problems or crises. It used to be that we could listen with some comfort to our grandparents when they said, "Time heals all wounds." And although there is truth in that statement, although time does seal over and diminish pain, and can give us the breathing room in which to seek solutions or come to terms with inner growth, we can take little comfort from such ideas in today's world—time is a commodity in short supply. Because the rate of change is so rapid today, because we are presented with so many options, few of us have time to adjust to crisis on a normal timetable. Thus, in our world, it is more necessary than ever before for us to know how to analyze and deal with personal crisis.

Problems, Emergencies and Crises

It is helpful to be able to distinguish among a problem, an emergency and a crisis. As one man we interviewed put it, "A problem is something I can see how to handle when it happens, and I'm confident I can find an answer to it. But crisis, well, with a crisis I don't know the answer, there's no ready-made solution to it." If Phil is told by the dentist that he will have to undergo extensive treatment for his gums or his teeth will fall out, he's got a problem. It means he'll have to fit numerous dental appointments into his working schedule over the next several months. And it means he'll have to juggle his budget in order to be able to pay for the treatments. But these are problems he knows how to deal with; they have a ready-made solution.

If Phil's visiting mother-in-law falls down in the bathtub and breaks a hip, he's got an emergency on his hands. But again, he knows how to deal with it. Both problems and emergencies can be dealt with by using resources we already have or recombining known methods in some new way to solve the problem. But few of us have any knowledge of the means for resolving a crisis. In part this is because a crisis requires new behavior and we don't know, can't possibly know, what that behavior may be. But it is also because we may not know enough about the *process* of going through a crisis.

Problem solving involves the reapplication of the already known. You can solve a problem on the basis of your already existing assumptive state, or world view. But crisis directly challenges your assumptive state and almost inevitably calls for a change in that state. To resolve a crisis we have to reorganize ourselves, changing our attitudes and our behavior. All of us have certain established sets of attitudes and behaviors— they are variously referred to as perceptive sets, mental sets, feeling sets, emotional sets and resultant behavioral sets. The way you brush your teeth or fry an egg is part of your personal behavior set—and so is the way you react when someone praises you or challenges your opinion or asks you to do a favor for them. Thus the assumptive state for the individual is equal to the sum total of all his sets, which were formed in the first place by the interaction between the person's inner self and his life experience, and by his ongoing interaction with the environment, since both the environment and the self are processes and continuously changing.

When crisis strikes, the old assumptive state may no longer be a sound basis on which to act. To solve the crisis we usually have to change our behavior sets and develop a new assumptive state. We all know that we have to change certain behavior sets, adding and subtracting and modifying them when the situation around us changes. If we move from a New York apartment to a Los Angeles suburb we have to reorganize our behavior patterns, developing new forms of action that correspond to our new environment. You take subways and cabs in New York, but in California you drive a car—you cannot live without a car.

Let us take another example—a new child arriving in a family. The young husband and wife have lived together for several years. They have fully enjoyed their life together, but the husband has become very dependent on her as wife and companion. The baby comes and suddenly there is a crisis for the husband. His assumption has been that he was the most important person in his wife's life. He is still a most important person, but the couple must now expand to take the needs of the infant into consideration. Much as the husband anticipated the baby, although he thought he knew what was involved, he finds it different from what he expected—he feels left out and it makes him angry and confused. His assumptive state has been challenged, and to meet the crisis he must change his state. It may take a short time or it may take years for this adjustment to be made.

In crisis, many people first try to use their old behavior sets in attempting to resolve their situation. Since a challenge to their assumptive state is involved, the old sets will not work—some people have to find that out for themselves, while others recognize the fact from the beginning and move on to seeking new ways of dealing with the crisis. The young husband in our example tries to use the old sets first, and when they don't work, he begins to send hidden messages about his frustration to his wife. "Where are my socks, why don't I have any clean shirts?" he may grumble. "Why do we always have to wait for dinner?" What he is really saying, of course, is that he feels left out, that he has not yet changed his assumptive state to include the baby in it.

In the case of this husband, the challenge to his assumptive state is not a major one, and the resulting crisis can perhaps be solved by mustering new combinations of the old sets of established behavior. The young father will learn, hopefully, that his needs have to be meshed with the child's, and that he can expect new kinds of responses, new expressions of love from his wife, responses that include the child. By forming a new configuration of his behavior sets and reorganizing the elements of his existing assumptive state, he can perhaps solve the problem and grow to some extent.

But usually in crisis, and often when the challenge is a major one, even recombining the old sets won't work. The magnitude of the crisis may require that we develop some new behavior sets, integrate them with the old and arrive at an entirely new assumptive state. If your wife is having a baby and you lose your job at the same time, a major readjustment will be necessary. If we divorce or are divorced we will have to find new ways of viewing our world and our relation to it; in future man-woman relationships we may have to drop some of our old behavior sets and develop new ones. For many people retirement brings on a similar shock, making entirely new sets of behavior necessary to the achievement of continued growth and fulfillment.

When we develop new behavior sets in response to a crisis, we expand and grow. In rising to the crisis, searching for and developing new ways of dealing with life, we become better able to deal with any number of other possible situations more readily. The greater and the more sophisticated our repertoire of behavior sets, the more capable we become. This is one of the ways in which crisis works to our benefit, and why we should not fear it. Crises are an inevitable part of being human—but each crisis we face up to and solve makes us stronger and makes it easier for us to face other inevitable crises in the future.

Many people, when faced with a crisis, confuse cause with effect. Finding themselves in crisis, they tell themselves that they have failed. And since they have failed, they conclude, there is no point in trying anything else. They become convinced that their crisis is evidence of an inability to succeed. They turn their crisis into a cause for inaction. But their crisis should be a cause *for* action, for changing and growing, not for hanging back in fear and defeat. If a young woman tries to become a professional actress and fails, it doesn't mean that she is a failure as a person, or that her life is a failure. It simply means that, at that particular point in her life, becoming an actress was not the best direction for finding fulfillment. The fact that she failed at being an actress shouldn't be a cause for deciding that she can't succeed at anything—it is merely an effect of one choice that she has made. There are many other possible choices to be made in the present and the future, including acting at some future time. Instead of taking her crisis as evidence of defeat, she should *use* it to explore the other options open to her, to discover aspects of herself that have been lying fallow, and to try another approach to fulfillment.

Crisis involves risk; it is a time of danger. But it is also a vehicle for growth. If we refuse to take the risk, then we lose not only what we used to have (for we are beyond the point of going back) but also the future. Crisis is a time of testing—but it is also a time of renewal. Once we emerge on the other side of crisis, once we have shifted gears, we find ourselves filled with

renewed strength and courage. People who saw someone
during a crisis when he walked around with slumped
shoulders, gray face and harried expression, now find
him changed. "How marvelous you look," they say.
And he looks marvelous because he *has* changed.
It is through the meeting of the challenge of crisis that
we measure up to life, and more than that, measure up
to ourselves and our best potentials. Having conquered
one crisis, having run the rapids, we know that when
we meet the next one we will be better equipped. Next
time we will not be so afraid, next time we will know
better that out of the pain and confusion can emerge
a better, stronger self.

Coping

Most of us cope with life. To cope means to squeak
through, like getting a C on an exam. We don't cop
out, we don't fail, but we don't win any gold stars,
either. When we say, "I just can't cope with it any
longer," it means we throw up our hands in despair
and retreat. Coping is a middle way, lying somewhere
between advancing and retreating. We look at our children, as they weave their way through the strange mating
dances of adolescence, and we say, "Another year or so
and they'll be through that stage. I guess I can cope with
it that long." Coping does not give us a positive sense
of utilizing all our resources, of really coming to grips
with a problem, or of controlling and determining the
situation (especially not our children). Coping is getting by.

To grow through a crisis is a very different thing
from coping with it. Coping has a place as a form of
pre-crisis problem solving, on a short-term basis, but
if we merely cope with a crisis it will defeat us. With
crisis we have to go beyond coping. Yet coping can be
helpful in the early stages of crisis, as we try to maintain our equilibrium. Coping is useful in making the
best of a bad situation at a given moment. Coping can

make us feel better, and it can give us a breathing space until we are ready to face the crisis head on. But it can't solve the crisis for us.

Dr. Karl Menninger, in his book *The Vital Balance,* speaks of *coping devices*—those short-term regulatory devices we use to deal with everyday stress. Some of the mechanisms he describes, along with others, can be listed in various categories.

Physical Reassurance	Venting Your Emotions	Substitutes for Action
Eating	Blaming others	Rationalization
Drinking	Taking it out on	Talking it over
Smoking	loved ones	with friends
Drugs (from pot	Psychosomatic	and family
to tranquilizers)	illness	Watching
Sleeping	Crying	television
Exercise (tennis,	Cursing	Going to the
golf, jogging,	Laughing it off	movies
etc.)		Going on a
Work (cleaning		buying spree
the attic, gardening, etc.)		

All of these coping devices can be used to avoid facing the crisis, and often are; some of them, on the other hand, can give us the kind of momentary reassurance we need while we gather our strength to deal with crisis.

We all know that once in a while a good cry does a world of good—it won't solve our problems but it certainly makes us feel better. Being touched and held by a loved one, sharing coffee, hot tea or a drink, or smoking a cigarette at a tense moment can provide us with short-term relief. We can use exercise to avoid a crisis, like the man who plays golf all the time in order to put off a confrontation with his wife; or we can use exercise to let off steam and get our minds working on how to solve a problem or a crisis. Blaming others or developing psychosomatic asthma obviously isn't going to help, and may even make things worse by creating a second crisis on top of the first one. On the other hand, nobody can deal with crisis as effectively in a state of exhaustion as when they are rested—"sleeping on it" is still good advice.

For good or bad, however, we cannot *solve* our crises with coping devices. "If the objective is not achieved," says Dr. Menninger, "a higher price will have to be paid and devices of a more expensive kind will have to be called upon to maintain the vital balance." When coping devices are used to excess or for too long a time, they become *avoidance devices*. And when we avoid the crisis, we prolong it. Like letting a symptom go too long before going to the doctor, it's tougher to treat. Eventually we will need to move beyond mere coping to actively dealing with the crisis. We then begin to shift gears.

There is a story about a woman who was forced to flee the Nazis during World War II. It was difficult to know what to do or where to go, and time was at a premium. But in this crisis, the first thing she did was to go to a pastry shop, where she sat and drank a cup of coffee and ate one of the richest pastries she could find. *Then* she was ready to escape the Nazis. Coping thus can provide us with a cushioning effect. It gives us comfort when we sorely need it. If we do not use these coping devices to escape the necessary confrontation with the crisis, then we can use them in conjunction with the development of a *crisis-solving set*.

FORMING A CRISIS-SOLVING SET

POINT 1:

It is not the nature of the crisis itself that determines its impact but rather our attitude *toward it.* Our attitude is influenced by a number of factors: (1) the extent to

which the person's current assumptive state is based
upon myths or fallacies such as the maturity myth and
the guarantee hang-up; (2) the extent to which the
individual really knows what he or she wants; (3)
whether the change is self-induced because the individual is seeking such change or it is forced upon him
by external pressures; and (4) whether or not the
individual has a strategy for dealing with change. These
factors in turn affect the duration of the crisis, which
we call the *crisis span*.

When we are confronted by crisis, we filter the external events that give shape and form to the crisis
through our psychic lens. Whatever passes through that
psychic lens is affected—indeed altered—by our personality, character structure, life history, opinions, and
our internalized value system. Thus the backdrop
against which the crisis is played out is our inner self,
and it is not *what* we see that counts, but how we
perceive what we see.

POINT II:

All of us have a different crisis potential. What may
be a crisis for one person is merely a problem for
another. In Latin America the loss of a maid for some
middle-class women is a real crisis, because everyday
life, household tasks and status depend on the maid's
work. On the other hand, for a young American career
woman who is constantly juggling the immediacies of
household, job, and children, the loss of a maid is only
one of a series of problems to be dealt with. A job
change may become an opportunity for one man, yet
devastate another.

All of us have different resources to draw on in crisis;
some have more, some less. Some people may have a
strong ego that enables them to solve crises more easily
than those of us who are less well integrated and organized. The more experienced we are with crisis, the

better we *can* deal with it—the growth potential in crisis means that we can constantly enrich our resources.

Because we have different resources we react differently to different crises, and to similar crises differently at different times. A lot depends on your feeling and emotional state at the time. If you are under stress from other quarters when crisis comes, then you may find it more difficult to handle. There are, of course, crisis-prone people—the women who fall apart when the washing machine breaks down, the men who have a screaming fit when the slightest thing goes wrong at the office. There are also those who develop pseudocrises as a way of gaining attention, people a friend of ours refers to as the "wallowers." They seek one-upmanship through crisis, always telling you how bad it is, how they can't cope, how they have more misery than you. They may not in reality be that disturbed or disoriented at all, but they make a career of crisis and it becomes their chief mode of communication with others.

POINT III:

We can learn to distinguish between different types of crisis. There are *catalytic* crises—those that are precipitated by external events. Your apartment building is torn down, or your husband is leaving you and you have no job skills to help support yourself, or your employer calls you in and says, sorry Bud, but in two weeks it's over, not because you've failed to do your job properly but because a government contract has been canceled.

There are *recognition* crises—those that are provoked by some internal cause. The first sign of such a crisis may be a general but deep-seated dissatisfaction. Then follows a realization that your old ideas about your relationships, or your work, are no longer good enough. "Crisis?" said a blunt investment counselor. "Why that's what happens after a period of sheer boredom." But there is something other than just boredom that brings on an internal recognition crisis, that pushes us beyond the point of no rturn.

Catalytic crises, those from outside, hit suddenly out of nowhere. Recognition crises, those from inside us, may also hit suddenly, but usually they have been building for a long time. We may know something is wrong but put off facing it until finally we can do so no longer and must recognize the crisis or come to a standstill. Or we may not have felt that anything was wrong, with the awareness of crisis descending upon us like a revelation. As a general rule, it can be said that the longer the recognition crisis has been building the harder it will hit.

POINT IV:

Sometimes we are faced by more than one crisis at once; when that happens we must sort our crises out and deal with them one at a time. Usually, in fact, when there are several crises at once, they are interrelated. For instance, Peter K. had a job with a large corporation. The corporation had offices all over the country, and in the first ten years of Peter's marriage to Barbara they moved five times, as Peter was assigned to different branch offices in different cities. Then, for the next four years, they lived in Boston, a city that both Barbara and the children liked very much. Peter was informed that he was to be reassigned once again. Barbara said, "No, this just can't go on any longer. If you accept the new assignment you'll just have to go without us. We're staying here." The children who were now in school and had made large numbers of friends didn't want to move either. And the question for Peter was one of deciding which of several crises to deal with first. He was fed up with moving around the country himself, but if he refused, the chances for further advancement within the corporation would be cut back. If he went ahead he would be giving up his family. The crisis he found most devastating, personally, was the idea of living without Barbara. But it became clear to him that the family crisis was solvable only if he dealt with his career crisis. Since the thought of quitting his job with the corporation—crisis though that would be—was less disturbing to him than losing his family, he decided to face up to the job crisis first. He didn't want to leave the corporation, but the crisis of finding a new job with another company that was based in Boston was one he thought he could deal with. The crisis of separating from his family was beyond him.

In this case, the most important crisis, the one that Peter found most disturbing, was *not* the one to face up to first. For another man, under different circumstances, his career might have seemed more vital to him than his family. Such a man might have gone in the opposite direction from Peter, hoping that his wife was just bluffing and would in the end agree to the move. Thus sorting our multiple crises involves knowing or finding out what you really want most. Until you have made that decision, it is difficult to deal with multiple crises.

POINT V:

Don't panic. Panic is too often our first reaction to crisis. But panic can be kept within bounds if we know what kinds of *anxiety symptoms* we can expect in ourselves when crisis hits. Psychologists have described three crisis phases for individuals faced with severe bereavement; the same phases may occur in other kinds of crisis situations as well.

(1) Physical and psychological turmoil. Disturbances in body function (indigestion, insomnia, palpitations), and of mental mood and intellectual control. You are likely to feel lousy and find it difficult to think straight.

(2) A painful preoccupation with the past. For instance, the man who begins to feel that he has "wasted" the best years of his life in a job he hates, is likely to

spend much time belaboring the past, sometimes blaming others for his predicament, at other times running himself down in a self-diminishing way.

(3) A period of remobilization of our resources, with activity in some direction. This is the point at which we can begin to shift gears, leading on to resolution of the crisis and the achievement of growth.

Obviously, the faster we get to this third phase of crisis reaction, the more quickly we will be able to shift gears. Yet many of us get hung up on the first two phases, both of which contribute to a feeling of panic. If we do not experience the truly awful feeling of panic, we may at the very least experience the discomfort of anxiety. Some people do not need a major psychological crisis to experience panic; the contemplation of anything new or unconventional is anxiety-provoking. Yet all of us are familiar with the anxiety we experienced as children facing our first day at school or going to the dentist for the first time. Even as adults the dread and anticipation of the dental chair is frequently worse than the experience itself. But once familiar with what happens after the first few days at school and once reassured (if not *quite* comfortable) after our visit to the dentist, anxiety vanished and we developed, even as children, a mastery over the situation. Knowing what to expect prepares you for knowing how to meet it. Knowing you are not alone helps too. No one lives without some anxiety. Even our supermen astronauts feel anxiety; but they have learned to contain their feelings and think about solutions to problems. They have learned to utilize relationships with their fellow astronauts for support in their times of stress and decision. Few of us can be as controlled and steady under similar circumstances, but if we know that anxiety symptoms are likely to occur in crisis or change we can learn to ride through it, knowing that these feelings will dissipate with mastery of our situation.

POINT VI:

Discover the crisis question. In every crisis we not only reach a point of no return, but we also move beyond certain questions. If a man is sitting in his office questioning himself as to whether or not he should move to another apartment building, and then the building he lives in burns down, he is beyond that question. He is beyond having or making a choice in response to that question. He can't deliberate or vacillate any longer. He *has* to move. When we find ourselves in crisis we may not have been *consciously* asking any questions that pertain to that crisis. But there is always a question implicit in the crisis, and if we can find out what it is, it can be of great help in illuminating the direction we should move in now.

If a man is fired from a job, the crisis question might be, Did I really like that job, was it good for me? He may or may not have asked this question consciously of himself before he was fired. The answer to that question no longer means anything in respect to the old job—by being fired, the man has moved beyond the question. But the answer to that question can mean something in respect to seeking a new job. It can help him to decide what kind of job he now wants. Similarly, a woman who suddenly becomes a widow has an implicit question about her life with her husband that she may or may not have asked: Can I live without him? Can I be an independent person? Once again, she is beyond this question in regard to the life she previously had, but it has a great deal of relevance to the life she will now be making for herself. Thus, by exploring the implicit crisis question, any of us can better understand the changes ahead.

POINT VII:

Go into the crisis. By going into the crisis we mean experiencing it fully, not avoiding it, not trying to defuse it. In order to make a breakthrough to an under-standing of the real nature of any given crisis we must keep asking questions. We must face up not just to what we feel, but ask why we feel it. If we take into account the fact that our perception is altered by our personality and character structure, life experience and attitudes, then it is just one step to asking the questions that lead to the real nature of the crisis: Is there anything about my personality that should make me feel the way I do? What past events in my life have a bearing on what I'm feeling now? Is my attitude preventing me from seeing the problem clearly? What is needed of me to change? In what ways can I change?

These are not easy questions, and we can't expect to come up with answers in the first few days, or even weeks. But if we make the effort of asking them, and if we keep asking them, we will accomplish two impor-tant things. First, we will be discovering the true nature of our crisis, making it possible to begin the process of shifting gears. And second, we will be making the crisis work for us, because in the course of asking such questions of ourselves we will be learning more about who we are and want to be. Not everything we learn will be immediately applicable to the crisis at hand, but the more we know about ourselves and our relation to the world around us, the more we will grow and the easier it will be to grow.

By going into the crisis, opening ourselves fully to it, we may experience considerable discomfort at first. But those who come through crisis with real change and growth are often those who seem to take crisis the hardest.

POINT VIII:

Don't make snap judgments or look for immediate solutions. Many crises will seem to demand immediate decisions and actions. We may be inclined to strike out blindly after the first shock and panic—or even during it. But don't panic or take rash action. Stop everything for the moment. Recognizing that your perceptions will be altered or impaired by the first anxiety symptoms, it is clearly not a good time to make quick decisions.

If your wife, after years of strife between you, demands a divorce one night and asks you to leave the house, what do you do? Certainly you don't go charging off the next morning to find an apartment and sign a two-year lease that afternoon. More likely you will take a hotel room or stay with a friend for a few days while you get your bearings, until you *know* what direction you want to move in. Or you may decide to sit it out until both of you consider this action more fully.

During the first hours or days of crisis, it would seem wise to ask yourself if what you're doing, the action you're taking, will have short-term or long-term effects. If it's going to have long-term effects, think again—you may not be ready to make that kind of decision yet.

POINT IX:

Do find someone who cares and who can listen to you. When crisis strikes, this point may be the very first one to take action on. Don't panic; stop short, don't do anything rash and do seek out someone to talk to. It may be your mate or someone in your family or a best friend. There is no need for secrecy in our time of deepest need. Just by talking to someone we can defuse our anxiety and clarify some of our confusion and hurt. At times of crisis we especially need the affectionate support of people who care. But this does not mean someone who will insist upon telling you what to do. It does not mean someone who will smother you with compensation, telling you you're perfect and everybody else is wrong. You need a person who cares for you and who can understand you in a compassionate way without offering immediate pat solutions or telling you what to do. Only you can solve your crisis. Other people can help you, but they can't solve your crisis for you. Since they may be able to see your situation more objectively, they *can* give you a different viewpoint. You may pick up clues from other people by asking them about how they handled their own crises. They can't give you an exact model to follow, because they are different people. But you may find some things they have to say about their own solutions to their own crises can be applied to yours.

You may feel that you need professional help and fortunately today there are many helping professionals who understand the nature of our personal and social crises. Crisis intervention centers are located in some major hospitals and mental health centers; they provide many techniques for immediately coping with the crisis. In a variety of ways, therapists can help us meet our crises in positive ways that promote growth. But even the best professional cannot solve your crisis for you. All they can do is to help *you* to solve your crisis for yourself.

POINT X:

Try something new. You are now ready to begin shifting gears. Trying something new is equivalent to the step of experimentation in shifting gears. The points we have been making in these last few pages apply primarily to the early steps in the process of shifting gears: awareness, evaluation and exploration. Now it is time to move forward, to take action and to grow through our actions.

To realize our full potential as human beings we must continue to grow throughout our lives. And crisis, unsettling though it may be, gives us our greatest opportunity for growth. We grow in many subtle ways even when our lives are at their smoothest. But when we are in crisis and our entire being is focused on resolving the crisis, we can take a great leap forward. When we want to learn a new language, or how to drive a car, or to use a pocket calculator, we make a conscious effort to change and to expand our skills. With emotional habits, it's harder to learn something new, but the rewards can be enormous. Not only can the conscious effort to change lead to a resolution of the particular crisis, it can also lead to a new sense of one's self and a new confidence. We grow by meeting our crises head on, by letting go of our past ways of looking at the world and finding new ways that expand and enrich our interior selves.

Crisis is a distilling process out of which we can emerge more completely ourselves. Like metal tempered in fire, the impurities can be burned off. We can come through the ordeal true and clean, with the vital core not only intact but tempered to a greater strength. As a friend said to us, "I only truly know someone in a crisis, and then I know him in a minute." But not only can we know others most truly when they are in crisis —we can know ourselves most truly in crisis if we take advantage of it fully and make it work for us by exploring ourselves as deeply as we can.

CHAPTER SIX

Nothing Is Wasted

The Journey Is Just the Beginning

The painful preoccupation with the past that many of us experience when we arrive at a point of crisis or necessary change can become one of the greatest obstacles to shifting gears, to moving forward and experiencing growth. We say to ourselves, "If only I had done such and such, I wouldn't be in this pickle." Or, "If only I *hadn't* done such and such, everything would be OK."

Peter B., for instance, has just lost his job with a brokerage firm for the simple reason that the firm has closed its doors, a casualty of the falling stock market. He doesn't blame himself for the firm's failure; of the dozen brokers in the firm, he was one of the three who was doing a profitable business. But he does blame himself for not having taken another job that was offered him three years before. An old friend was at that time founding a company to develop, manufacture and distribute high-priced and high-quality stereo components. He asked Peter to join the new firm as treasurer. It would have meant taking a cut in his income and he wasn't at all sure that the fledgling firm would be a success—so Peter turned the offer down.

Since then, because of the advanced engineering of their product, the company has in fact become a great success. Looking back now, Peter berates himself for having made a "mistake." If only he'd taken that job, he wouldn't be in crisis now—or at least that's what he tells himself. And he's spending so much time kicking himself that he's not getting ahead with the business of facing up to his crisis. Instead of trying to discover the way to his future, he's spending all his time thinking about what might have been.

Let's take another example. Susan F. quit college after two years and took a secretarial job to help put her husband Jack through law school. They waited to have children until after he passed his bar exams and joined a Cincinnati law firm. The children are now teen-agers; Susan's primary role for the past sixteen years has been as housewife. But now Jack wants a divorce. He has been having an affair with another woman for over a year and he wants to marry her. Susan is not only in crisis, she is on the edge of despair. It is not just that her marriage has fallen apart— she and Jack haven't really been communicating for some time. What depresses her most is that she has "wasted" half her adult life on him. She remembers how reluctant she was to quit college, twenty years ago. And now she can do nothing but bewail the fact that she did quit. "If only I'd insisted on finishing," she says, "the whole thing might have been over before it began. I might not have married Jack at all— and I wouldn't have wasted all these years on him."

Both Peter and Susan feel that they made wrong decisions in the past, that their current crises are based on past mistakes. Peter is convinced that he wasted the golden opportunity of his life. Susan feels that she has wasted not just opportunity but life itself. Instead of dealing with the crisis at hand, growing through it and going on to a new life, both are caught in a whirlpool of regret.

When we arrive at a point of crisis like Peter's and Susan's, a point of no return at which change becomes essential, we have reached the end of a particular inner journey in our lives. New experiences lie ahead, experiences that will bring us further growth and a changed vision of ourselves as individuals: a new assumptive state, in fact. But the more time we spend regretting the journey that has brought us this far, the less time we will have to experience the future.

We can make Peter's and Susan's situations clearer by analogy. If you are traveling in Europe and cross the English Channel by boat on your way to Paris, you could easily encounter rough seas. But once you reach France, the more time you spend lamenting the rough journey, wishing you'd taken a plane instead and thinking about your queasy stomach, the less time you will have to enjoy your stay in Paris. Since you can't change the decision now anyway, common sense should tell you to forget about the rough journey and make the most out of what lies ahead.

But although most of us can apply common sense to this kind of limited situation, a great many people find it difficult to extend the same kind of sensible approach to their lives in general and to crisis situations in particular. Like Susan and Peter we berate ourselves for not having taken a different path at some point in the past. We dwell on the supposedly wasted years and lost opportunities. But what we are really doing is using the concept of "waste" as a rationalization for not doing anything to solve our crises. As long as you keep on thinking that the solution to your current crisis lies in the past rather than in the present, and that you failed to seize upon that solution when it was open to you, then you can continue telling yourself that there's no point in mustering the courage to move forward into the future. Time spent in regretting missed opportunities makes us triple losers: we can't change the past, we lose present living time and we affect the future.

We have this reaction in crisis for a number of reasons. In part it is due to the length of time involved in the buildup of many crisis situations. When Susan looks back over her life and places the blame for her present crisis on her decision to give up college and marry her husband twenty years before, she is taking the view that half her adult life has been a mistake— a view that obviously is going to have much greater impact than feeling that one should have taken a plane instead of a boat across the English Channel. On the other hand, the impact of the crisis situation makes it even more important to concentrate on the future, on what you *can do now* rather than on *what you did then:* bewailing your bad boat crossing can ruin your first day in Paris, but bewailing twenty years of your life can undermine the next several years, and perhaps the rest of your life.

The maturity myth also plays a part in our feeling that the past has been wasted. The myth leads us to believe that we can eventually be home safe, and when we find out that we aren't, we feel cheated. Feeling cheated, we may look for someone or something outside ourselves to blame, as Susan blames her husband. Or, like Peter, we may tell ourselves that we acted foolishly. Either way, we once again become mired in the past instead of seeking answers and new directions in the present for the future.

But an even more basic reason for our tendency to fix our attention on the past rather than on the future when we are in crisis is that most of us simply have no idea of what is involved in the psychological growth of the human being. Not knowing what psychological growth consists of, how can we possibly know how to use our experience to help us grow?

As human beings, how do we grow?

How We Grow

Knowing how we grow is fundamental to mastering our own life strategy. Understanding the processes of growth, whether they occur through crises or through the many other stimuli to growth, will make it easier for us to recognize what happens in relationships with others, what happens in crisis, why it is necessary for us to shift gears and how to facilitate the growth we need.

We grow according to certain definite and recognizable patterns, which we can see quite easily in our physical growth from infancy to adulthood. But psychological growth, which is at the heart of shifting gears, is not so easy to see or to put our finger on. Yet it, too, follows certain patterns, involving a definite process and taking on recognizable forms. These patterns and processes, common to all living organisms, and apparent in our psychological and social growth as well as our physical growth, have been brilliantly presented by George T. Lock Land in his recent book, *Grow or Die*. In this section, we have drawn freely on his concepts in explaining how the patterns of human psychological growth apply to our own concept of shifting gears.

Growth is transformation. We watch the young infant with round face and as yet unetched features develop and transform through childhood, adolescence and into manhood. He occupies the same body in infancy and manhood, but he has grown—recognizable in feature but greatly transformed. He has taken in nutrients from the outside world and through his genetic and hormonal mechanisms has transformed these nutrients into an adult body. Here, transformation and growth is acutely visible—we *can* see it happen. At the same time as his body grows, two other kinds of transformation are taking place: socialization and psychological growth. Socialization we can also *see,* to a considerable extent—the child becomes toilet trained, learns to say "please" and "thank-you," begins to use a knife and fork, etc. But we find psychological growth much more mysterious because we cannot so easily or apparently see the results of such growth in concrete form. We can see it only in words, behavioral manifestations, attitudes. One child is neat and well-mannered; another child in the same family is messy and rebellious. And we wonder why.

Yet our psychological growth occurs according to the same patterns as our physical growth. For our bodies to grow we must have nutrients (food); we screen these nutrients for what we can use and absorb, digest and assimilate them, and reorganize the elements to change and develop our form. We do the same thing as part of our psychological growth. We seek nutrients (information) from the outside world. We then screen this information, selecting what is useful to us and rejecting what we think is harmful. This screening process is called *selective perception:* at a cocktail party, for instance, we screen out other noises around us in order to be able to hear the words of the person next to us. Pain and pleasure, plus our memories of these, influence or distort these perceptions and the way we receive and store information. We digest and analyze this information, breaking it down into manageable units. Finally, we reassemble or synthesize this information for use in extending or projecting ourselves into the outside world (by speech, actions, etc.).

When we project ourselves into the outside world, we test our information against it. The world gives us *feedback,* positive and negative, nourishing and nonnourishing. A nutritive environment which encourages our positive expectations gives us not only feedback, but "feedforward" into positive and expanding growth. According to the response we get, we modify or regulate our future acts of growth. The responses we get become new information, and the cycle begins again. Thus we are in a constant process of exchange and interaction with the world around us, either in interpersonal relationships or in relationship to objects, situations and experiences. Growth, then, involves ". . . incorporating parts of the environment into our system and extending ourselves into it—creating an interrelationship."

Within this general process three separate forms of growth have been outlined by Land. As infants, we grow first by *accretion.* We are all *me,* trying to engorge our parents and everything else we come into contact with. There is no real reciprocal exchange with our environment. We try to take everything outside us and make it the same as what is already inside us. Then we go on to *replicative* growth, which is accomplished by copying and imitating. We strive to become *like others,* or to associate with others that are *like us.* We absorb and digest only the information that already matches what we know and discard anything that is sufficiently different. We have become more selective than in the stage of pure accretive growth, in which we try to absorb everything. But there is still only a limited exchange with the environment; there is no striving to create something new beyond becoming like something else or manipulating it to be like us.

The third pattern is *mutual growth,* which is a real reciprocal exchange of growth with the outside world, a self-extension through sharing. By not only sharing commonalities but also sharing and learning from differences, two individuals can provide mutual feedback to one another. Whether it is in interpersonal relationships with a spouse, a friend, children or business associates, whether it is with ideas, objects, a course of learning or a simple diversionary enjoyment, the same process applies. By connecting with shared similarities *and* reaching out to exchange differences, we are then able to make new combinations within ourselves, to change, to grow and to relate to the outside world in a new way.

We utilize all three of these forms—accretion, replication and mutuality—in our individual growth. Each one is a step building on the other towards expanding growth. Accretion is pure self growth; replication is growth *through* others; mutual growth is growth *with* others, putting it all together. If we replicate successfully, it verifies our behavior and reduces our fear of sharing growth with others. Thus each form has a place in our pattern of growth, though it should be obvious that mutual growth is the most beneficial.

Accretion is important in the early development of the infant, and occasionally we learn and grow in this way as an adult—when, for instance, we suddenly get the feeling that a song or a poem was written "just for me." This kind of response can easily be carried to excess in the adult, however. We all know people who constantly seem to be saying "me, me, me." And since their desire to have the whole world relate to them, and only them, can't possibly be satisfied, such people often become deeply frustrated. Lacking real exchange with the world around him, the "me, me" individual sometimes retreats into alcoholism or drugs. Or, more commonly, this totally self-absorbed person needs to possess or be possessed, has a drive for power or needs to be dominated.

Replication can also be useful to us as adults—up to a point. If we want to learn the latest dance step, or decide to take up chess, we start off by emulating others, by replicating the actions of someone more experienced than ourselves. We copy people we admire or influence others to copy us in any kind of behavior—love, achievement, social interaction. And in so doing we grow to some extent. But if we build our entire lives around emulating others, becoming as much like the Joneses as we can, or demanding, for example, that our spouse or children be exactly like us, we become slaves to replication, giving up our individual selves to a numbing conformity or authoritarianism. Thus it is only when one form dominates our patterns that growth is turned into nonproductive channels.

For the adult, then, mutual growth is the healthiest and most rewarding kind. The environment about us, our community, our family, our groups, our world is not just a vast terrain from which we pull food for our bodies and information for our psyches, it is an integral part of us and our growth. When it prevents the conditions of growth, when it presents us with a bewildering number of options and shrinking values, we, and our growth, are affected. To the degree that we are selective and seek out and give positive and nutritive feedback, to the degree that we guide our own and others' growth and make a conscious and concerted effort to interact with the environment, to that degree we will survive in a form we want and with the values we cherish. "True mutual growth," as Land points out, "is shared rather than 'self actualization.' It is only when we realize each other fully that we grow to the heights possible in man."

What Souvenirs Are You Collecting?

Knowing how we grow, we can see more clearly how crisis affects growth, and how the active search for growth can help to resolve a crisis. To begin with, all learning is cumulative—from infant groping and exploring, through childhood training, schooling and play experiences, and later the selective learning that comes from family, sibling and peer relationships. You may forget incidents, you may give up learning or using certain skills, but as we all know, once you learn to swim, even if you don't swim for five or ten years, you will be able to if you have to. We often do not appreciate the significance or value of something we have learned until much later, when the mosaic of our lives, of what we have learned, becomes larger— then suddenly, an almost forgotten piece of information falls into place and takes on a new meaning. Nothing is really wasted—it remains only to emerge in the new awareness of growth in and of our self.

Information is a nutrient—you are, in knowledge as in body, what you eat. Just as some of us eat better foods than others—trying a greater variety of foods, taking care to choose foods with a high nutritional

value and a good balance of protein and vitamins—so
some of us seek out information of greater variety
and with greater use potential. Others may want to eat
nothing but meat and potatoes, or have an unfortunate
fondness for junk foods and TV dinners. But whatever the quality or diversity of the information we
seek out and make part of us, there is always far
more for us to draw on than we are consciously
aware of at any given moment. In crisis, we have both
a special need and a special opportunity to sift
through our knowledge about the world, looking for
those pieces of information that can be of use to us
in resolving the crisis and moving forward into the
future.

Yet, instead of doing this, many of us tend during
crisis to remember chiefly the "mistakes" we have
made. Susan, faced with the crisis of her husband's
request for a divorce, is caught up in remembering all
the bad things that ever happened to her. She is looking for mistakes—and the chief mistake, as she sees
it, was giving up college to marry and help support
her husband in the first place.

Susan is collecting souvenirs of the past, souvenirs
of the inner journey she has made up to this point in
her life. What kind of souvenirs is she collecting? All
the bad ones. It is like coming back from a trip to
Europe with the bill from a restaurant that over-
charged you instead of with the decorative menu
from the restaurant at which you had a superb meal.
See how I was cheated, she is saying, instead of, See
what a good time I had.

These negative souvenirs are not going to help Susan meet her crisis. And they are based on a false
premise to begin with. The action that Susan took all
those years ago, giving up college and marrying Jack,
was not a "mistake" at the time. True, she was reluctant to quit college, but after weighing the question, she decided that that was what she wanted to do.
That was what she did do, and to suppose that if she

had done something else everything would have been all right is to indulge in fantasy and avoid the realization that no one is perfect and everyone, including Susan, can make errors in judgment and wrong turns. One could even question the whole concept of "mistakes," for they become mistakes only in retrospect.

Susan is not going to learn anything about what to do *now* by lamenting her supposed mistakes of the past. It would be better for her to look clearly at *why* she labels them mistakes. Analyzing why and how she made her decisions and, more importantly, what her actions and feelings were in carrying out those decisions can be much more profitable. We learn from our mistakes only by first accepting them, analyzing them and having confidence in ourselves to move on to new kinds of action. We learn even more by recognizing and acknowledging our successes.

Instead of concentrating only on what she might have done wrong, Susan could resolve her crisis easier by seeking out what she did *right,* by discovering in her past the things that gave her satisfaction and a sense of growth. As a mother, for instance, she has the most intimate kind of knowledge of human growth—she has nurtured, cared for and helped her children grow. That experience of parenthood has given her a unique experience in learning. No other occupation in the world offers us a similar opportunity for observation, involvement and shared growth. There may be many aspects of her relationship with her children that are pertinent to her own present situation. *That* is what she should be looking for in her past—the information, the nutrients, that can be helpful to her *now.* What's more, she has undoubtedly learned more as a wife and mother than she realizes. Unfortunately, our society assigns a low status to the occupation of housewife, but that low status is a false estimation of the capabilities and resourcefulness that any housewife must bring to her role if she is to be successful at it. Management skills, competency, diligence, patience and innovation are part and parcel of the homemaking role. And from these past uses of her capabilities, Susan should also be able to draw support and help in seeking to resolve her crisis.

To concentrate only on her supposed mistakes is to negate her past altogether, throwing out the good with the bad. When we devalue what we have learned and experienced, and ignore the ways in which we have grown, we are in effect throwing away the very tools with which we can build a life strategy or shift gears.

Nor will Peter gain anything by kicking himself for not having taken the job offered him three years earlier. When we turn down an opportunity it is usually for one of two reasons: (1) we feel there is more risk than potential reward involved in it, or (2) we are not ready to take that kind of step. Peter rejected the job with the stereo manufacturer because he thought it was too risky. He could well have been right. So there is no point in remorse. Susan now feels that she would have been happier if she had finished college and embarked on a career of some sort. But it was far more difficult for a woman to have a career twenty years ago than it is now. And, in fact, when she quit college, Susan wasn't at all sure what she wanted to do with her life. For most of her friends, getting married and having a family was the chief objective—if she had turned Jack down, most of her friends would have told her that she was not only making a mistake but was plain crazy. Twenty years ago, Susan probably was not ready to follow an independent course. Now she is. And today's climate offers her unparalleled opportunities for picking up a new second life. Women are moving into the mainstream of American life from all directions, beginning new careers at forty and fifty and at all ages opening up areas traditionally closed to them.

When we are in crisis it does us no good to look back and cry "mistakes and waste." Instead, we should try to turn off the emotional faucet. Turn off the self-deprecations. You need your energy for building the future. The journey you have taken so far is only the beginning; for all of us, some parts of the journey will have been pleasant and some unpleasant. But pleasant or unpleasant it is *your* past and all of it is part of you and can be used in the future. What is past is unalterable; only the present and future can be *lived*. Cut off the "if onlys"—they can't be used, they can only prevent you from making the most of the present and building for the future. Concentrate on living "now for now," to repeat the concept we discussed in *Open Marriage.*

If we can change our mental set from the typical "oh what a waste of time," negative attitude about people and experiences to a more positive attitude that allows us to ask, what have I learned from that person or experience, what is the potential good that can be discovered, then we can *utilize* the past in dealing with our crisis or devising a strategy for the future. Susan's life with her husband is not wasted—it is a resource from which she can develop a full awareness of her present situation, discovering for herself the crisis question. For Susan the question may be something like, Don't I need something more than my husband and family to fulfill me? Now that her husband is asking for a divorce, she has moved beyond the asking of that question. Moving on to answering that question in a way that will unfold her own potentials and her own self-development will be a growth-producing step. It will involve her with new ways of discovering her inner self in mutual growth with the world around her.

The only way out of crisis is through growth. Not growth by accretion, by trying to make what lies outside into "me"; not growth by replication, by copying what somebody else is doing; but the kind of growth that involves a mutual exchange with the world around you, in which you learn by exploring similarities *and* reaching out for differences. Such growth integrates the past with the future. You take from your past what is valuable, you learn new things in the course of shifting gears, evaluating, exploring and experimenting, and then, by making the decision, taking the step, and letting go of the parts of the past that are not useful, you move on to a new level of growth and of knowledge. And each time you grow, the more knowledge you have, the more knowledge you can have and the more growth you can achieve.

In crisis, it may seem to you that your life structure is a rambling hodgepodge of disconnected, unrelated, narrow windowless rooms—the building blocks and beams may seem cockeyed, jerry-built and hardly worth saving. But you can salvage the materials and start all over again with a new design. Now, using the materials you already have in a new way, you can construct the kind of building, the kind of life, that meets your needs, your hopes and your dreams. The building blocks of the past are not wasted; they are the raw materials out of which you build the future. But if you stand around bewailing the shape of the old structure instead of getting about the business of rebuilding it, you can waste the *future*. Rebuilding requires effort and courage—knocking apart the old structures to get at the usable raw materials is uncomfortable, even painful, but when the ground is leveled and the view beyond is clear, the excitement of building anew takes over.

CHAPTER SEVEN

Centering and Focusing

The Crisis of Elena and Edward

At 1:30 A.M. the phone rang. The building superintendent at the apartment house where Edward's seventy-nine-year-old mother lived alone was calling to tell them that they would have to come pick her up: she had wandered out into the street in her dressing gown and refused to return to her own apartment. Elena and Edward, in their late forties, lived nearby. Two years before, when Edward's father had died, they had brought his mother, Maria, from Florida to be near them in Pittsburgh. Over the past several months they had become aware that Maria was becoming increasingly senile, and that she was simply too disorganized to cope for herself. Always affectionate, but volatile and compulsive, Maria was now more cantankerous and independent than ever. Edward and Elena had tried a number of stopgap responses to the situation, which, given Maria's personality, did not work. The phone call from the superintendent precipitated the full crisis. But let them tell the story:

Edward: "What could we do? A decision had to be made—did we bring her into our home, which was what we really wanted to do, or did we put her in a nursing home? She was no longer able to take care of herself. She lost her money, let strangers in off the street, burned herself when she was cooking, and she constantly shifted around every object in her apartment all day long. Somebody had to be with her twenty-four hours a day. We couldn't afford a nurse at home. So who was it going to be? Elena or me? Our daughter Jane was in college, and our son John was married and living his own life. With the kids gone, Elena was working part time and going to graduate school for her degree—she was taking up where she'd left off when we were married. It was a terrible decision and I'm still not happy with the outcome."

Elena: "It seemed as though there was only one right decision. We should have taken her in with us, where she belonged. It's unthinkable in a Latin family to send your mother to a home—which was the only other alternative. My family is on the West coast, Edward is an only son, and most of Maria's friends were dead or lived in other parts of the country. But we had to think about what it was going to do to us. Ed loves Maria but they've never gotten along. She was always a difficult person to live with. She drove him crazy when she was rational, and now she wasn't even that. It would have destroyed Ed. I'd spent my entire adult life taking care of Ed and the children. I have no regrets about that, it was a great life, but now I needed to do some things just for myself. The real question was whether what we could give her was worth the frustration and unhappiness it was bound to cost."

Edward: "We'd be giving her love she can't get in a home—but for how long? In the long run we would have had three basket cases instead of just one. I didn't think we could survive it. Frankly both of us realized that we were not equipped, either physically or psychologically, to care for someone in her condition much as we wanted to. So we went to social service for help, and placed her in a home near us. We visit her, but it isn't the same thing. But we just couldn't see that the alternative was one we could cope with."

Elena: "That decision was the hardest one we ever had to make, and it's cost me more emotional wear and tear than I can tell you. I still feel guilty about it. I loved Maria and I appreciated everything she had done for me in the past, but I'd given as much to her as she had to me. At this point I just had to say that my needs and Edward's needs were important too. There just wasn't any right answer to the problem, but after looking at the situation from all sides, we came to the conclusion that the alternative we chose was less destructive than the other."

Elena and Edward have lived with their decision for several years now. It still pains them at times to think about it; they still feel guilty. But they also feel more strongly than ever that it was, under the circumstances, the best decision they could make, indeed the necessary decision. No life decision of this nature that any of us makes can be right or best for everybody. Anytime we move forward, anytime we make a major decision, it will cost us something. At times it may cost us pain and guilt. But if we do not move forward, if we refuse to face up to the costs of life, we become living dead, cease to grow and in the long run cause ourselves and others even greater misery.

Our crisis culture, in which so many changes are taking place in our values, our relationships and our family structure, has created new kinds of problems for all of us. The large, tightly knit family of fifty years ago would not have had to face Elena and Edward's crisis. When there are large numbers of relatives living within close geographical proximity of one another, some kind of accommodation can usually be worked out among various members of the family to share the burden of caring for an aged parent, so that all family members have some freedom of movement for their own development. But in today's mobile and urban society, with its smaller families living in small apartments scattered across the country and isolated from the rest of the family, traditional solutions are often impossible and we find ourselves compelled to make much more difficult decisions about a wide range of problems.

If we are to solve some of the crises our contemporary society forces on us, we must learn to put ourselves right into the *center* of that crisis, to come to grips with situations as they are and to see things clearly enough to make a decision about the course of our lives.

These decisions will invariably affect others. If we put ourselves in the center of the crisis, if we focus on the problem clearly and accept responsibility for what we do, our decisions are more likely to affect others in a positive way. As Edward discovered, "We had to come to grips with ourselves and realize that what we did, despite our feelings of guilt, was probably better for Maria. Her real need in her condition was for professional care. And, in fact, since she has been there, she has improved and even recognizes me occasionally when I visit."

Elena added, "We almost went ahead and took Maria in anyway, in spite of our conviction that it would be a disaster and regardless of the consequences to ourselves. But if we had, it would have been primarily because we were afraid of feeling guilty about putting her in a home. And it just seemed to me there was something cowardly about that—I mean if you can't accept responsibility for doing what you know is the best thing, then you're not worth much to anybody, are you?"

Many of us though, would not have been as willing as Elena and Edward were to accept the responsibility for their own actions. Many make a practice of doing or not doing things because we are afraid we will feel guilty or that other people won't approve. We stand on the periphery of events swayed by the externals into making decisions that may seem "right" at the time but which ultimately may turn out wrong for everyone.

It is only when we begin to know ourself and are in touch with our own center—only when we decide that we truly count—that we can give in a truly supportive and loving way to others. Until we know our own needs we cannot judge or deal with the needs of others closest to us. Love and support that are given out of guilt and a sense of sacrifice can only turn sour. If we lose our sense of self then we also lose our ability to connect fully and compassionately with others. When a man gives up a job that is causing him conflict, even though the new job he chooses pays a lot less and means that he can do less financially for his family, the end result is still a better husband and father—what he is giving, though it may be less in material terms, is given out of his own fulfillment and thus has greater value. A jilted lover or spouse who finally manages to find his or her own center and meaning in life becomes a less dependent person and one more capable of intimacy and giving in his next relationship. The end result for responsible and caring divorced parents is not only happier parents, but children who no longer suffer uncertainty, fear and torn allegiances, children who thrive better with confident and productive separated parents than with miserable and unstable ones who stay together.

Thus centering is not a matter of being self-centered in the old, derogatory sense; it is a matter of finding our stable center of self so that we can then give freely and openly to others out of our own fulfillment. Many of the choices we have to make in our crisis culture are bound to be ones that create some unhappiness and dissatisfaction; many times a decision will not seem to be the best for everyone. But we can make these confrontations with life decisions an opportunity for growth and finding our connectedness with life.

Edward and Elena's situation points out one important use of centering in the midst of crisis. Another use of centering is to promote our awareness in the first step in shifting gears as a preparation for change. Susan, mentioned in the previous chapter, will have to find some new direction in her own life if she is to resolve her crisis now that her husband wants a divorce. To do this, she will first have to concentrate on herself. She will have to center on *her* needs and desires if she is to make some kind of meaning out of her future life.

Like many adults, Susan has probably gone through life making decisions, learning and living without much thought about her inner self. Instead of spending time on remorse, she should begin the process of getting to know herself and finding that inner balance which can direct her toward growth.

Centering

Each person's life is important, but we cannot see that importance in its true light until we learn to recognize ourselves as the center of our lives. We are of little value to others if we cannot be of value to ourselves. Being centered on your individual self gives you the solid base you must have to work out your crises and problems. As Fritz Perls, the author of *Gestalt Therapy Verbatim,* has said, "Without a center, everything goes on in the periphery and there is no place from which to work, from which to cope with the world. . . . This achieving the center, being grounded in one's self, is about the highest state a human being can achieve."

Centering is the process of becoming aware of what *you* really want, how *you* really feel, what *you* really need. It is the process by which you come to know your essential self—your center of being which gives you a feeling of balance in life. Centering helps you to feel in place in life, and being centered is feeling confidence and security in yourself. A man who recently changed from corporation life to greater freedom and satisfaction in free-lance work explained that "being centered for me is having left behind the old anguish and the old restraints about conforming to someone's else's expectations. It is being able to travel through life without having to touch base with all the old landmarks and signposts that used to make me feel secure. I *am* in place with myself because I am at home with myself."

To use a very simple analogy: being centered is like riding a bike. The feeling of knowing your center of balance and feeling sure of yourself is the same. Now riding a bike doesn't take much; almost anyone can do it. But you must get it rolling and risk falling before you can experience balancing. No one can do it for you; *you* must find that inner sense of balance for yourself. Having once learned it, you never forget it and your mastery of the bike enables you to move that bike in the direction you want to go. Having once learned to center, you find that inner sense of confidence and belief in yourself that enables you to be more flexible, yet more certain that you can manage your decisions, actions, crises and growth in a positive way.

To center involves getting in touch with three different aspects of the self. One aspect is that part of the self which responds to life out of feelings and emotions. What are we, how do we act and what kind of *feelings* direct our actions? Knowing and recognizing ourselves as we are is the first step to changing to something we may want to be.

Another aspect is getting in touch with that part of the self that is not consciously organized. This is the psychic reservoir from which we draw our creativity: our memories, feelings, dreams, fantasies. This is the raw material of the self, rich with as yet un-

formed connections; if we can make this raw material
known to ourselves, can get more fully in touch with
it, we can begin to form those latent connections,
drawing upon them not only for greater individual
creativity but also as a means for becoming fully involved with others and the world around us.

The third aspect of the self is the will. This is the
force from which we derive the energy to act. This
kind of will is not to be confused with willfulness or
being headstrong. It is rather the *strength* behind our
actions, the directing center of the self. Many of us
recognize or feel the full force and power of our will
only when we are in a survival situation in which we
must act instantly. It is the force we are talking about
when we speak of a critically ill person's having "a
strong will to live." All of us have will, but we must
constantly reaffirm it, find it anew, in order to choose
freely how we want to direct our life and development.
Whether we must find it quickly in a crisis, or are able
to nourish its development slowly in small steps before
we try to make a change, it is essential to our growth.
"Only when the individual is in full possession of his
will and is fully conscious of it," says the psychoana-
lyst Arieti, "can his self flourish and grow."

When we become aware of our feelings, inner resources and our will, we can not only grow through
crisis and find our purpose in life, but we can also do
the things we want to more effectively. Ray Bradbury,
the science-fiction writer, once commented, ". . . I
would say that the days in the one year when I learned
to trust my passion, my emotions, my hungers, my
hates, my loves, my first needs, rather than the blind
god reason, was the day I began to write good short
stories." This sense of trust in our inner selves is being
centered.

There are a number of techniques that can help us
in learning to center, but before we discuss them, let
us return for a moment to Edward and Elena. They
were able to solve their crisis over Edward's mother

with some confidence in their decision, if not without pangs of regret and guilt—because both had gone through personal change. In recent years, both had shifted gears: Edward from a high-paying sales job he disliked to a less remunerative position teaching mathematics and Elena from housewife and mother to working for her degree in child psychology. Both of them had learned to center and to recognize their emerging needs for new kinds of involvement and fulfillment—Edward because he realized that stress and competition gave him little satisfaction and Elena because she needed a new purpose in life and an affirmation of her individual self.

Centering can not only help you find a new direction in life, but it can also help you feel confidence in your self no matter how your life changes or what direction you take. Julie, a young college teacher, discovered this one summer. "I guess you can say I discovered my own uniqueness," she said. "I accepted my plusses and minuses—my good and bad traits, and I learned to appreciate them. For the very first time in my life I realized that *happiness lies within me*. You know, every year I panicked going through the fear of not being reappointed. I don't have tenure and I used to see myself on the breadline if I lost my job here. Now I say, So what if I am not reappointed. There are other alternatives, other colleges. My happiness lies within me, and I can take that happiness with me wherever I go—even to Morton's chocolate factory, if that's what I want." How one finds this sense of internal consistency and security will vary from individual to individual, but the following suggestions may help you to find your own way.

Centering Techniques

Centering, getting in touch with our true selves, is something we must basically do alone, by ourselves. Being alone gives us the ability to make contact with the deepest parts of ourselves. As long as we are pushed and pulled by forces outside ourselves we can never become the center of anything except those demands, obligations and expectations. We need time in which we can turn off the outside world and quietly get to know ourselves, to experience our thoughts as our own, and to formulate our own questions. The following techniques all have to do with making use of our aloneness to discover our true centers.

(1) *Don't be afraid to waste time.* All of us need time to do nothing. Within limits, "wasting time" is not only healthy but useful. The idea that it is bad to waste time is a stifling hand-me-down of the puritan work ethic. We waste time anyway, but we feel guilty about it. Other cultures—those of the Mediterranean countries for instance—find laughable the injunction that wasted time is lost time. The people of such cultures are able to waste time joyfully, without guilt, to take pleasure in those times they spend doing nothing, hanging around the fountain or sitting in the sun in the courtyard or plaza. If you always feel guilty when you aren't doing something "constructive," you will have a hard time getting in touch with yourself. People who can't waste time without feeling guilty inevitably wind themselves up tighter and tighter, worrying their problems into the ground; they lose perspective and perform their "constructive" tasks less efficiently in the end. "Wasted time" isn't really wasted —it's just unstructured. And it is in our unstructured moments that we are most open to the unconscious reservoir of creativity that exists in all of us.

(2) *Daydreaming can be very productive in helping us to center.* Daydreaming is mental drifting and wandering, at times unfocused and at times going over the edge into fantasy. If we are open enough to let ourselves experience our daydreams fully, they can tell us a lot about ourselves, about the desires we ordinarily censor out or keep under wraps. In daydreams you innovate, imagine, conjure. Daydreams are not reality,

but they can give you clues to things you may want to make into reality. As the eminent Yale psychologist Jerome Singer has said, "The ability to make believe and to day-dream is a cognitive skill which helps make people more creative, more flexible in solving problems and better able to postpone immediate gratification in favor of long-range goals." So why not daydream to learn more about yourself? Why not rekindle childhood dreams and open up the possibilities for letting them guide you to where you may really want to go?

It is only a step from wandering in our daydreams to the point where something clicks and we focus on one of them. Consciously examining a particular daydream can serve to put us in closer touch with our unconscious wishes, desires and hopes. We can then begin to *direct our daydreams,* not merely following their course, but pushing them in new directions to see where they will take us. When we begin to direct our daydreams we are taking a step in planning a change in our lives. By concentrating on and directing our daydreams we not only nourish our hopes but begin to draw upon our inner resources, and our creativity as well as our will.

Directing our daydreams gives us practice in projected problem solving, and planning to implement these dreams can increase our motivation and bring the pleasure of anticipation.

(3) *The real key to centering is checking things out with yourself.* It has been said that you can best know a man by the questions he asks rather than the answers he gives. The answer we give today, based on the best current information, may not be adequate tomorrow when additional or conflicting information comes to light. Even the supposedly final, often sacrosanct, answers of science are constantly being updated as new information becomes available. For human beings, whose lives are a *process,* growth and change will inevitably bring different answers during different

phases of adulthood. But in arriving at the answers that are the best possible ones for us at a given period of our lives, we can ask the same kinds of questions whether we are shifting gears at thirty or at fifty or seventy.

During this period of questioning, of checking things out with yourself, try to dispense with all the *shoulds* and *oughts* in your life. Try to postpone judgment of yourself, eliminating words like *good* and *bad* and *worthless* and *valuable,* and concentrating instead on your pure response.

There are a number of ways of going about asking the questions that are essential to the centering process. One of the best approaches has been presented by John Stevens in his excellent book, *Awareness,* from which we have drawn in the material below.

To begin with, complete the sentences "I need . . ." and "I want. . . ." Make a long list for "I need" and then a long list for "I want." You may find it easiest to write them down. Examine your feelings about the things that you said you needed. Do you really experience them as a need, or can you begin to "realize the difference between something that you really need, like air and food, in contrast to other things you want that are very pleasant and nice, but not absolutely necessary." Couldn't you survive without most of them? You may, as John Stevens suggests, experience a feeling of lightness and freedom once you have realized that "some of your 'needs' are really only conveniences and not necessities." Then examine your "I want" list and compare the two. When we begin to see a *need* as a *want,* our feeling about it becomes much less desperate. Your needs tend to control you, to "own" you, while you control and "own" your wants. Thus every need you can see freshly as a want begins to come under your control, becomes a choice rather than an imperative. And when we have a sense of choice and control we can more easily move forward to fulfill our wants.

Another pair of sentences to complete that can give you insight are those beginning with "I have to . . ." and with "I choose to. . . ." Make your list for each one. Then try replacing the "I have to" sentences with "I choose to." Add the reasons why you "choose to." As we begin to take responsibility for our choices, we can begin to see new possibilities for self-determining action and new reasons for our behavior. Other statements you might experiment with are: "I can't . . ." and "I won't . . ." or "I'm afraid to . . ." and "I'd like to. . . ."

Very often in asking these various questions we will discover that many things that we begin by saying we need, or that we feel we have to do, are really things that other people have *told* us we should need or ought to do. And we've gone along with what we've been told, without really thinking about it. But if we are to discover our true centers as individuals this is exactly what we must think about. Look at your lists again, and ask yourself, Who told me I needed that, or that I have to do that? Did I tell myself? Or did somebody else tell me? If somebody else told you, then it is even more important to check things out with your *self;* do you "own" your values and responses or are they simply borrowed from somebody else? If you don't own them, they own you—which means that you are really owned by somebody else.

In order to begin to own ourselves, and to prevent other people from owning us, we must be able to say *yes* or *no* because that is the answer we want to give rather than because it is the answer the other person wants to hear. It can be a revealing exercise to examine a situation in which you said *yes* or *no* and really wanted to say the opposite. Many of us find it difficult to say *no,* ending up not only with loss of self but with our commitments stretched so thin that we can't do anything effectively. Some people say *yes* because they think it will make them look better, or that they will be rewarded for agreeing (this form is so prevalent that it has contributed a phrase to the language: the yes-man, of the sort that surrounds business executives and politicians, to the public's endless cost). Other people say *yes* simply because it is the easiest way out; they chiefly don't want any trouble, and often after they say *yes* they fail to carry through (your landlord, plumber and auto mechanic may fall into this category).

Why are you saying *yes* when you would like to say *no?* Why are you saying *no* when you would like to say *yes?* To help you find out, take a recent situation in which you felt ambiguous about your *yes* or *no.* Ask yourself, What did it do *for* me to say *yes* (or *no*)?, What did I gain by saying *yes?,* What did I avoid by saying *yes?* Now imagine yourself making the opposite reply in the same situation. Ask yourself how you would feel as you said it. Imagine what the other person's response would be. And then put yourself in the other person's position. Do you feel more powerful as yourself or as the other person? In that situation do you own yourself or does the other person own you?

Once you begin to own your self and your feelings in answering *yes* or *no,* once you begin to understand why you respond with a *yes* or a *no,* you are beginning to be aware of your self, you are involved in the processing of centering.

(4) *Free Flow Dialogue With The Self.* We can also experience our centers by being *open* to ourselves in moments of solitude and letting the dialogue with self flow freely into an examination of the inner-self —an examination of our hurts, passions and sorrows as well as our discoveries of strength. Often this free flow helps us to restore and reaffirm our trust and faith in our self, but quite often it brings an awareness of our essential loneliness. It requires courage, but such loneliness can be as Dr. Clark Moustakas points out, ". . . associated with a new truth that suddenly shatters old perceptions and ideas." It is this dialogue

with the self that ". . . precedes clarity of awareness, a sense of direction and action."

(5) *Discover your feelings by talking about them.* For this you need a special kind of person in whom you trust, to listen to your disclosures and exploration of self. The way that person listens to you and encourages you is of paramount importance. Encouragement does *not* mean probing or questioning. His attitude should be receptive, caring and nonjudgmental, if you are to center and find out more about yourself through his listening. It is not easy to find someone who can listen without coloring your feelings with his own or without leaping to interpretations before you have made them. But ideally, many of our intimate relationships in which we have respect and caring could help us to learn more about ourselves in this way.

We have experiences and we *feel* something about those experiences: perhaps our reactions to a boss's order, the way we shouted at our wife, our joy in being with someone, or our reactions to saying *no* at last when we really wanted to. The meanings of many of our experiences and feelings about them are undefined and vague until we can bring them into the light of our consciousness and express them. We discover what Dr. Eugene Gendlin has called the "felt meaning" of our experiences when we express them. Through disclosing ourselves to another person we can uncover these implicit *meanings,* and as they become a reality to us, we can move on to new meanings of the experience for us. We can own our *feelings* about the experience and in the process dissipate our tensions and anxiety about them. In this process of clarification we unfold, grow and move on to new understandings and discovery of ways to change. As Dr. Gendlin has so perceptively shown in his research, personality change can occur through this type of experience.

Focusing

The purpose of centering is to know yourself, to get more fully in touch with your feelings and your potentials so that you can have a feeling of owning and directing your life. But it is not enough just to center. We must also learn to focus on something outside ourself. The purpose of this process is to make connections between your inner self and the outer world in order to enter into a meaningful exchange with life around you.

There is a famous illustration used in gestalt psychology which demonstrates the importance of focusing:

If you concentrate on the two outer, shaded segments of this picture, you will see two human profiles facing one another. The white segment in the middle becomes the background. But if you concentrate on the white center, the shaded segments become the background and you see a vase instead of faces. Thus, it is instantly apparent that we, as individuals, can *choose* our focus. Just as we can choose to focus on either the faces or the vase in this picture and make it the center of our attention, so we can change our focus in relation to any object, situation, idea or person.

Many people in today's world, however, living in a culture which presents them with a bewildering array of options, try to focus on too many things at once. If you try to focus on both the faces and the vase simultaneously you will find that it is impossible— your focus alternates from one image to the other. Unfortunately, that is what many people do in their lives. They alternate between options, unable to make a *choice* between one focus and another, and ending in a state of indecision and frustration. Most situations in life are not as clear-cut as the illustration of the vase and faces above, but are less confusing once we decide what *we* want to focus on.

Focusing means concentrating all your attention on one particular thing, bringing it into sharp relief in order to clarify your relationship to it and to become involved with it. When we concentrate our attention on a particular object, person, endeavor or problem we bring all our energy to it, we become completely absorbed by it, shutting out extraneous and irrelevant stimuli. We are surrounded by irrelevant stimuli in today's world, and if we try to deal with all of them at once, we find ourselves unable to deal successfully with any of them.

Many of us find ourselves caught in more than one crisis at once. We are overloaded with decisions that must be made. There seems no way out and we simply want to turn tail and run. It is at this point that focusing becomes essential. Take one crisis at a time —they are all related anyway, since they are yours. Concentrate on that crisis, relate only to that problem at the moment. Ask yourself the centering questions ("I need" and "I want," etc.) in respect to that particular problem and forget the others for the time being. By trying to consider all your problems at once, you can only end up in a muddle. But if you separate them, taking them one at a time, a natural progression will unfold, making it possible for you to arrive eventually at an overall perspective.

Focusing in the Larger Sense

The importance of focusing, however, does not lie only in its use as a practical tool for resolving a problem or crisis. There is a larger sense in which focusing, together with centering, is the key to productive fulfillment and finding a purpose in life. In order to achieve a wholeness as human beings we must invest the self that we have discovered, through centering, in the projects, relationships and jobs that we choose for self-fulfillment. That investment of the self in the external world is a matter of commitment, of truly giving ourselves to what we are doing.

Focusing in its largest sense means becoming intensely involved in something, and it is no different whether it is in an idea, a job, painting a picture or developing a friendship. It means becoming a part of and entering into an exchange with whatever you are focusing on. Most of us have experienced being so involved in and taken up with something that we completely forget ourselves in the experience. It might be a drama on the stage, a detective story, having sex, repairing a watch or making a soufflé. Or it could be anything we have a passionate interest in. In that moment we become totally immersed in the situation, fascinated and absorbed by it. We can experience this same sense of involvement in many aspects of our lives if we are aware of what it means to focus.

When you focus on a task or an idea, it means giving all your attention to it, looking for the similarities to and the differences from other experiences and feelings you have had, looking for ways you can bring something of yourself to it and being open to what it has to offer you, trying to find new ways to relate to it. These are the connections that stimulate our involvement with an idea or a job and through which we expand and grow within it. When you finally choose a focus everything falls into place and you discover, sometimes with surprise, that you can use many past experiences, resources and facets of yourself within the framework of that focus. You become passionately involved in it only when you do make the effort to find these connections and fully engage yourself in it. Whatever you choose to focus on will help you to grow and to understand the process more fully. And centering on yourself can help you to make this choice.

Let us return to the case of Edward and Elena. Their decision concerning Edward's mother was made on the basis of knowing their inner selves. Edward, in the process of centering, had discovered that he needed greater satisfaction and self-fulfillment in a less stressful life; Elena had discovered that she needed something beyond her role as housewife. But they had done more than find a new center. They had projected it into an interaction with the external world in their commitment to something outside themselves. Edward had focused by changing careers and devoting himself to teaching; Elena had focused by committing herself to a course of study in child psychology that would eventually lead to a new career.

It is not enough just to center. If a person centers on his inner self without at the same time finding a focus on something he can become involved with and give something to he may become merely self-centered, able to maintain his sense of self only by manipulating other people. The self-centered person refuses to accept the responsibility for his actions, and rationalizes them instead. He is not truly committed to or involved in anything outside himself. Elena and Edward accepted responsibility for their decision. They were aware of themselves *and* of their connection with life, of the ways in which they could grow through giving. In his teaching Edward was not simply fulfilling his self, but giving his self to others in the process. And Elena was studying child psychology not merely to satisfy her new sense of self, but also in preparation for imparting her knowledge through helping others in the future.

To focus in the larger sense, however, does not mean that we must be actively involved in helping other people in the way that a teacher, a doctor, a social worker or a fireman is. For instance, in the last few years there has been an active interest in the plight of blue-collar workers in such occupations as steelworking, automobile manufacturing and other assembly-line jobs. These workers have been protesting that the way in which their work is organized is both dehumanizing and intolerably boring. It effectively prevents them from having any kind of focused interaction with their jobs: you can't very well interact with a fender or a metal ingot after all. Furthermore, their need to be involved and respected as persons was ignored. Experiments in a number of factories, suggested by the workers themselves, have demonstrated that there is another way to set up the work patterns in such industries which does allow a sense of interaction. In several factories, workers have organized themselves into teams. Instead of one man doing nothing but attaching automobile fenders and the next man front bumpers, teams of four or more men work together exchanging jobs from hour to hour. Instead of being controlled by a foreman, the men decide among themselves who will do what when. And because they now have a chance to interact with one another instead of merely with nuts and bolts, they have developed an entirely new focus, a new attitude toward their jobs. They have become *involved* in a personal way with the job and with their coworkers. An increase in both efficiency and in personal job satisfaction has been the result. For the workers the benefit is increased self-esteem and a sense of self-determination. For the employers, the benefit is greater productivity on the job.

To achieve wholeness then, we must know more about ourselves and what we need and want by centering, but we must also put ourselves into action by focusing on a course of action or a goal outside ourselves. If you tend to focus on the outside world and a goal that someone else by way of the maturity myth has chosen for you, then there is bound to be a time when conflict will develop between that outer goal and your inner self. Similarly, if you pay too much attention to yourself and are merely self-centered, there is bound to be conflict between you and other people in both your professional and personal relationships—and a feeling of emptiness because you are not really involved with something outside yourself. Centering and focusing are like two sides of a coin. Each side is integral to the coin. Without each side there can *be* no coin, no wholeness. Similarly, we cannot grow or change without true involvement in the outside world. "The whole self," writes the philosopher Dr. Maurice Friedman, "is not what I am aware of when I am simply self-conscious. . . . Our wholeness is most there when we have forgotten ourselves in responding fully to what is not ourselves." The moment of interaction is the moment of growth. We become more ourselves in our actions and interactions with the world: with people, with jobs, with ideas, with objects, events and projects we enjoy as well as with crises and problems we must confront and grapple with. Vitality in life and our ability to grow and shift gears exists only in our confrontation and full engagement with it.

The Awareness Wheel

The way in which we bring together our external focusing and our internal centering is of vital importance—relating in a meaningful way what we have focused on to what we have inside ourselves provides the *connection* between the self and the larger world. Making these connections not only allows and encourages growth, but also gives us a sense of security. If we concentrate entirely on the external world, and that world changes (which it inevitably will), we have nothing to fall back on. Concentrating solely on the inner self, without reference to the realities of the world around us, makes it impossible to deal successfully with the changing world. It is the *feedback* between focusing and centering that *gives meaning* to our actions. And when our actions have meaning, we feel a sense of security. When the feedback mechanism breaks down, so does meaning, and without meaning we feel lost and afraid.

This feedback system, which we mentioned in the section on growth, affects our basic interaction with the world around us. We can explore our part in this feedback system in a more detailed way, showing what happens inside ourselves in our responses to the outside world. On its simplest level this system is in operation all the time, in every communication we have with other people. Although growth often takes place in spurts, these sudden leaps forward are based upon all the experience, all the communicating, that has gone before. So that if we understand better how moment-to-moment communication takes place, we will have a better grasp of how focusing and centering play their parts in resolving our crises.

To show you what happens inside our *self-system* during communication, we are drawing on a program for improving communication in relationships which was developed and researched at the University of

Minnesota Family Study Center. To help the couples in this program an *awareness wheel* was developed. Its primary purpose was to demonstrate how and why we respond to communications from another person, but we feel it is also applicable to all our responses to the outside world. The process is the same, whether the triggering action is your mate saying, "Please pass the butter," or asking for a divorce, whether someone jostles you on the subway or the company you work for closes down. The process by which we make external events meaningful is the same. The purpose of examining this sequence of internal events is to help

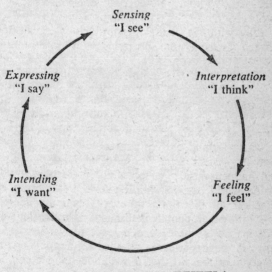

THE AWARENESS WHEEL*

FIG. 6

*Adapted from *Alive and Aware: Improving Communication in Relationships.* Interpersonal Communication Programs, Inc., Mpls. Mn., 1974.

you become aware of what happens inside yourself before you respond. If we can better understand what happens to us and become fully aware that *we* are at the center of our responses, we can then understand more clearly how to change.

Moving clockwise from the top of the wheel, we can explain each of these steps in the following way:

(1) *Sensing:* *All* information comes to us through one or more of our senses: sight, touch, smell, taste or sound. For convenience' sake, all the senses are represented on the wheel by the statement, "I see." We see our child running out into the street in front of an approaching car. Or we hear our husband yelling from another room, "Come here, Mary."

(2) *Interpretation:* The data or information, the things we "sense" from the outside world, are then interpreted. Our interpretation may take the form of an impression, an assumption or a conclusion. Sometimes the interpretation may be very direct and clear, as when our child runs out in front of a car: we immediately know that he is in danger. On the other hand, if our husband calls, "Come here, Mary," we may hear those words as a command, an appeal, a request or an exclamation of excitement, depending upon the tone of voice and the circumstances. But our interpretation may not be based on the tone of voice and the circumstances as much as it is on our own mood. If we are in a bad mood, and are centering on that mood to an extent that makes it difficult for us to focus on anything outside us, we may hear the words as a command when they were intended as an exclamation of pleasure. To the act of interpretation we bring our past and present feelings, our experiences and our perceptual sets. We may interpret correctly or incorrectly. Most foul-ups in communication and most misunderstandings between people occur between the act of sensing and of interpretation. Even our sensing is screened, and perhaps distorted, through

our perceptual filter—that particular way in which we view our life.

(3) *Feeling:* We experience a feeling as we make an interpretation. This, too, is related to our past experiences and behavior sets. We might, for instance, interpret "Come here, Mary," as a command even though it was really an exclamation of excitement if we were always imperiously commanded—and expected to obey without question—during our childhood. If so, our feeling may be one of irritation or resistance. If what we heard was an exclamation, and we *have* interpreted it correctly as that, we may have a feeling of anticipation or shared excitement. Frequently, of course, we may repress our true feelings. We are trained through socialization, suggestion and pressure to deny our true feelings about many things that we sense and must interpret. Sometimes we repress our bad feelings, our anger when we are pushed in a crowd, or our hurt when someone says something rude about the way we look. At other times we repress our good feelings of joy, excitement and affection; American men, for instance, are taught to repress their feelings of sentiment and affection as being "unmanly," just as American women are taught to repress feelings of assertiveness as being "unfeminine."

(4) *Intentions:* Based upon our awareness, we have intentions. When, in reaction to our child running out into the street, we see, interpret and feel, intention follows almost instantaneously. We want to save him from the danger. When we hear "Come here, Mary," our intention—whether it be to respond verbally, to hurry into the other room or to ignore the call—will be guided by what happened previously during the cycle, in the interpretation and feeling steps. To ignore the call, to screen it out, is an intention even though it brings the cycle to a halt. Sometimes we have to screen things out—you can't respond to everything, after all. Then no further action is necessary. If you are in the middle of a telephone call when your

husband yells from the next room, or you are lifting a
twenty-pound turkey out of the oven, it is very likely
that you will screen out his voice, at least for the
moment.

(5) *Expressing:* We then put our intentions into
action. (If we intend *not* to respond, we keep quiet,
which is also action in this sense.) We act immediately
to snatch our child out of danger. In responding to
"Come here, Mary," there are a greater number of
possible actions open to us. Throughout this sequence,
in fact, we are making choices: about how to interpret
what we sense, whether to deny or accept our feelings,
what kind of intentions we will adopt, and how to
express our intentions. Most of these choices are made
unconsciously in ordinary communication. When we
are in crisis, however, it is important to become consciously aware of what is happening to us during these
steps in the awareness sequence.

Recognizing and being aware of these steps should
make it possible for us to see more clearly how focusing and centering work, and to understand the importance of these two interacting processes. For instance, when we hear the words "Come here, Mary,"
from the next room, we can choose to focus or not
on this external stimulus. If we do not focus on the
tone of our husband's voice, we may misinterpret
his meaning. Our misinterpretation *could* lead to an
eventual argument with him because we have misunderstood. On the other hand, if we do not focus on
him because we are holding the hot pan with the
turkey in midair, we are quite rightly putting our
emphasis where it belongs. What we are doing at that
particular moment requires our full attention—and
we can assume that when he discovers why we didn't
answer him, he will understand. We are being selective
about what we will focus on, because at that moment
it is more important to center on our own self. We
hear his voice, but it only takes an instant to check
out with our self whether or not to respond.

If we do respond, then it is important to *focus* on his tone of voice, and then to *center* on our interpretation of what we hear if we are going to succeed in making an appropriate response. In crisis, the importance of achieving this interaction between focusing and centering is raised to the highest degree. If we refuse to face up to our crisis, to focus on it sufficiently to become fully aware of it, we will only prolong it. We are also delaying the completion of the awareness sequence when we ignore the words "Come here, Mary," but in this everyday situation the delay may be of minimum consequence. The same kind of delay applied to a crisis—whether it is the sight of our child running into the street or the loss of a job—may be of maximum consequence. It may make things a great deal worse. Thus, in crisis, focusing on our problem becomes of much greater importance than usual.

But centering also becomes of greater importance in crisis. After we have focused on the crisis sufficiently to be fully aware of it, to be ready to face up to it, we must begin interpreting it. This interpretive step on the awareness wheel corresponds to the steps of evaluation and exploration in the shifting gears process. In order to interpret the crisis successfully, we must center on our inner selves, asking ourselves what we really want, what we really feel and how we can act in new ways that will help us resolve the crisis. And while in ordinary communication we may move rapidly, almost instantaneously, through the awareness sequence, in crisis it may be necessary to focus and then center several times as we progress through each step of the sequence. Each time we do this the two processes provide feedback for one another, so that each time we are able to focus on our problem with a little more precision and to center with greater understanding of the inner self.

This process can be just as important in *any* change in our lives. When we are confronted with change or the challenge of something different many of us ignore or suppress our internal responses, or we respond spontaneously and automatically out of habit. We *re-act* instead of *acting* or being aware of the way in which our feelings influence our intention and direct our actions. Instead of responding immediately in old patterns, in rejection of something that is different, we can use our understanding of this sequence to discover what is happening inside ourselves. We can stop and examine our *re-actions* at any point in the sequence and for the first time, perhaps, make them intentional *actions*. If we are to confront change and grow, if we are to open up to these possibilities within ourselves for growth, we must begin to think and to know why and how we act—to open up to the possibility that things outside us may be different and for a good reason. To re-act out of old habits and defenses to something different because we are afraid to see or recognize the reasons for them or the value of them is to deny our possibilities for growth. It is the open person who is willing to confront himself in the meeting with life, the one who is willing to grapple with change and go through the effort and pain of examing his senses, feelings and interpretations of events, who is able to grow. Personal change comes only through confrontation with a reality different from ours.

When our feelings, our inner resources and our will are explored and used in consort with one another, we experience a sense of wholeness. Yet the benefits go beyond simple wholeness, for each of the elements of the self then enhances the others in a continually expanding, synergic way. The resulting synergic power makes it possible for us not only to make better, stronger decisions, but also to achieve harmony both within the self and in relation to the environment in which we live.

The process of focusing and centering, then, can

help us reach the point of being able to proceed to a decision about how to move forward and change, and how to resolve our crisis in a way that promotes maximum growth.

CHAPTER EIGHT

Decision-Making

Priorities

Steven T. was in his late forties. More than twenty years earlier, fresh out of business school, he had gone to work for his father-in-law, a garment manufacturer. His plan had been to work with his father-in-law's company for five years, to gain experience, and then to strike out on his own. But before those five years had passed, his father-in-law's business partner had died. Steven's father-in-law was the creative brain of the company, but his partner had handled the financial end. It was clear that if the company was to continue, a new treasurer would have to be found. Reluctantly, Steven had agreed to take on the job. He and the company had prospered, but as the years passed, Steven became increasingly aware that he wanted to do something different with his life. When his father-in-law died at seventy, still working, Steven decided that it was time to make a change if he was ever going to do it.

Steven had always felt a special affinity for academic life—his grandfather had been a high-school principal and several aunts and uncles had been teachers, at both the high school and college level. It seemed to him that his business expertise would suit him admirably for the position of treasurer in a private school or college, where hopefully it would also be possible for him to teach a course or two on the side.

At this point in his life, Steven began to center on himself in a new way. He knew what he wanted for himself in very concrete terms. Almost certainly he would make considerably less money if he embarked on the new career he envisioned for himself. But money was not a first priority. The first priority was to find a position that would satisfy him more fully, and in different ways. On the other hand, there was his family to consider. He had two teen-aged children. The first priority for them was an education that would make it possible for them to make the most of their lives. At that time, the family lived in a Connecticut town that had a first-rate public high school, one of the best in the country. Steven knew that his possible new career might take him to a town or city where no such comparable educational facilities were available.

There was also his wife, Janice, to consider. For fifteen years they had lived in the same house. The house itself was extremely comfortable and attractive, but what made it special was not only the feeling of a warm home Janice made for him and the children, but also its gardens. These were Janice's work. On their two acres of land Janice had lovingly created a small botanical paradise, nurturing flowering trees and bushes from all over the world. There were a rose garden, an Oriental rock garden, an extraordinary asparagus bed, raspberry and strawberry patches. Janice's work had been featured in national magazines several times, and Steven knew how much it meant to her. Aside from caring for her family it was her first interest.

Knowing that a move to another part of the country would interfere with the priorities in the lives of both his children and Janice, Steven hesitated to change anything. But he had spent twenty years orchestrating his life according to the priorities of his children, of Janice and of her father. He felt deeply that it was only fair that he now have a chance to exercise his own priorities. For years he had known that his true self could be fulfilled only by circumstances other than those in which his father-in-law's company placed him.

At last, he told his family that he had decided to make a change. He talked to Janice first, telling her of his own needs and suggesting that if whatever new job he found took him to another state, they could keep the Connecticut house, that he would take a small apartment in the new town or city, and that Janice could join him as often as possible. Then he talked to the children, suggesting that if they did not want to go where he was going, he would try to find boarding schools for them where they would be happy. If his new job were in a neighboring state, they might even be able to continue in the local school, and he would fly home on weekends. "I told them I didn't know quite how it would all work out. But I wanted them to realize two things. The first was that I cared a great deal about their happiness and their needs. And the second was that I also had a right to my needs. I said I'd do everything I possibly could to protect their needs while I was pursuing my own, but that if I didn't find another way of life for myself I wasn't going to be much use to them anyway."

Steven's family surprised him. To begin with, Janice said that although it would make her very sad to leave that house and the gardens she had put so much into, she would want to go with him. Aside from the fact that she wanted to be with him, the challenge of creating a new garden someplace else appealed to her. The only stipulation she made was that they wouldn't sell the old house to anyone who wouldn't care whether her garden lived or died. Steven's children said simply that they'd thought for two or three years that he ought to do something else—they'd known he was unhappy.

Since this story has a happy ending (a doubly

happy one, in that the job Steven found was with a college only twenty miles away), we would like to emphasize that this is a true case history. The fact that it is true is not important so much for the fact that happy endings do indeed exist, as it is for the fact that Steven hesitated unnecessarily for more than a year before telling his family of his need for something new. When your needs are authentic, and when you are a compassionate person with a full recognition of other people's needs and priorities, the chances are that the people you care about will be more ready to understand than you might expect.

In making a major life decision that also affects others, most people will find that their pattern of response will probably fall into one of the four following categories:

(1) Those who know their own needs and priorities and are also aware of the needs and priorities of others.

(2) Those who know their own needs and priorities but whose first concern is the approval of others.

(3) Those who are uncertain as to their own needs and priorities and look to others to tell them what to do.

(4) Those who know their own needs and priorities and simply do not give a damn about the needs and priorities of others.

The first type of person will act to fulfill his own needs, but will do so in a mature, responsible and compassionate way, attempting to make the reasons for his action as clear as possible to those he cares about, and looking for ways in which to protect the needs of others. Steven is a prime example of this first type. The second type will make a decision in which he puts his own needs second to the approval he seeks from others. He will try to find out what other people would like him to do and will look for ways to fulfill his own needs on other people's terms. This may work in the short run, but in the end he will end up back where he started—with his needs unfulfilled. Such people, because they are unwilling to take the risk of making a definitive decision, of fully shifting gears, often create additional crises for themselves, and are constantly trying to catch up with their true selves. Basically they want to have their cake and eat it too; they will never succeed in realizing their full potential until they summon up the courage to shift gears completely and accept the responsibility for doing so.

The third type, uncertain of his own needs, has not yet learned to center, and is out of touch with himself. He is easily manipulated by other people, ever-ready to conform to the values and priorities of others. He never feels truly secure because he has placed the meaning and purpose of his life in the hands of others. Unless he takes charge of his own life, he will live in constant fear of change, both in himself and in the world around him.

The fourth type is, quite simply, dangerous. He does not care what happens to other people, so long as he has what he wants. Because he does not take the needs or feelings of others into account he may be good at making decisions, but the decisions he makes are often destructive. He victimizes those who are uncertain, manipulating them for his own selfish ends— usually rationalizing his actions and believing that he is really helping the people he attempts to control. He always knows what is "best" for everybody—and that's what is best for him.

All of us respond in each of these four ways at one time or another. There is not one of us who hasn't made a self-centered decision on occasion, and rationalized our reasons for doing so. There are times when it may even be necessary to tell the rest of the world to go jump in the lake—it is only when that kind of pattern comes to dominate the individual's life, when a majority of his decisions are self-centered ones, that he becomes a real menace to the rest of us. Such people unfortunately tend to find their way into positions of power, precisely because they are so ruthless in making decisions. But most of us are more likely to err in the opposite direction; not knowing our own priorities, we fall back on the will of others to see us through or, seeking the approval of others, we do what they want us to do even though we *are* aware of our needs.

But if we can't expect always to achieve the fully mature response—acting on our own needs and priorities while retaining a compassionate awareness of the needs and priorities of others—we can always *aspire* to achieved in full, but the higher the standards we set for ourselves, the closer we come to realizing our potentials. All of us know people who have achieved more with limited ability than others with seemingly greater talent—and the difference between them is the level of aspiration and commitment they bring to the task. The true genius of human beings is their ability to transcend their limitations through the combination of aspiration and commitment. Only by centering upon our true needs do we recognize our full potential; only by focusing upon the fulfillment of that potential through action do we extend ourselves beyond our limitations.

Priority-Establishing Techniques

This book as a whole is concerned with understanding our individual priorities and their relation to the changing world in which we live. Many of the concepts we have discussed in previous chapters have a direct bearing upon establishing our priorities. An understanding of how the maturity myth affects you, knowing that there are different phases of adulthood in which you will need different kinds of fulfillment, learning how to free yourself from the idea that the past is "wasted"—all of these concepts are integral to establishing your priorities.

We have also previously discussed some specific techniques that you can use. In Chapter Four we touched on the possible uses of the time management techniques of Alan Lakein in discovering which of your present commitments can be trimmed back to make room for the fulfillment of new needs. In his book *How to Get Control of Your Time and Life,* Lakein suggests dividing the components of your life into "A," "B" and "C" lists, in order of their importance to you. Upon reflection, you may find that some items should be shifted from one column to another. Any new element that ends up in the "A" column should be acted upon—even, we would add, if it seems to conflict with some other "A" priority. If it is important enough to be in the "A" column, it deserves your full commitment. The fact that it conflicts with a holdover from the past is simply an indication that you are at the beginning of the process of shifting gears; your old need reflects the status quo, and although you may be reluctant to let it go, the new need represents the future and the path towards growth.

Dr. Sidney Simon has alternate suggestions for determining your priorities which he has developed for use in his values clarification courses: one of these is to make a list of your top priorities, say a baker's dozen, then subtract five that you could live without, and finally subtract two more that it would cause you hardship to let go but which you could do without in an emergency. The techniques discussed in Chapter Seven in regard to centering are also readily adaptable to making a determination of your priorities. Whatever method you use (and you may come up with one of your own), we do strongly urge that you get out a pencil and paper and write your priorities down. Verbalizing them is one way of concretizing them, but to write them down inevitably brings greater clarity. Depending upon the nature of the problems or crises facing you, it can also be useful to make such exercises a joint project with your husband, wife or lover. If the other person knows what you are doing from the beginning, the fact of your concern for him is fully established and a comparison of your priorities can reveal problem areas that can be discussed openly before they reach a crisis level. Sometimes it can be advisable to exchange priority lists while agreeing in advance not to discuss them until the next day.

But whether you are making up a priority list on your own or in conjunction with a loved one, try to be openminded in considering alternatives. After all, these are not things you have already made a decision about—you are merely seeking the information you need to base your decision on. Explore the unfamiliar, include one or two wild possibilities straight out of your daydreams. Make it clear, if you are drawing up a priority list to exchange with someone else, that you have put in some far-out possibilities. The other person may not think they are that strange, after all; in fact, the seemingly "impossible dreams" that you each come up with may be surprisingly similar and open up a whole new area for down-to-earth consideration.

Values

In order to fully comprehend the nature and meaning of our priorities, however, we must also know what our values are. Values differ from culture to culture; but they also differ from individual to individual within a given culture. We can see this clearly in a very simple example in the idea of "first come, first served." In England and America, if we go into a butcher shop we expect to be waited on in the order in which we arrive. The butchers take care to notice that order, and if someone tries to jump his turn, either the butcher or another customer who was there first is likely to point out the facts of the situation. In some countries, on the other hand, it comes down to the one who can shout the loudest getting served first. You may have been in the butcher shop for ten minutes, patiently waiting to get someone's attention in the midst of the hubbub. Suddenly, from five feet behind you an old lady in a black shawl who has come into the store that very moment bawls out her order over the heads of those in front of her—and more likely than not, she'll be served before you are. In some countries, line jumping is the expected thing, a kind of game that some people are better at than others.

However, there are some Americans who constantly try to muscle into lines, and people in other countries who regard their countrymen's behavior as disgraceful. Such people do not share, at least in this regard, the general cultural values of the society they live in.

In today's crisis culture, then, we have a double problem in discovering what our values really are. Not only may our personal values diverge from the general cultural values of the society, but those cultural values themselves are changing at an unprecedented rate. When our personal value sets have been shaped by and in the context of societal norms that no longer exist, we are inevitably in trouble. And in the crisis culture, the "norms" seem to change almost yearly. That is the real basis of what is called the "generation gap"—our children do not understand or choose to live by our values for the simple reason that those values are no longer reflected in the culture at large. It isn't that today's children are more rebellious; rather they are being formed by a different culture from the one that formed their parents.

Cultural *themes,* like "first come, first served," are the *shoulds* and *shouldn't*s of society in general. We don't get up each day and repeat to ourselves the themes and values by which each of us lives, of course. Yet our actions and reactions are determined by the value system we have incorporated into our inner selves. But in today's world the values we have internalized often turn out to be at odds with what is going on in the world around us. When our educational system in many urban centers is a shambles, when teen-age gangs and grown-up junkies run wild in the streets, when people are murdered at midday *after* giving up their money to their assailants, we can't very well tell our children to try to cope with the world on the basis of the values that most Americans lived by only two or three decades ago. The old standbys for the transmission of values are becoming less meaningful all the time. Most of us now have to live with two sets of values—those we would hope to live by, and those new values that are the result of techno-cultural revolution and its impact upon every facet of our lives.

To show just how much things have changed, let us examine the Boy Scout Law, which incorporates twelve value ideals that expressed our "social" values fifty years ago. The Law reads that a scout is: "Trustworthy, Loyal, Helpful, Friendly, Courteous, Kind, Obedient, Cheerful, Thrifty, Brave, Clean and Reverent."

But what do these values mean today? How can we talk about trustworthiness when top government officials tap the telephones of their own aides? When loyalty leads directly to Watergate, can we be sure that loyalty is a good thing? How can we speak of helpfulness when dozens of people hurry by while a young woman is murdered on the street? Is it possible to be friendly with your neighbors in the cities of America anymore? If you're courteous and kind you are frequently snubbed or even taken advantage of. When obedience to corporate and governmental orders means lying to the public, when thrift means cutting back on medical care for the aged, when bravery is tied up in our minds with Vietnam, how can we even talk about being clean or reverent?

Most of us would like to believe that these and other values are still operative, but the majority of them have been distorted and misused so many times that our entire culture has become unsure of its own definitions of what is right and good and in which situation. Thus what we have to do is to make the values we choose meaningful to us personally first and then hope to make them meaningful for the group. Once we took all our values from the group without question; now we must reaffirm the meaning of these values for ourselves. And even as we make our own values, we may need a second or subsidiary set of "coping values" that allow us to function in the world in which we live. Thus our task is twofold: (1) to develop a set of coping techniques, and (2) to look for ways to reinforce and reaffirm our basic and universal human values in the face of change.

If the church is weakening, if the schools are failing, if the most basic building block of our society, the family, is breaking up—where are the values to come from?

Are we to model our own values on those of television shows? Are we to walk the streets in apprehension day and night? Are we to resign ourselves to the conclusion that nothing can be done, to relegate ourselves to the societal jungle without hope of change and simply pray for personal survival? Some may think this is the only course. Yet, as individuals, we can initiate constructive change and redirect the downhill trend of our culture. We can restructure our values, blending the old with the new, and design, or at least prepare, for those that will inevitably come. We can work out life values that build human dignity and minimize the guilt and shame built into our puritan ethic. We can work toward growth values that can create in each of us a vital, centered self.

Some hopeful experiments are being carried out. In some early childhood education programs, for instance, the teaching of morals and values is integrated with the presentation of factual knowledge and skills development. These programs reflect much of the old and some of the new values, including:

courage	conservation	personal efficiency
freedom	health	initiative
honesty	perseverance	reliability
cooperation	courtesy	friendliness
respect	tolerance	understanding

Mainly, these values are oriented toward *group* interaction, the common good of community and society—the word *love* is missing, as are many others.

Abraham Maslow has listed certain values, which he calls Being-values, as basic to our growth and development in self-actualization:

wholeness	perfection	simplicity
aliveness	richness	effortlessness
goodness	uniqueness	playfulness
justice	beauty	reality
truth	honesty	autonomy
self-sufficiency	completion	

For attaining a centered self, and for then focusing that self in commitment to something that is larger than the self, we feel that all the qualities and values of Maslow's self-actualizing person are significant, as are those values that make for creative and enhancing group interaction.

In addition to the lists above, we feel that the following values and qualities apply directly to attaining a vital and centered self capable of growth and interaction with others:

SELF	OTHERS	CREATIVITY
self-acceptance on all levels	love and liking of self and others	acceptance of challenge
self-confidence	tenderness	awareness of self and life as
identity	generosity	process
strength	compassion	acknowledgement

adaptability	kindness	of fear without
flexibility	cheerfulness	being con-
		trolled by it
responsibility	gentleness	imagination
commitment	genuineness	experimental
		attitude
sense of humor	integrity	inventiveness
optimism	respect	curiosity
spirit	openness	spontaneity
privacy	respect others'	ingenuity
	privacy	
independence	caring	transcendence

We have made this brief exploration into values for the simple reason that while everyone talks about the need for values, a great many people really don't seem to be able to say what values are. What's more, with the exception of Maslow's work on the values of the self-actualizing person, there is very little literature on the subject. Our values, in the most basic sense, are what we find worthy about other human beings and in ourselves. They are our codes of conduct, our preferences, our beliefs and our ideals. The values we choose to emphasize guide our perception, thinking and feeling both about ourselves and our environment —and our environment includes people, ideas, things and places as well as Nature in its total sense. Some values may be changed, modified, dropped or added as we grow through time, as we change and as society changes. For instance, in these times of electronic surveillance and computer print-outs on a man's entire career, many people feel that privacy is becoming a more important value than it has ever been.

Any decision we make will be a reflection of what we value. If we value the expectations and opinions of others more than our own, our decisions will reflect that fact. If we value ourselves and our responsibility to both ourselves and others, our decisions will reflect it. Muddy thinking and mixed feelings produced by a conflict of goals and uncertain values will result in decisions that are hard to carry out and to live with later. But if we clarify our values and practice centering, we can focus on making decisions with which we feel comfortable, and in which we have invested the commitment of self.

Some of the *ways* we choose to put our values into action may be unique, drawing upon our individual creativity—but they are bound to be a result of the values we have chosen for ourselves. Go over the lists of values we have set down in these past few pages: which ones are most important to you? Choose ten of them, or fifteen, that hold a particular meaning, a particular worthiness for you at the moment. Then in making your various decisions in life, check back against those values. To what extent do alternative solutions to your problems or crises fulfill the values you hold paramount? The alternative that is most completely congruent with your chosen values will be the one you will find most fulfilling in the long run, even if it presents more practical difficulties in the present.

The Decision-Making Process

Most of us in our daily round of living tend to respond to situations, people and things in fairly consistent terms, based upon our life experience, our lifestyle and our behavior sets, all of which are in turn based on our values and priorities. A crisis however, presents us with a situation in which we have gone beyond the point of resolving the matter on the basis of the past—we must find new ways to orchestrate our lives if we are to move forward successfully. We must develop a new assumptive state, a new life stance, which means changing our priorities and often some of our values as well. While there are only a given number of basic human values (which we have tried to clarify in this chapter) the combinations of those values which we choose as individuals can change con-

siderably in the course of our lives, depending upon
the phase of adulthood in which we find ourselves as
well as the particular challenge we are facing. If the
phase we are in leads us to feel that our central task is
to define ourselves in terms of society, then the values
we have listed under the heading *self* on our chart are
likely to be the most important to us. If we are involved in self-exploration, then the values under the
heading *creativity* may be uppermost in our consideration. If we are seeking to commit ourselves to something larger than ourselves, then the values under the
heading *others* may be our chief concern.

At all times, whatever phase we may be in, we will
be drawing to some extent on all these values—but the
ones we put at the head of our list will change as we
change and as the world we live in changes. In making
a decision in a crisis situation, then, our awareness of
the priorities and values involved is crucial.

If we go shopping in a department store without
knowing just what we want, we may have a feeling of
frustration, we are "at a loss" as to exactly what we
want. We may flounder in this indecision and go home
to think about it some more. Or we may take the easy
way out and let a salesman or a shopping companion
influence us. If we make a purchase under these conditions, we invariably find out later on that the other
person's choice was wrong for us, and that we have
made a mistake. We can return the item or take the
loss.

Such haphazard behavior and unproductive decision-making unfortunately is not limited to shopping. The same pattern is often followed in making
much more serious life decisions—whom you decide
to marry, what career you will follow, how you invest
your money, who your friends are, how you spend
your time. But in these decisions it is usually impossible to return the item for credit. If we are unhappy,
we stumble through the decisions we made, making

the best of them, but inwardly blaming others or the times we live in.

Yet if we really examine the situation, we may realize that most of our unhappiness with decisions we make stems from the fact that we have relinquished our autonomy—our *own* part in making them. We give up this autonomy in many ways: by being influenced by others more than ourselves, by not seeking adequate information relevant to *our* needs, by not knowing our values and priorities, by stubbornly resisting change or by sinking into a rut and making a "decision" by default. We do this not only in our life decisions but at many choice points in our everyday life. Not all situations we meet in our daily lives seem like a crisis; yet, they, too, may require a decision about change in our attitude. They may not be as highly charged emotionally as our major life changes, but the process of decision-making is the same. What do we do, and how do we react, for instance, when our boss ignores our latest accomplishment, our son wants to leave college, our daughter of eighteen wants to live with her boyfriend, our wife wants a separate vacation, our husband suddenly wants to take flying lessons? As parents, spouses and individual persons we meet change today around every corner. Some of us use these opportunities for reassessing our position and for personal growth. But many of us try to stand pat and defend our positions because old habits are easier than going through the process of examining ourselves, evaluating the situation and making a decision (which could be against change as well as for it). With our children we fall back on authority, with mates we fall back on "love," and with other situations we fall back on habit and custom. And when we reach an impasse we deploy every defense at our command—tears, battle, authority, sacrifice, rationalization *and* indifference—to avoid the confrontation with the fact that *we* might have to change our view-point and look at things in a new way.

Yet each confrontation with change in our lives can be an occasion for thinking about decisions and actions, and opening up to change. Whether we come up against a personal crisis, a change in life plan or these daily events, we should approach decisions consciously aware of our part in them and how we can turn them to advantage. Successful decision-making in any aspect of our life starts with awareness and is a process we can learn. The following suggestions will help you understand and develop this process:

(1) Know your values and your priorities.

(2) Seek information that is relevant (center on your individual needs and resources; focus on the resources in the world around you and the alternatives to which you can or want to commit yourself).

(3) Explore these alternatives and try to discover new ones.

(4) Imagine the consequences of each alternative to help you evaluate each one. Rank-order them if necessary.

(5) Make your choice (centering and focusing continue to be important here).

(6) Examine how this choice *feels*.

(7) Develop a contingency plan in case your first choice doesn't work out.

(8) Be willing to take the risk.

(9) Realize that important life decisions require commitment and some continuity in time.

(10) Realize that your decision can be changed or modified. If you make the "wrong" decision you don't have to stick with it at any cost, but you do have to be committed to it long enough to test it thoroughly.

Seeking relevant information is important. Get all the data you can about the situation, the circumstances, the possibilities. If you try to decide and something isn't clear, wait until you get more information and repeat the process. Open yourself up to gathering information in those areas you may never have considered before. In the process you are enlarging your knowledge and perhaps finding relevant factors that will strongly influence your decision. But, at some point you have to stop and make your decision. No matter how much data you try to get, there will always be some unknowns in the situation. No one ever gets complete or perfect information.

How do you find alternatives? Some will be readily apparent either through habit or convenience. But in change or crisis, it is the new alternatives we want to explore. Opportunities cannot be taken if we do not perceive them or look for them. In exploring new alternatives, some problem-solving techniques developed by industry and corporations might be valuable. After all, if they come up with new and profitable solutions, so can we in solving our own personal problems. One of these techniques is the familiar think-tank, brain-storming approach to solving problems. You throw in all kinds of crazy wild ideas along with the practical, obvious ones. The basis of another creative system called Synectics involves looking at your problem in such a way as to make the strange familiar and the familiar strange. You can use another of their techniques by training yourself to look for analogies—how one thing is *like* another, even though they may be as different as a bee and a tree. They are similar, of course, because each has a life cycle: each is born, grows and dies. Everybody knows how they are different; the challenge is finding how they are alike. We can use these techniques in thinking in new ways about almost anything as well as in finding new alternatives and options that we may not have thought of before. Get out of the rut of accepting the usual paths or the tried-and-true solutions that society has set out for us and begin to discover your own creative solutions. Instead of thinking in a linear logical way, from *a* to *b* to *c,* try to think sideways—or even upside down. If it works, or suggests a new way of looking at your problem, it doesn't matter how silly it is. Think of an illogical solution, something that may not work, but which may be valuable in pointing out something else different that *will* work.

How do you choose from among the alternatives? One way is to examine the consequences: What will happen *if* you do so and so? Imagining yourself in certain alternatives may rule them out as being risky or unproductive—or, maybe, very exciting.

Having done all this preparatory work, start thinking of how you feel inside. No matter how well outlined or thought out the process is, the most important part of any personal decision is the human element—sit back now and ask, How do I really *feel* about it? This is the purpose of centering and getting in touch with yourself. "When faced with alternative courses and choices about my future," says Ray Bradbury, "I always ask my stomach, not my head, to decide. The head may rationalize . . . convince one to take a job that is really wrong, but the stomach knows, feels, smells Sickness, if you are wise enough to pay attention to it." Trust your gut feelings sometimes, no matter how logical another alternative seems. Use your head to find an alternative that sits well with your stomach. And realize that we are too often swayed from taking a risk by our rationalizations and our need for approval. Forget your fears of imperfection, failure and loss of opportunity which often cause indecision and trust your feelings and intuition—along with the information you've gathered.

Choice means eliminating all the alternatives but one. Too many options may be confusing but the better you know yourself the easier it will be to eliminate those that are not right for you. Life is full of exciting and wonderful chances. But to make the most of any given chance or choice you must give yourself fully to it. If it doesn't work out, choose something else. We realize that the process we describe for making a decision may sound very rational but it is actually not so simple. In making decisions people will be beset by many considerations that are *not* rational. People are impulsive, emotional, moody and, sometimes, delightfully illogical, and no strategy or plan is ever followed perfectly. But what these suggestions can do is give you some ideas on how to attack the problem and how to get a handle on decision-making.

We will be exploring the last three steps in the process more thoroughly in the next chapter, but we mention them here because to make a mature decision some awareness of their importance is vital. You can make a decision—and then never put it into action. Thus a preliminary awareness of the need to take the risk and commit yourself to action has a strong bearing on the process of reaching your decisions. In addition, the knowledge that we can always shift gears again often gives us the courage to make tough decisions that we might be tempted to shy away from.

There are two categories of decision-making that we should be aware of. First, there is the decision that we make all alone, as Steven did in the case history at the beginning of this chapter. A majority of the fundamental decisions of our lives are ones that we have to make alone, and we have emphasized that necessity throughout this book because the maturity myth and other societal pressures too often lead us to go along with somebody else's determination of what we should do and be. But there are also consensus decisions to be made, within the family group for instance. If we are moving from one locality to another, the decision to take the new job that requires the move may be one that we make fundamentally alone—because we feel that it is essential to our own fulfillment and thus to our relationship with our mate. If both partners in a marriage have careers, then decision by consensus takes on a greater meaning.

One couple we knew recently faced the problem of a career conflict. Mark is an expert in computer design; Janice is a doctor specializing in cancer research. They both had jobs in Chicago, but then they were simultaneously offered new positions, Janice in Boston,

Mark in Pittsburgh. In both cases, the new jobs appeared to be just what they were looking for individually. But if they were to continue their marriage on a normal basis, one of them would obviously have to give way to the other's needs. The research position that had been offered Janice gave her an opportunity that simply could not be duplicated anywhere else in the country. And while Mark's job offer was an extremely good one, there did exist a number of other companies doing similar work, two of which were in the Boston area. So, by consensus, they agreed to go to Boston where Janice could take up her unique opportunity. She accepted the position, and within three months Mark had found a job in the Boston area that was the equivalent of the one in Pittsburgh.

A consensus decision does not, of course, mean that one person simply capitulates to the other, or that one person allows the other to make the decision for him or her. Consensus is not a matter of abandoning the needs of the individual self, but of weighing the particular circumstances. It means that both have examined the possible solutions and agreed fully on the best one for the moment. In the case of Janice and Mark, for instance, there may well come a time in their lives when their positions will be reversed. In reaching a consensus decision of this kind, all those who are involved must be aware, and prepared to openly recognize, that it may be necessary to shift gears again at some point in the future.

In the case of secondary decisions—those that do not directly involve our life stance and our assumptive state—we can include a greater number of people in the decision-making process. Thus, although one parent alone may have to make the basic decision that necessitates the move to a new town or city, the rest of the family can certainly be included in deciding which of several possible apartments or houses they will live in. The same is true of vacation plans, etc. In fact, if each individual is encouraged to make clear not just *what* he thinks the family should do but also *why* he thinks so and what his choice *means* to him, a great deal about the nature of decision-making can be learned by everyone involved, and constructive patterns of communication and understanding can be established that will be helpful in facing major life decisions at other times.

Two other suggestions may be helpful in making your decisions:

1. *Find your best time for decision-making.* For each person this will be different: for some it may be walking alone at night, for others during a morning shower. But whenever it is, each of us has a best time. Know your hours of weariness and low ebb when you tend to distort and exaggerate problems. Choose your strongest and most optimistic time to make a decision.

2. *Go into your problem when it is hot—but cool it before you make a decision.* This timing is different from choosing the best time to make a decision, because it is for a different purpose. This is centering and focusing on your problem when your gut feelings tell you something is bothering you. You may be in the midst of your heaviest work load or with a houseful of guests, but something is bugging you—an earlier phone call or an argument. This is the time to face it. It is, as a friend told us, "picking up the problem when it hurts the most," and working on it. It may help you to see and feel other aspects of the situation which you might perhaps overlook later when you have cooled off. The courage to confront a problem when it hurts the most will help you to clarify some issues and feelings. But use the "hot" approach only to *explore* the problem. Use the "cool" approach to *redefine* your problem and make a decision about it.

The Decision-Making Cycle

At this point the awareness wheel that we presented in the previous chapter can be expanded to take in

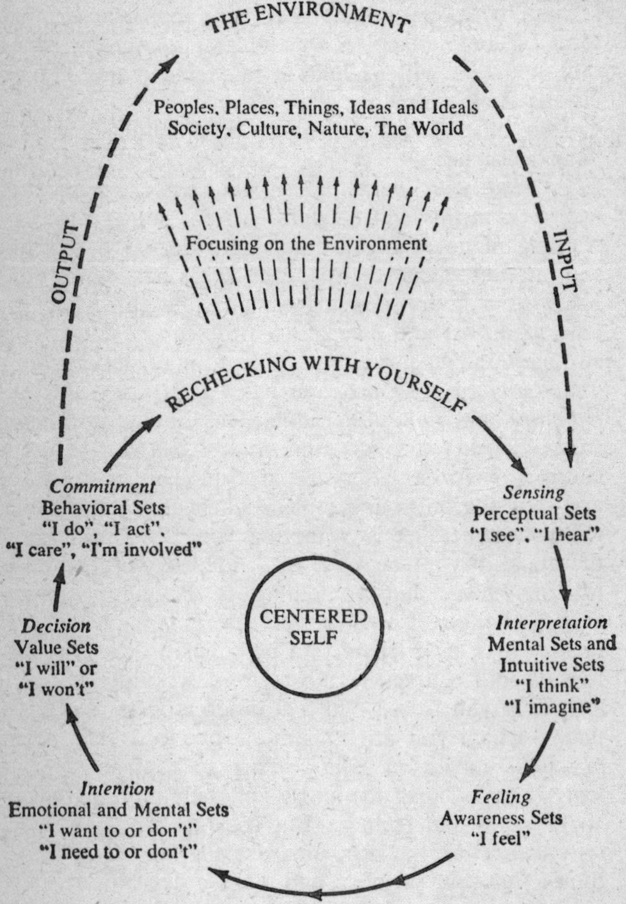

THE ENVIRONMENT

Peoples, Places, Things, Ideas and Ideals
Society, Culture, Nature, The World

Focusing on the Environment

OUTPUT

INPUT

RECHECKING WITH YOURSELF

Commitment
Behavioral Sets
"I do", "I act",
"I care", "I'm involved"

Sensing
Perceptual Sets
"I see", "I hear"

CENTERED
SELF

Decision
Value Sets
"I will" or
"I won't"

Interpretation
Mental Sets and
Intuitive Sets
"I think"
"I imagine"

Intention
Emotional and Mental Sets
"I want to or don't"
"I need to or don't"

Feeling
Awareness Sets
"I feel"

THE DECISION-MAKING CYCLE
FIG. 7

what we have learned about the decision-making process. This expanded model represents the decision-making cycle (see Fig. 7).

The decision-making cycle involves the first four steps that we learned in the process of centering: sensing, interpretation, feeling and intention. But decision-making involves the two additional steps shown on the model. Being centered can help you to understand the first four steps of this cycle. The decision step has been discussed in this chapter. But, as we have noted, it is not enough simply to make the decision; that decision must also be put into action. In many cases we may reach a decision but still hesitate to fully commit ourselves to it. At that point, instead of our decision becoming "output," we may need to go through the cycle once again, bypassing commitment for the moment and rechecking things out with ourselves further.

All decisions involve input from our environment as well as what we add to this information from our inner selves. The information and data we gather and receive from the outside world—about our alternatives, our relationships and feedback from others—are important in carrying through the sequences of the decision-making cycle. But *your* input is equally as important. It is *you* who interprets all the input and makes the decision. Being centered, focusing on your area of involvement and going through the process of decision-making can help you to see areas where you might become more open to change and to finding new solutions. We may have to go through the cycle, or parts of it, several times before we are finally ready to commit ourselves to action. But eventually if we are to resolve our crisis, if we are to grow and to change, that final step must be taken.

CHAPTER NINE

Commitment Means Action

Taking Risks to Gain Security

We all hesitate to take risks. Risk-taking, like change of any kind, is a step into the unfamiliar. Faced with the unfamiliar we hesitate on the brink, our mouths dry, our hearts pumping twice as fast. Human beings have always felt this way. From earliest times, man has feared the unknown; through the eons he has built elaborate systems of ritual and beliefs to deal with his fears and with the exaggerated fantasies that the unknown provokes. But although man needs security and does everything he can to maintain it, he also needs challenge—and because he has been a risk-taker and problem solver for two million years of evolution, risk-taking has become a part of his nature. The tension and the ambivalence between his need for security and his need for challenge provide the dynamic for growth and life. It is because man has responded to the challenge and has taken risks that he has evolved into the dominant creature of the earth. And so what we have is a paradox: in order to maintain his security, man has to take risks. Real inner security comes only from the constant reaffirmation of ourselves, of our competence and capability, through action, involvement and challenge.

In terms of shifting gears, it is through *taking the step* that we truly grow. It is not enough to make the decision. Until you implement your decision, you have not shifted gears. Until you act on your decisions, they are only wishes, only a matter of "I would like to." Self-realization and self-actualization mean just that: realizing ourselves in action. To think or feel something is only the beginning. Until we say what we think or do what we feel, we have not committed ourselves to those thoughts or feelings and cannot realize their full meaning or their full potential.

You find yourself in crisis. You face up to the existence of the crisis, achieving awareness, which is the first step in the process of shifting gears. By focusing and centering you refine that awareness, evaluating your situation and exploring possible alternatives. You make a decision to change, to seek a specific new path to self-fulfillment. But if you stop there, you have not shifted gears nor resolved the crisis. To resolve the crisis you must now take the risk of committing yourself to action, of testing your competence in a new situation.

The Commitment to Action

What does it really mean to commit ourselves to something? There is in all of us a deep need to feel involved in the world out there—it is expressed in our need for both intimate relationships and social encounter, the need for self-esteem, the need for competency and productivity, the need to feel connected in a vital way to life and to have our actions count. But involvement comes only through commitment to some kind of affirmative action. It is what we choose to do that determines the nature of our commitment.

We may, during one phase of our adult lives, commit ourselves primarily to defining ourselves in societal terms, concentrating our energies on external goals—job, family, material advancement. At another period of adulthood, we are likely to find ourselves in a different phase, committing ourselves primarily to the expansion and extension of our inner selves. Or we may commit ourselves to something larger than ourselves, like the retired major we mentioned in Chapter Four, whose new career as a teacher not only brought him more personal fulfillment, but also gave him a sense of contributing to making the world a slightly better place than he found it. But whatever phase we may be in, and whatever we commit ourselves to, the act of commitment follows the same basic pattern.

Commitment is a matter of how we look at things. The clearer we can see our involvement with life and our connection to it, the more our commitments become meaningful. The following story illustrates this important point about commitment: Three bricklayers at work were asked what they were doing. The first man explained that he was putting one layer of bricks on another and smoothing concrete between them; the second man explained that he was building a wall which would be part of a large structure of so many feet wide and so many feet tall. But the third man said, "I am working on this building which will be a school for children, where they will learn and play." As the third bricklayer shows, commitment is basically an attitude toward what you are doing and the meaning you give to it. His vision was larger, his connections more meaningful.

Commitment means making a choice and giving ourselves *time* to involve ourselves with whatever that choice is. If a man is offered three different jobs, he must make the decision to take one of them. One job may pay more, another have more potential for advancement, and a third seem more in line with the man's particular talents. Whichever one he accepts, the man is committing himself to that job for the foreseeable future. That does not mean that he can never change jobs again, can never shift gears, but it does mean that for now the man is going to put the other two jobs out of his mind and focus on the job he accepts, for now he is going to devote his time and effort to that job, he must commit himself to it wholeheartedly, must allow himself to become fully *involved* in it.

To be fully involved means entering into a relationship with whatever commitment we choose, whether it is a job, a personal relationship or creating a work of art. *Relationship* is the essence of commitment and through working at this relationship we give and extend ourselves, learn and grow. Commitment means accepting the limitations—routine, materials, hours, personality—both of ourselves and of the other we are committed to. It is only by accepting these limitations that we can *transcend* these limitations through growth —stretch them and grow.

An artist accepts the limitation of his material, whether he chooses wood or stone, neon tubing or oil paints. A sculptor, for instance, respects the basic integrity, the unique qualities, of the raw piece of wood he has selected. He begins to work on his piece of sculpture, investing himself, his concentration, energy and creativity in his action. Out of this commitment emerges an entity, a work of art, through which both have been transformed: the piece of wood into a new form and reality, the artist into a new realization of himself through striving for a new expression of himself. Our personal relationships or commitments offer us growth in the same way. By involving ourselves with another, by caring and respecting the basic integrity of both persons in the relationship, by being willing to change and learn from our differences as well as our similarities, we transcend our limitations and grow.

It is the same when we choose to commit ourselves to a project, idea or career. We must care enough to give our best to it, to look for new ways of growing within that commitment and for extending our limitations by both giving of ourselves and being open to receiving and to an exchange. In a relationship, commitment is being involved to the point of finding an authentic response, a commitment to caring with time enough to find the essence of self and the other in our actions and thoughts. In our involvement in a job or project, it is the self that we discover, that benefits and grows through the experience. And, by giving our best to it, we discover and become aware of the potentials of the job or endeavor. If we don't give our best, we are not really committed, and we will certainly fail to make the most of the potentials in the job or relationship.

When we make a commitment, we cannot hope to derive greater satisfaction, or feedback, from the job or relationship than we are willing to give to it. Sometimes, of course, we find that no matter how much we give, no matter how committed we are, the job or relationship is simply not providing feedback or satisfaction to the degree we feel we need. If so, it is time to shift gears. But we cannot justifiably arrive at the conclusion that we are dissatisfied if we do not give fully of our best to the job or relationship in the first place. If we fail to truly involve ourselves, to give ourselves, then we cannot hope for satisfaction.

When we commit ourselves fully to a new course of action, when we take the step, we bring our total selves into play—our past experiences (including some that may have seemed "wasted"), our developed abilities, our latent or hidden capacities. It is as if the act of commitment itself releases these capacities and makes it possible to utilize many resources we were unaware of. But we use these parts of ourselves in new ways, reorganizing and reintegrating the various parts of ourselves to apply to the particular focus we have decided on. And as this reintegration occurs, we grow, inevitably. The degree to which we grow will depend on how much of ourselves we bring to the commitment, will depend on the level of interaction and exchange we can stimulate between our inner selves and the external situation or relationship to which we have committed ourselves.

We can see the importance of commitment and its contribution to growth in one of the commonest of work situations. Two people, men or women, are hired by the same company at the same time for jobs at the same level. They may be secretaries, filing clerks, assistants to a department manager—whatever. Both of them may think they deserve a better job at higher pay with more responsibility. But they have two different reactions to this feeling. One does the job half-heartedly, even sloppily, making his or her resentment known in many small ways. That person obviously is not going to be quickly promoted and will very likely move on to another job someplace else where the same pattern is likely to be repeated. He is uninvolved wherever he goes. The other person, despite his or her reservations, becomes fully involved and committed to the job, looking for the aspects of it that are interesting, looking for ways to do it better, more efficiently. That person's commitment usually comes to the attention of his or her superiors, leading to a promotion, a more fulfilling job and better pay. And in the course of committing himself or herself to the job, by entering into a real exchange between the self and the task, the individual will grow, will learn things about himself, will enhance his or her self-esteem, and be better prepared for the more responsible position that comes with promotion.

In today's world a great many people say, "Why bother, everything is lousy anyway, why should I commit myself—to anything?" This reaction is easy to understand, of course. Our national leaders hardly provide us with inspiration. Our employers seem more concerned with profits than with the quality of work we do. Everything seems temporary. And because we live in a crisis culture in which values are constantly changing, in which yesterday's belief is today's delusion, it is hard to know what we should commit ourselves to. But in fact we can find our own values, ideals and goals worth living by only through commitment, only by doing.

We define our values by what we do. Self-realization takes place only through what we do. Self-realization is not ". . . an end in itself or a form of being preoccupied with oneself," as Dr. M. Friedman points out. "It is the movement of the person through time, the response of the person to situation, the interaction of the person with event." Through action, through the commitment to action, through taking a step and engaging life in a new way, we grow, and our hidden inner resources unfold and emerge through these actions. No one can lead you into taking the step. That is the final point at which *you* have to act, alone. Ultimately you have to take the risk, you have to complete the shifting gears cycle by taking the step into new action and commitment.

Half Steps

Our commitment to a new course of action can take place by half steps. This approach was the one taken by Tom, whose story we related in Chapter Four. Recognizing his dissatisfaction with his life-style and the demands of his New York City construction business, he had evaluated his situation, explored the alternative possibilities, and found what he thought he wanted in upstate New York. He was ready to take a step toward a new kind of life, but he didn't want to take it all at once. First, he wanted to experiment, to take some half steps. He bought a house upstate, and moved his family there; but at the same time he kept their New York City apartment and commuted back and forth. While investigating the business opportunities in the area around the new home, he continued to run his old firm in the city.

Tom's experimental approach to a new way of life left him with an avenue of retreat. It gave both him and his family time to adjust to the changes they were making, so that the process of shifting gears was carried out gradually over a period of time. But, even taking such half steps involved a considerable degree of commitment. You aren't really taking a half step if you simply dabble with one solution after another for a few days at a time; dabbling of this sort can be useful if you are still involved in focusing and centering, but to take a half step you must commit yourself to at least a limited investment of time. You may give yourself a year or more, as Tom did, or six months, or even two or three months. The difference between the half step and the full step, between conditional commitment and complete commitment to a new way of life, is a question of time. With a half step, you say to yourself, "I'm going to try this for a specific amount of time, and see if it works." With full commitment, and a complete shifting of gears, you say, "I'm going to live this way for an indefinite length of time, for as long as I feel happy and fulfilled." With a half step, you know that in six months or a year you will have a further decision to make: Does this way of living in fact work? With full commitment, that decision is behind you: yes, it will work.

There is also another sense in which we can talk about half steps. Many of us, in our past experience, have done or learned things that we can make use of to greater effect in the future. We described earlier the case of a woman who had majored in fine arts in college and had always been interested in interior decorating. For the first twenty years of her adult life, however, she had been a housewife. After her children were grown, she decided that she wanted to extend herself into the outside world, to develop a career. Her previous training in fine arts, together with her lifelong interest in decorating, constituted a half step she had already taken toward a possible career. That experience had not been wasted; it was simply that she hadn't previously realized its significance.

Most of us have taken half steps at various times in our past. One former television executive we know used to haunt local auctions in country towns, buying up what looked like broken-down pieces of junk. He would cart them home in the back of his station wagon, strip them down to the original wood, repair and refinish them. In his early fifties he lost his television job in a corporate reshuffle, and for the past ten years he has been putting his expertise about American furniture to use in a well-known Madison Avenue antique shop only twenty blocks from the sky-scraper where he used to work. Other men have used their supposed "hobbies" to create new careers for themselves in such diverse areas as photography, running a boatyard, becoming a golf instructor and opening a rare-book store. We all hear and read about such people constantly—but we simply conclude that they were "lucky" instead of looking for such half steps toward a new career in our own lives.

Women, because of the low status accorded the housewife in our society, are even more likely to think they have no talents that are marketable, talents that can be turned into a career in their later life. In fact, though, many women have even more potential half steps to choose from than men do. We know numerous women who have turned so-called domestic arts into lucrative businesses. One divorcée parlayed her ability to knit into a national mail-order firm; the handmade sweaters, shawls and scarves she sells are produced by hundreds of women scattered across the country. Another woman who spent years working for nothing as chairman of her local society for the preservation of historical buildings learned so much law that she decided to become a lawyer herself. Any woman who has managed to successfully run a household, balance a family budget and bring up children has taken half steps toward several possible careers, whether she knows it or not. Many thousands of such women have already put what they have learned as housewives to work in new careers in teaching, business and the arts. And most women have the potential to do the same.

When we want to change our lives, then, when we want to shift gears, the first thing to look for is often the half steps toward a new life that we have already taken without recognizing them. We may not be sure which of those previous half steps is the right one for us to pursue. If not, then experimentation is in order. We can try out a possible new career on a part-time or free-lance basis to discover whether or not it is suitable for us, whether or not we are both good at it and happy with it. Or we may find that, having already taken a half step in the past, we are prepared to take the leap and commit ourselves fully at once.

Taking the Leap

Taking the leap does *not* mean rushing blindly into a new course of action without stopping to think. The man whose fiancée elopes with some one else is simply asking for trouble if he turns around and marries some other girl he hardly knows a month later. The "on the rebound" syndrome is not the means to the successful solution of any crisis. However, once we have become fully aware of our situation through focusing and centering, have evaluated and explored the possibilities and reached a decision, it is often possible to take the step all at once, commiting ourselves completely to action as soon as the decision has been made. We may wish to eliminate the half steps and take the leap directly into our new mode of life.

The more self-confidence the individual has, the higher his self-esteem, the more likely he is to feel sure that his decision is the right one. His confidence is likely to be greatest if his decision involves a new goal toward which he has already taken a half step in the past. But sometimes we have no choice. Circumstances may force us to take the leap. We may be offered a job and told that a yes or no answer is required in two days. We may see a house for sale in the country; if we don't take it, it may be snapped up by the next people to look at it. In either case, we either have to take the step or not take it. No experimentation, no half steps are possible. Our reaction to such situations will depend on whether or not we have already progressed far enough through the shifting gears process to be prepared to make the decision and take the step simultaneously. If we haven't progressed that far, the pressure of circumstance may serve as a kind of goad that speeds the process up. Our feelings of deep dissatisfaction may be that primary circumstance or motivation. Or we may find ourselves vacillating, unable to make up our minds—in which case, obviously, we would be very foolish to take the leap.

But today many people are dissatisfied enough to take a leap in regard to life changes. They are "breaking out," as one author expresses it, of traditional paths to make their own way in radically different and original life-styles. A young suburban banker and his wife move to Canada to manage a country store in a frontier town; a corporation executive leaves to do freelance writing and live in the mountains; a young couple in advertising decides to join a cooperative ecological farming community. In these, and similar cases, there are no half steps. Such a leap requires an immediate involvement and commitment. The risk may be greater, but so may be the satisfaction and fulfillment.

Rebuilding on the Same Ground

Living in a time when change is extremely rapid and options are increasing in quantity if not in quality, the solutions to our personal change and crises often take dramatic forms. We shift gears not just from one job to another but from one career to another; we move not just from one street to the next but across the country. A man who was an aeronautics engineer in California last year turns up running a ski lodge in Colorado this year. The woman who was a Virginia housewife last year turns up as a St. Louis newscaster this year. These sometimes surprising case histories make good examples through which to explain the process of shifting gears: the fact that they are dramatic makes them easier to understand. But it should be remembered that it is also possible to shift gears in less obvious, quieter ways.

It is perfectly possible that the housewife down the street who ran off to New York and is now living with a painter in a Village loft hasn't shifted gears at all. In that bohemian loft she may be waiting on her new boyfriend in a more subservient way than she ever did on her supposedly male chauvinist husband back in Middletown. She hasn't shifted gears, or faced up to her problem, but just transferred her problem to a more exotic locale. On the other hand, the couple who have lived next door for twenty years and still do, may have shifted gears without your really noticing. If you think about it, you may recall that this suburban couple didn't seem to be getting along a few years back; their friends were wondering about the possibility of divorce. Now, though, everything seems to be all right.

What this couple has done is to shift gears, not by changing careers or drastically altering their life-style, but simply by discovering themselves anew in a new kind of relationship to one another. Outwardly they may seem to be living much the same life they always have, but inwardly they have changed. They have learned to communicate with one another more openly, to respect one another's right to privacy, allowing one another more room in which to develop their in-

dividual identities. If you look closely, you will notice
that they do more things independently of one another,
that they talk *with* rather than *at* one another, that
they have a new attitude toward one another.

We will be talking more fully about relationships
and the shifting gears process in a subsequent chapter.
At this point, though, it is important to make it clear
that shifting gears can be accomplished in an intimate,
quiet way between people without recourse to drastic
changes in life-style. Such drastic changes can and will
be the necessary answer for some people. But there
are others who will find that they can shift gears in a
way that allows them to *rebuild on the same ground.*
The steps they take in order to shift gears may well be
subtle ones that an outsider will hardly be aware of.
The external elements in their life are likely to remain
much the same, but their attitude toward them and
each other will be different.

If our attitude changes, in the course of shifting
gears, then the same job, the same mate, the same
surroundings can seem as fresh as a new job, a new
mate or new surroundings.

Helping Aids

There are several points to keep in mind in respect
to taking the step. These aids can help you combat the
fear of taking a risk, the fear of committing yourself
to action:

POINT I:

Breaking through the risk barrier. Many of us remain paralyzed even after we have come to a decision
because we are afraid of looking foolish, afraid of
what others will say about our actions. Even though
you have begun to check things out with yourself, you
may still be unduly guided by what others might
think. Taking a risk is frightening precisely because it

means taking a stand for yourself, putting your "reputation" on the line and, in many cases, flaunting tradition or propriety.

But there comes a time for each of us when we have to have the courage of our convictions, the courage to act. The first time we say no, for rational adult reasons, to an authority figure—teacher, parent, boss—may be the first time we truly become an individual. And this is something we may have to repeat throughout life—dumping our concern over what others will say and taking a stand for ourselves. If we worry to excess about being liked by others, or being "perfect," we never live our own lives or really know ourselves. Often, instead of losing dignity, you are likely to gain respect by standing up for yourself and doing the thing you feel is right.

"They called me crazy when I painted the icebox," said Sanford Darling, who picked up a paintbrush when he retired at sixty-eight and began covering his furniture with vivid primitive landscapes and scenes of his travels and childhood in Wisconsin. He painted chairs, stools, even wastebaskets. He covered the entire outside of his house with such scenes. Crazy as they called him, this man's desire to express himself, and his unconcern for conformity, have brought him both pleasure and fulfillment in a new area late in life. And even though he lives in a quiet mountain area, his unconventional paintings have brought eight thousand visitors to his doors over the eight years since he started painting. He enjoys not only his involvement in recreating his memories, but also the contact with his visitors; through the paintings that cover every surface of his house, he gives these strangers a guided tour of his life.

At other times our hesitation in taking a risk may be because we are afraid of failure or of the unknowns in the situation. "What will happen *if*," we ask ourselves, "if I don't succeed, I don't do it well, or if something happens that I can't handle?" When the risks involved in a given situation are such that you feel anxiety, one way to break through is to ask yourself this question: What's the *worst* thing that can happen to me? Exploring the realistic possibilities can be reassuring, precisely because they are never so bad as your unfocused imagination led you to believe. Balance this out by asking yourself, realistically: What's the *best* thing that could happen to me? Weigh one against the other before you assume the risk is too great.

POINT II:

Focus on past successes to bolster confidence. In our society, in which success and failure are measured by others' standards, and in which the lure of homogenized comfort and homogenized conformity deprives us of challenge, the fear of taking a risk has become almost endemic. Measuring our successes by how well we achieve the goals that others think worthwhile often gets us in trouble; doing the "right" things may well be wrong for you. It is not a success for you if marrying the "right" person (according to your parents and friends) has led to a relationship in which you are abjectly mismatched. Achieving in the "right" profession, chosen for you by your parents, may be giving you ulcers or high blood pressure and affecting all your relationships negatively. Success in other people's terms, then, may mean only frustration for you in terms of doing the things you really want to do. Trying to please everyone and be liked by everyone, the syndrome so prevalent in our culture, is a self-destructive loser's game. Growth and fulfillment start with the centered self, depend on the commitment of the self, and are ultimately evaluated, for better or worse, by the self.

Measuring our successes by others prevents us from recognizing our real private successes. One man we know of, when asked to list his successes for a personality assessment test, couldn't think of a single thing he had done right or he had been a success at. This is ridiculous, of course—but not uncommon. If each of us would sit down and list the times in our life when we have done something to *our satisfaction*—ours, not somebody else's, and to the point of personal satisfaction, not perfection—we could use that list as a resource to build our confidence for taking a new step, to reassure ourselves that we can do it. Try to remember the times you have solved a problem, created something or achieved a goal according to your own desires, something that *did not* depend on the approval of others. Forget your "failures," the times you haven't measured up to someone else's expectations, and focus on the times you have been successful for yourself. Then taking the step will seem less risky.

POINT III:

Use imaging to forecast your own success. Every successful athlete—and especially those in individual sports like track or swimming—uses imaging, but they call it "psyching themselves up." Our minds are powerful tools and we have it in our power to imagine being a success, to imagine that we are what we want to be. Basically, this is a technique for fostering a positive self-image. Imaging is not just daydreaming, or wasteful fantasy. It is taking a real-life situation, although one you are not yet in, and thinking yourself in that situation. Rather than destructive imaging, which is remembering failures in the past, concentrate on potential successes. The way in which we think about ourselves, after all, often becomes a self-fulfilling prophecy. You are not only *what* you do, but what you *do* is a result of what you think you *can* do. If you think, "I can't do this," or "I just know this isn't going to work out," if you are not committed or involved, the job *will* turn out badly—whether it's managing an office or opening the lid on a jar.

Imaging can also be used to take ourselves over the hurdles in a kind of dry run. You can think of the possible pitfalls, of the disappointments that a new endeavor may bring, and of ways to deal with them if they occur. Just as the professional golfer goes over the lay of a golf course in his mind, making himself aware of the sand traps and water traps, so we can use imaging to prepare ourselves for the potential trouble spots along the way. You will then be better able to cope with the bumps that will come, in some cases avoiding them altogether, in other cases riding over them to the success you want. Of course, if you find yourself concentrating unduly on the trouble spots, then it is time to go back to imaging the rewards, to concentrating on the aspects of the situation you know you can handle particularly well.

POINT IV:

Maintain some anchor points. Whether it be a small Caribbean island you treasure, or a small summer cottage, or a special fishing cove, or an old farmhouse in Vermont—a place where you can go for peace, quiet and a change of setting—try to maintain some anchor points in the midst of change.

In a psychological sense we also need such anchor points in order to mobilize our resources when everything happens at the same time. Especially, when you are making changes in your own life, whether by half-steps or by plunging in, don't try to change everything at once. If your marital relationship is shaky, your oldest son has just dropped out of college, and your daughter is marrying a young man you disapprove of, it is not the time to make a major career change. You already have three crises to deal with—that's enough for this point in your life.

We need stress and tension in life to give us zing and motivation, but too much at once, as recent studies have shown, cannot be tolerated. If too many life changes occur at once, your stress score mounts up, and something is bound to give, usually your physical or mental health. Thus we must learn to make a judicious assessment of how much change we can take at once. As we discussed in the chapter on how to make crisis work for you, it is important when you are faced by multiple crises at once to confront them one by one, devoting all your attention to the resolving of one before you move on to the next—unless, of course, they can all be resolved by the same means. The resolution of a crisis demands change—and we can only take so much change at one time.

If you are changing your career or going through a relationship crisis, keep some things stationary. Return to and maintain some customary activities, old friends or familiar habits where there is little stress for you. These oases of nonstress can give you respite from stress, comfort and a feeling of stability. In addition, some anchor points often tie in with making changes by half steps and are similar to contingency plans. Tom, you will remember, moved his family to the new house he had bought upstate, but for more than a year he also kept their old apartment in New York. That old apartment was, in the midst of change, both an anchor point and a practical tactic in his strategy for change.

CHAPTER TEN

Creating Your Own Challenge

Reaffirming Your Competence

Creating your own challenge gives you the opportunity to purposely test yourself in new situations—and then return to the old problems with renewed vitality and vigor. Although you may wonder why in the world you need another challenge when you haven't been able to solve the problems at hand, there is sound therapeutic value in creating one. In creating a challenge you set the limits of the test based on your own estimation of your potential. The risks you are taking are self-determined. Thus the created challenge is of a completely different nature from the crisis situation that has been precipitated by uncontrolled circumstances. Those challenges we create and take on for ourselves become our touchstones of growth, our proving ground for inner potentials. They enable us to discover our competence. Thus, challenge provides a step toward maturity and the self-confidence that we can meet life on our own terms.

We have touched on some aspects of the created challenge in earlier chapters. In our discussion of centering, for instance, we talked about the therapeutic value of learning to say *no* when asked to do something that you don't want to do, and suggested beginning on a level at which you can bring yourself to refuse someone else's suggestion, be it neighbor, wife or boss. The point of that particular exercise was to help you to center on your own needs, instead of always trying to please others—the result of such centering being an increase in your self-esteem. But while the point of the exercise was to center on yourself, the technique was one of creating your own challenge.

The creation of challenges of this nature for ourselves thus becomes an escape hatch through which we can succeed in prying ourselves loose from a personal behavioral rut. When we go on a diet or decide to stop smoking we are also creating our own challenges, in order to escape from a condition or a habit that we know is bad for us. These are ordinary, everyday created challenges—but there are others that can help us to deal with crisis. Crises, as we have noted several times, are very much tied up with *attitude*. For instance, Louise, a woman in her mid-forties, was recently divorced. Her children were grown and leading lives of their own. She did not have to worry about money, but she found her new single life unbearably empty. For a few months she managed to keep herself seemingly busy by having lunch with friends several days a week, going to art galleries and movies, endlessly prowling through department stores and playing bridge every other night. But although she was "busy" she was not occupied. Her life still seemed empty.

The obvious answer to her crisis was to become involved in something that interested her and that could give a new focus to her life. But she had married her husband straight out of college and had never held a job. She was convinced that nobody would want to hire her for anything but the most menial job—and that even if they did she wouldn't be able to handle it.

Then one day in the supermarket she ran into a neighbor who ran a nursery school. This woman, Miss B., was extremely harried and upset. Her mother, who lived in another state, was due to return home from the hospital following a major operation. Miss B. wanted to be with her mother for a week or ten days, but couldn't find anyone reliable to take over the school— it was shortly before Christmas, and everyone seemed to have plans they couldn't change. Louise, on the spur of the moment, said, "Well, could I help?" Her offer was gratefully accepted, and although Louise almost immediately had second thoughts and began worrying about the things that could go wrong, felt she couldn't back out. Besides, she'd brought up two children of her own—that was one thing she did have experience with. Louise thus created her own challenge.

The ten days she spent at the nursery school were difficult and tiring, but her confidence increased almost daily. After this experience was over, Louise realized that she would make a good teacher, and that she had a special kind of experience that could make her exceptionally useful—one of her own children had stuttered badly as a child. She took some courses in speech therapy and now holds a job that gives her not only a sense of her own worth but of commitment to something larger than herself. Her crisis is long past— but she sometimes wonders what might have happened to her if she hadn't tested herself, her competence and her unused capacities in those ten days at the nursery school. That self-created challenge was the escape hatch by which she found her way out of despondency and purposelessness.

Jolting Yourself Out of a Rut

The created challenge can also be used to get ourselves moving when we know that we ought to be seeking change but can't seem to take the initial step. Jim, for instance, had a good job with a consulting firm that paid him sixteen thousand dollars a year. After four years, though, the work had become repetitive and sometimes boring. He wanted to look for a different job that was more fulfilling, used his artistic abilities to a greater extent and had more potential for the future. But he procrastinated and found it difficult to really commit himself to any kind of action. He kept his eyes and ears open in hopes of stumbling across a job that was more to his liking, but he was very busy with the job he had, and he still liked it reasonably well—it wasn't really driving him up the wall, as he put it. Besides the money was good.

On the other hand, Jim saw a crisis coming. He wasn't climbing the walls yet—but another year and he would be. He wasn't unhappy at this point, but he wasn't happy either. And he knew he wouldn't be happy until he began doing something that gave him more satisfaction, that used some of his other talents and abilities. "The sooner I really face myself," he said, "and admit the fact that I really don't like what I'm doing, the better off I'm going to be in the long run. I'm really hedging in every direction." He decided that the only way to galvanize himself into action was to face up to his situation. So he simply quit the job he had, creating his own challenge—even his own crisis—forcing himself to look for something he did find fulfilling.

Thus, creating your own challenge can be used to get a jump on a potential crisis. Obviously, creating your own challenge on the scale that Jim did is going to create additional problems as well. You must have a considerable degree of self-confidence to take such a step. But the problems that accompany a self-created challenge are ones that you have taken on knowingly and can plan in advance for. Even if there is an element of risk you are prepared to take it. Such problems are bound to be less oppressive, less severe, than those that take us unaware, unprepared, and emotionally at our weakest. If we have the courage to create our own challenge, to *make a risk* for ourselves, it means we are at our strongest. And the best time to face a crisis, like the one that Jim brought on himself, is when we are at our strongest. If he had just drifted along for another year, getting a little more depressed and frustrated as time went on, he would have been at his weakest when he finally faced up to the fact that he couldn't stand things as they were any longer. The more strength we have, the easier it is to change—and thus to create our own challenges when we are at our strongest can save us from greater problems in the future.

Jim and Louise demonstrate how we can create challenges out of the fabric of our day-to-day existence. Others, however, need to find distant settings, a greater stimulus, a tougher testing ground. Prying yourself out of a rut is, after all, relative. A man we interviewed already has a high-geared business life full of challenges, yet he chooses dangerous sports such as shooting the rapids as new testing grounds. "The challenge has to be strong enough to make me forget my own business challenges, one that will shock me out of my normal thought patterns. To be completely absorbed and involved in the experience I need something completely different with new danger and risks."

A familiar and exciting challenge people create for themselves is setting off on a voyage of testing and self-discovery in unknown areas and exotic lands. Here the necessity to develop new behavior and to meet the unknowns is more compelling. New situations and strange circumstances call upon new resources. Decades ago the young man traditionally went to sea. Today we create new horizons—Chichester sails the ocean alone, housewives skydive, a young woman drives across Africa, a young man teaches children in Ecuador, a doctor joins a hospital team in Tanzania, a sixty-year-old couple joins the Peace Corps, a young psychologist works with migrant farmers, a couple back-packs into the Canadian mountains. To create our own challenge by striking off into strange lands or undertaking unusual tasks is more dramatic than letting things happen or responding to familiar opportunities.

And creating a special challenge in another area has special values. We discover new resources and competencies we could never have realized we had in our ordinary situation, simply because the old situation did not call upon them. Sometimes we discover a new direction in life, a career or interest, which we implement upon our return. At other times, greater insights are gained which change our assumptions about ourselves and our ordinary existence. As an example, an archaeology professor we know, who had not been in the field for many years, was offered an opportunity to join an expedition to search for lost cities in the northern Andes. Since it meant thirty days on horseback in high mountain jungles and scaling 3,000-foot cliffs in search of ancient tombs, it was something he thought twice about at the age of forty-eight. Yet, accepting this special challenge not only brought him a renewed sense of competency, reaffirmation and excitement in life, but it also significantly changed his assumptions —*and* those of his adolescent sons—concerning the whole concept of "maturity." As he said, "I gained a new perspective on my life and future. Instead of feeling I was on the down-swing and a relic of the maturity myth, that experience gave me a new zest in life. I got a kind of elation at meeting that challenge, especially at my age, and I found that it wasn't age but spirit and courage that counted."

Those challenges we create for ourselves can represent another stimulus for growth and learning apart from crisis—and they certainly need not be as daring as archaeological exploration or skydiving. Challenges occur in the simplest events and places. They can be scaled to our needs and capabilities. In fact, our personal relationships can provide more challenge and opportunity for growth than the most daring exploits. The day-to-day confrontation between parent and child, and between husband and wife, provide the impact of challenge and a powerful stimulus to growth, if we are open enough to accept it.

The Meaningful Challenge

Ironically, our society, which creates so many unwanted crises, fails to provide sufficient meaningful challenges. In most primitive societies, past and present, various trials and rites of passage between adolescence and manhood and between levels of status in the adult hierarchy make it possible for the individual to test himself against common societal standards. Our society lacks such generally recognized challenges, lacks common standards. In fact, homogenized and mechanized modern-day society increasingly diminishes the number and variety of challenges open to us on an individual level. Part of our fascination with beauty contests, professional sports and Academy Award ceremonies is that through them we can vicariously experience a kind of challenge that is denied to most of us individually. But vicarious challenges are not enough—if we cannot personally experience challenge and grow through it, it has no real meaning to our inner selves.

Societal conditions that restrict our opportunities for personal challenge impel us to seek out new ones for ourselves. Nowhere is this more apparent than with youth in our society. They travel the world with a knapsack, drop out of school and create new life-styles in order to provide an authentic experience for self-affirmation lacking in the traditional slots open to them in an urban and corporate existence. Out of a compelling need for challenge they create their own contemporary odyssey. No matter our age, life is in a very real sense an odyssey we all must undertake to find ourselves.

There is a desire and a need in all of us for challenge. When society does not provide such challenges, when we begin to feel stale and tired, we must often create our own challenges to get ourselves moving again. Gordon Rattray Taylor has said, "When a much longed-for goal is achieved . . . the glow fades, and we begin to launch fresh plans, to set fresh goals. And as we look back, we see that much of what now appears to us as happiness lay in the struggle. . . . It is for this reason that men sail boats, climb mountains and take on other challenges, including intellectual ones."

But in our society we have become confused about the difference between crisis and challenge. There are so many crises that we must deal with, and often do not know how to deal with, that the idea of challenge has come to seem frightening to many people. As a result many of us spend a great deal of time avoiding any challenge, let alone creating one for ourselves. And obviously some challenges are better avoided. If you can't swim four lengths of the local pool without becoming winded, it would clearly be foolish to take on the English Channel. But if we avoid *all* challenge we cease to grow; we remain aloof from life. The more challenges we meet, the more we grow and the greater the future challenges we will be able to meet successfully. The man or woman who spends all his energy in avoiding challenge is fighting a losing battle against growth and change. We must have challenges to grow, and we must grow to become fulfilled. Without challenge we become frustrated and dulled. If we do not test our competence, if we do not prove ourselves to ourselves, we inevitably become despondent. The mistake so many of us make is to try to prove our competence in terms of what somebody else thinks we should be doing, instead of in terms of what is most meaningful and rewarding for ourselves. Creating our *own* challenges, rather than measuring ourselves solely by the challenges that circumstance and the will of others impose upon us, can help us to escape the arbitrary limitations of the maturity myth and the confusions of the option glut. With each challenge we create for ourselves and succeed in meeting we come to *know* ourselves more thoroughly. Thus, we have the task ". . . as long as we live," says Friedman, "of going on probing, testing, authenticating—never resting content with any earlier formulation. However true our touchstone, it will cease to be true if we do not make it real again by testing it in each new situation. This testing is nothing more nor less than bringing our life-stance into the moment of present reality." Whether they are reaffirmed through change, crisis, or created challenge, our touchstones will develop as we develop in interaction with the world. Every day offers us an opportunity to see some aspect of life in a novel way, to expand our vision. Thus, shifting gears is not only a way to resolve crisis or plan a life change, it is the process of meeting life *each day* with a courageous attitude open to whatever may come that gives us a chance to grow and a willingness to shift our perspective and enlarge the dimensions of our life. We learn how to center and focus better. And we learn how to shift gears at our own pace and according to our inner needs instead of merely in response to crisis.

When any of us begins to say, Now what? when we have reached the goals we previously set for ourselves or have come to feel that those goals no longer make sense, what we need is a new challenge. Whether you are a housewife with grown children, a man or woman who no longer finds your career fulfilling, or a young person just starting out on the journey of adulthood, to ask, What now? is to tell yourself that it is time for a fresh challenge, time to shift gears.

CHAPTER ELEVEN

Relationships

Toward New Kinds of Relationships

In the past our relationships provided us with a fortress of security. We belonged to a certain class, to a family, to a church—all of which demanded from us the replication of certain habits and beliefs and kinds of behavior while at the same time providing the ritual necessary to sustaining those habits and beliefs. The paternalistic and authoritarian nest provided us with an all-supportive context from which we interacted with others. Because that context was based primarily upon conformity to external demands and seeking the approval of others, it created in us an often excessive dependency, but it was at least comfortable and snug and secure.

We had a feeling of belonging both to kin and geographical location, and our needs for security, self-esteem and recognition were bolstered by these social and territorial roots.

The fact that changes in our world have shattered this context for our relationships makes it difficult and sometimes impossible to interact successfully with others in traditional ways; yet we still retain our needs for belonging and security and comfort. But in our contemporary world of crisis and change we need something more from relationships than an all-supportive context with built-in dependency. We need relationships that can help us to grow and become *self*-supportive at the same time that they provide a feeling of belongingness. The crisis culture, as we have shown, has awakened new needs in the inner self and has created a compelling necessity for us to become more self-assertive, self-determining and self-supportive. We must shift gears, discarding the old concept of relationship as all-supportive, and developing instead a concept of relationship as giving us the capacity to be self-supportive. Our relationships today can only be vital and sustained to the extent that they give us the courage and strength to grow: each of us receiving from others the support necessary to our growth and giving back to others the support they need for their growth. Only then can relationships sustain the pressures of a world in rapid change.

In a crisis culture in which the old supports have broken down, our needs for self-development have become primary. But unversed and uneducated in the ways through which we can grow psychologically and emotionally into a new security in the self, we still depend upon the old relationship patterns to provide this security. We are blinded by the maturity myth and bewildered by the option glut. We enter adult relationships, especially marriage, expecting them to fulfill our dependency needs, expecting them to provide the same kind of security our parents once looked for in a different world. But what is even more confusing and devastating we expect our adult relationships to provide what *we didn't have* in our parental homes. Many of us have grown up in families in which our needs for self-esteem, self-confidence, love and caring were not sufficiently met. We go out into the world still seeking for the sense of self that our families did not fulfill for us, but we try to achieve that sense of self in the same kinds of relationships that existed for our parents (or failed to sustain them) and which are simply inadequate to the pressures of today's world.

Lacking a sense of self, we look for someone to make

up for the deficiencies in ourselves, someone who can play mommy or daddy for us. We frequently pick mates largely on the basis of our deficiency needs—those that were not satisfied in our parental home—and then when those needs are not fulfilled by the partner we choose, the relationship goes sour. Deficiency needs are bottomless wells that can never be filled by others. If you don't believe in your own competency, if you are afraid of life, and you marry a "strong" person in order to compensate for what you perceive as your lack, you can't possibly succeed in becoming strong by association. In fact you will probably only confirm your own weakness to yourself: "I told you so," you will say to yourself when your partner manipulates you and insists upon your doing things his or her own way.

Although others cannot fulfill our deficiency needs, we can free ourselves from them through personal growth, by seeking out the aspects of ourselves that are most individual and fulfilling those. The old dependent relationships stifle such growth and self-discovery. But that doesn't mean that we must run away from relationships in order to find ourselves—we just need new kinds of relationships. When we fail to understand that distinction, our relationships frequently become commodities, another aspect of the option glut. We computerize our matchmaking (using, ironically, the same kind of standards of compatibility that were employed by parents in the days of "arranged" marriages). We rent-a-date with someone we'll never see again. We wander endlessly from one uncommitted relationship to another, just as we do from one value to another and from one tempting life-style to another. Yesterday's marriage of convenience has given way to today's disposable relationship, neither one providing the intimacy and relatedness we so desperately need and want.

Man lives only through the relationship of his self to the world around him. His relationships, in the largest sense of that word—to intimate others, friends, community, government, work and ideas—provide the context and meaning of his life. Whether it is our basic need for a feeling of community with others, our need for a deeply personal and intimate relationship, or our needs for relationships to ideas, values and beliefs, the meaning of the self exists in counterpoint to the world around us. There is no purpose to self-discovery if we do not relate that self to others. As Maurice Friedman has said, "We are all persons, to a certain extent, by courtesy of one another."

We cannot grow in dependent relationships. But growth without relationships has little meaning. We do have needs for interdependency, which means sharing our dependencies and needs with others in a way that helps us to deal with these needs and grow beyond them. We do need emotional closeness, we do need to know someone cares for us, we do have a need to love as well as be loved and we also need to grow. Our freedom to grow, however, does not come from refusing to enter into committed relationships, but exists instead in the capacity to become ourselves within the relationship.

The new kinds of relationship we are talking about are essential not only to fulfillment and growth for adults, but also must be fostered between parent and child. The "generation gap" reflects the inability of both parents and young people to make a leap toward mutual growth together in the face of a changing world. Both have to learn from one another. The parents have greater experience; but the children, because they were born into the crisis culture, in many ways are more aware of its impact and significance than their parents are. Many parents, not understanding their child's emerging identity, are unable to provide the supportive respect for the growth of the child that is so essential. Others are so lost, so isolated, that they are unable to share themselves with their children. And the children—affluent yet shoplifting, each with his car but no place to go, with every material benefit but no purpose in life—feel unneeded, unloved and alone. Parents and children need one another in the same way that adults need one another—they need to be able to learn from one another, to share insights and growth. Parents need to care for their children in a way that helps the children to grow in self-supportiveness, in self-reliance and in the belief in their ability to grow and develop their full potential in a changing world.

Caring—The Essential Ingredient

One of the essential ingredients in the new concept of relationship is caring: caring for the self and for the other in a way that can help each to grow more self-supportive.

In our relationships with others we need love. But love is not enough. All the individual knows, as Maslow puts it, "is that he is desperate for love, and thinks he will be forever happy and content if he gets it." The individual doesn't realize beforehand that even after achieving love he will want to continue in search of additional kinds of fulfillment. While love is fundamental as a base for growth, there will be other emerging needs that cannot be met through love alone.

We also need basic compatibility in relationships. But, as with love, we have needs beyond compatibility. We cannot grow to be ourselves unless we have a relationship in which we not only share certain fundamental likenesses but also share and learn from our differences. Sharing and learning from one another's differences is not just a matter of tolerance for another's habits. "It is not just blind 'acceptance' that a normal person desires," says the psychologist Nathaniel Branden, "nor unconditional 'love,' but *understanding*." We need the active feedback and acknowledgment by our intimate other of our desires, our beliefs, our feelings and our emotions—and most of all each of us needs the other to "attach importance to the reasons behind our emotions."

It is this kind of caring that we need in relationships today. "Through caring for certain others," writes the philosopher Milton Mayeroff, "by serving them through caring, a man lives the meaning of his own life. . . . only the man who trusts himself to grow, who is not trying to force himself on to be something he thinks he is supposed to be, will be able to trust another person to grow." Everything in this book has been directed toward helping you to guide your own life, to become more self-assertive, and to be more self-supportive, self-determining and autonomous. And the essence of caring is to help those you love to do the same for themselves. By taking your own stance in life you become more yourself. By assisting another to take his or her stance in life, to become more himself or herself, you demonstrate how much you care for them —but at the same time you are caring for yourself. For as each of you becomes more himself, each of you has more of himself to give to the other in an intimate relationship. We cannot give out of our deficiencies, but only out of our strengths. The greater those strengths, the more we can give without diminishing ourselves or others.

Thus a relationship in which both persons are growing, in which both persons are capable of shifting gears, in which both persons are becoming more self-initiating, allows both to more fully experience their uniqueness and to grow still further. There is a delicate balance between our self-assertiveness and our caring that can be maintained only by respecting the integrity of the other. Each of us has an essence of self that constitutes our unique way of responding to life—a mosiac of our past and our future potential, our experience and our hopes, our reality and our imagination. Whatever this essence is for the given individual, when we care for another it is this unique quality in him that we are caring for. When caring exists, this center or essence expands and unfolds through change and growth.

Yet no matter how much we care for another, we cannot do his growing for him. In caring we become enabling factors in one another's growth, but most of the actual work of growth we must undertake on our own. Each person must work through his own style of self-development. For some this will be easier and the process will go smoothly, for others it may be more difficult. Sometimes we must care enough for the other not to attempt to rescue him from the legitimate pain that can accompany growth. "We show lack of trust by trying to dominate and force the other into a mold, or by requiring guarantees as to the outcome, or even," as Mayeroff states, "by 'caring' too much."

When a child falls and scrapes his knee, the mother who "cares" too much rushes in saying, "There now, don't cry, that doesn't hurt." The child knows all too painfully that it does hurt. How much more honest and caring is the mother who says, "There now, of course it hurts, no wonder you are crying, because those scrapes are painful. I know it must hurt, but soon it will go away and mend." This is honesty, sympathy, empathy, reality, courage, hope and caring all in one response. Caring is the pain we experience in seeing our child experience his first disillusionment, in letting him make his own mistakes, and in giving him the encouragement to go on growing. Caring in an adult relationship is helping each other to grow by receiving and not denying each other's authentic feelings. We cannot grow until we accept the feelings we do have, as ours. Until we know and accept our feelings and emotions we cannot grow into full emotional response. In a world where the maturity myth means being emotionally closed, we have been taught to restrain our emotions and to feel that something is wrong with expressing them. The child, as Nathaniel Branden points out, has learned ". . . to equate being 'grown-up' with being emotionally closed." Thus we care by helping each other to understand our emotions.

Caring thus is encouraging someone to do something he wants to do, not what you want him to do—encouraging him to act according to the way he feels, not the way you think he should feel. Caring is listening and trying to understand the hurt another person has, the joy he has, and most of all, caring enough to let him express it. Having this quality of caring helps two people to attain mutual growth.

Mutual Growth

A relationship of mutual growth is one where intimacy through mutual self-disclosure occurs, where there is respect for the identity, equality and integrity of the other, where there are flexibility, togetherness and aloneness. It is one where trust grows through a willingness to share joys and to work things out through open and honest communication. With trust we can open up to new possibilities and discoveries within ourself and the other.

With these qualities we become deeply involved and enlarge each other. We use our similarities (the things we feel an affinity to in another: habits, thoughts, feelings, idiosyncracies) as a basis from which to knit new self-extensions. We enlarge ourselves by learning and growing through exchanging our differences, and through this exchange and transformation of growth we create love.

When we perceive these differences as *desirable,* learning and growing through them, there is a joy and exhilaration in the exchange. But relationships are not always that simple. Each of us may perceive various differences, qualities or behavior in the other as *undesirable,* or we may perceive any change in the other as undesirable. But we also grow through grappling with the impasse these differences may bring. Staying with it through the impasses and growing through them requires courage, trust, honesty and effort; yet it is here, only in the honest confrontation of self with another through *time* and *change* in the intimate and caring relationship, that the greatest depths of personal and emotional growth can occur.

Love, growing out of this mutual extension and unfolding of each one's integrity through the help of the other, creates a bond through synergy. Each one's growth enhances and increases the growth of the other. In this type of "synergic build-up" two people can accomplish more growth together than either could individually, yet each maintains his autonomy—each augments the growth of the other, himself, *and* the relationship. This concept, developed in our previous book, we feel can best be expressed as: *I'm great, you're great, and together we're greater!*

All too often the reverse effect occurs. When one party in the relationship begins pulling the other down in despond, a negative involuted *synergic let down* is the result: each one's negative qualities or attitudes feed the other's back and forth in a diminishing spiral that can destroy the relationship.

Many of us have a great capacity for caring and yet it is not easy to develop or, sometimes, to find another person with whom we can have a relationship of mutual growth. Mutual growth is at times as painful and difficult as it is joyful and rewarding. But when both partners are trying, neither expects miracles or change to happen overnight. Each small step toward understanding enables us to take another, each step gives us more confidence in our ability to grow and our capacity to love.

The mutual growth of two people helping each other to become increasingly self-supportive through caring and synergy is not the same as the parallel relationship of two people who have become self-centered in their search for self-development. We sometimes confuse the two. In our crisis culture many people who have failed to find fulfilment through the false promises of the maturity myth mistakenly assume that the only alternate path is to become self-centered, rejecting intimacy and emotional closeness. Such people are so much in search of the self that they lose it. They transform their need for self-assertiveness into self-centeredness in a kind of superindividualism that ignores our needs for relatedness and interdependence with another. The philosophy of "you do your thing, and I'll do mine and if we don't make it together, too bad" is the result.

We can see the results of this philosophy all around us in the crisis culture. For some, living alone and liking it has become symbolic of a brave new independence. Sexual encounters become so casual and divorced from feeling that any person substitutes for another. Jobs and careers become only occupations performed with indifference and carelessness. Since the self-centered person does not relate with caring and is not willing to commit himself to the effort of mutual growth, he must find persons who match his current level of growth. They grow side by side, if there is any growth at all. When the going gets rough in the transitional periods between one phase of growth and another, they often feel it is time to drop the relationship and look for another person.

It is only through caring, then, both for ourselves and for others, that we can truly actualize ourselves, bringing our potentials fully into play. We must care enough about ourselves to find our own way of self-growth. And we must care enough about others to encourage them to find their own way. Mutual growth through caring, intimacy and synergy helps us to develop the kind of support that encourages the freedom of growth.

Intimacy

Intimacy is listening to another person's disclosures and caring about their meaning to the other person's growth. Intimacy is also caring enough to disclose yourself to others—making the effort and taking the risk involved in opening yourself up to another. Our culture has distorted the meaning of intimacy, however, by equating it with sex. Two erroneous conclusions stem from this distortion: first, that intimate relationships must include sex, and second, that having sex means you are intimate. Sex is, of course, one of the ways in which we express our feelings of fullest and deepest intimacy, but it is not necessarily an essential component of intimacy.

The essential component of intimacy is disclosure: my willingness to disclose myself to you, your willingness to listen to my disclosure, your willingness to disclose yourself to me, my willingness to listen to your disclosure. And it is this intimacy that enables us to share emotional closeness. Through caring and providing a receptive climate for listening to each other, we encourage our mutual growth and help each other to make self-discoveries. When we express our feelings, perceptions and experiences in words, they become clear in our minds and achieve a new meaning for us. In a climate of trust and caring we can be open enough to search for this new self-understanding and to share these intimacies. If we help each other to understand our individual and personal meanings and feelings in this way, we are helping each other to grow and to find new ways of action and interaction to further this growth.

When the full cycle of disclosure does not occur and caring and trust are not mutual, three types of unproductive situations might result:

(1) The person who is disclosing himself does not care about the person to whom he is opening himself. This kind of person's need is so great that he "tells all" without caring about how his disclosure will be received, how it will affect the person he is disclosing himself to, or whether the other person is capable of response. He is simply using the other as a receptacle—the receiver is an object.

(2) The person who is receiving the disclosure doesn't care. The receiver in this situation doesn't deserve the trust placed in him. Either nothing happens in the relationship or the receiver may use the disclosure against the other, either at the time of disclosure or later. And, the discloser, unless he is secure in himself, often feels vulnerable in this situation.

(3) Neither one cares about the disclosures of the other. There is really no intimacy at all. If one person discloses, it is a monologue; if both disclose, it is a duologue with neither one really having an effect on the other. If neither discloses it is an empty relationship based on casual and perhaps superficial exchange. When neither gives concern or compassion to the other or both lack the trust and courage to become involved —to risk caring about each other's disclosure—there is no real relationship.

These situations lead to a fear of commitment. And the fear of commitment leads to a rejection of relationship as a means to growth and fulfillment. Most of us, however, end up in tentative positions somewhere in between those above. We care, but we don't disclose; or we make limited and conditional disclosures. And that is fine. For we cannot be open with everyone. But in our closest one-to-one relationships, we need to have trust and disclosure in order to grow. When we do, it makes it easier for us to grow. For although each of us must do his own growing, the knowledge that his intimate partner cares about his growth frees the individual from fear of change in the relationship. As we become more secure in self—finding our center of self and shifting gears—we feel less vulnerable and are able to risk disclosures more openly with others without fear of change, rejection or loss.

There is also an intimacy we can experience with another which does not require words. Sometimes we are most with another in the moments of silence together through which we disclose an unspoken understanding of each other's feelings—whether these moments are ones of joy, awe, happiness, pain or anguish. This is an implicit knowing of each other. When one or both of us experience pain or doubt, this intimacy of silence and understanding is especially valuable for growth. Through it we can express our respect for each other's integrity and our essential separateness. We do not pretend to know the content of the other's thoughts, yet through our positive compassion and silent affirmation of each other we share an intimacy of understanding and closeness that transcends our separateness.

Intimacy thus experienced through disclosure and caring is an integral part of commitment and growth in a relationship.

Your Change, My Change

What happens, then, to an ongoing relationship when you begin to shift gears, to change, to find your own center, to solve your problems for yourself, to become more secure and make your own decisions?

As you change, there is bound to be a consequent change in your closest relationships. Your change may be threatening for a partner who is insecure with change. You may find yourself in a situation where the underlying message from the other is very clear: "You can't grow because I don't want you to. I'm too threatened because I am afraid of change in myself."

If this happens then you, yourself, have to make the decision as to which course of action is more important for you:

(1) to fall back (retreat) to your former position and not change;

(2) to split—if you reach an impasse and the situation gets too rough;

(3) to take the risk of change and work toward helping your partner change.

If you choose the first course it might be well to remember that in actuality one partner cannot hold another back from growth—unless you acquiesce. We are willing partners in controlled relationships. If you try to control him, you give up control of yourself. If he tries to control you and succeeds then you are willingly surrendering your own initiative and will to change. No one has the right to tell you you can't grow or change. If someone does then he is trying to defeat life itself. He is expressing his own fear, not yours.

If you choose the second and decide to separate, you are not alone, as our mounting divorce rate demonstrates. Broken relationships in all areas are becoming a national habit. This second course of action, to separate or terminate the relationship, has both its negative and positive aspects. If it is impossible to work out change because the anguish, resistance and bitterness is too great, then separation may seem to be the only course open to you. Inevitably two people change, even without conscious direction of that change; couples may have been mismatched to begin with and a life of tangled goals, great disparities in personalities, mixed hopes and damaged egos may have opened a gulf that can no longer be bridged. Nevertheless we should be aware that separation is too often just an easy way out. Splitting is much easier than facing our own self and dealing with the relationship we have. Blaming the relationship, blaming the partner or blaming the past can be a smoke screen against self-revelation. But none of us can control all the factors and circumstances in our lives, or the willingness of another to work through change in a relationship with us. Sometimes separation is necessary.

On the other hand, we all know people who have discovered a new self, or rediscovered their personal identity following the devastation of a divorce or separation. Such a crisis can call forth unknown resources and stimulate the courage to seek a renewed self. Years later some former wives and husbands are able to look back thankfully and say, "It was the best thing that could have happened to me." The tragedy is that such renewal and insight comes only after the relationship is lost and is no longer capable of being revitalized.

The optimum course of action is the third. Go ahead with your change, trusting that your newfound self and security can help you understand and gently encourage your partner to grow. Caring for ourselves and our own autonomy gives us the ability to see more clearly the other's needs in change and growth. Beginning to think and do and act for yourself should make it more possible for you to care for your partner, to help him to grow in his own way. By standing on our own feet, taking our own stance in life, initiating our own changes, we increase our ability to care for others. If caring and intimacy exist in your relationship, almost any change can be worked out—and will become another reaffirmation of your love and commitment.

Temporary Relationships

Temporary relationships are not to be confused with uncommitted relationships. We might as well get used to the fact that with our increasing mobility, temporary relationships are here to stay. In today's world there are temporary relationships, short-term relationships and long-term relationships. There are committed and uncommitted relationships. A long-term relationship can be uncommitted; a temporary relationship can be committed.

Commitment usually implies the dimensions of time and continuity in a relationship—time to get to know each other, time to go through the myriad experiences of life, having children, enjoying a new experience, meeting challenges together, knowing despair, joy, death, hard times and peak experiences. Nothing can duplicate this long-term knowing of each other. But there are other dimensions to commitment besides time.

If, by way of mobility, modern life forces us into situations where we no longer have the luxury of a long time in which to develop a relationship we must concentrate on finding the values and meaning in temporary or short-term relationships. Divorce, death, movement, location and circumstance increasingly diminish our chance for long-term relationships of every sort—whether it is with the vegetable man, the druggist, our employer, friends, family or mate. But temporary and short-term relationships are here to stay.

Because temporary relationships have a beginning and an end they have a special quality and value. You can relate to each other in a way you would not if you knew you would be seeing each other regularly over a long period of time. We should appreciate the freedom these relationships give us. They allow us to be more open and spontaneous, more insightful, less bound by conformity and less hidden behind the masks of our existence. We are new to each other, without a past except that which we bring within us to the relationship. We can gain new insights and perceptions of ourselves because we are in a new and unrestricted situation. In tempoary relationships you telescope your time—your past, present and future. Shedding the superfluous and superficial enables you to concentrate on what you have to share in that short time without the impedimentia of past experiences or the problems of the future. You exist in the intensity and meaning of the time you are with each other. We can be free of culturally determined preconceptions about each other, free of role-playing, of age, of sex and status. As one young woman said, "These relationships are exhilarating—you know you don't have to correct your faults and you can be your own real self, let it out."

But these relationships must also have a commitment to be meaningful—otherwise they may turn into encounters where each uses the other in a noncaring way instead of growing through the relationship. Despite the fleeting aspect of your time in that relationship you can be committed to respecting the integrity of the other and to the integrity and authenticity of your response. You can be committed to being most truly yourself, without artifice and without pretension, yet with devotion, attention and caring for the duration of the dialogue between you. In the three and four career lives that we can choose to have in the future, through out changes in life-style, occupations, location and interest, we should seek to develop the ability to make our short-term and temporary relationships more than superficial encounters and something of value in sharing and discovery.

The maturity myth has brainwashed us to overlook the value of temporary relationships and to believe that stable long-term relationships are the only ones that are of value and the only ones in which we can have commitment. But this is an attitude that can be modified if we emphasize the authenticity and the special qualities of temporary relationships. Long-term relationships do offer a kind of caring and an opportunity for development that no short-term relationship will ever offer us, no matter how committed it is. Each is different and has an integrity and value of its own. Knowing that mutual exchange is essential for growth, we can try to find it in any relationship, anywhere.

Friends

Good friends are rare. The care and nurturing of good friendships, while less demanding and less time-consuming than our primary relationships with significant others require many of the same qualities as those relationships: honesty, good communication, respect and caring. When we have made a good friendship, have shared in intimacy our profoundest thoughts, have earned the respect and affection that characterizes a real friendship, it can last through a lifetime. No matter the distance or time, there is a bond between us. We can hurdle huge gaps of time to revive the connec-

tions and bonds we had. We can be together or apart
as our separate needs demand; then once we are together again we can leap over the intervening space
and time and carry on where we left off—*if* we have
both been growing. Although some bond will always
exist between real friends, if, in the process of change,
one has grown and the other has not, if the interests
have diverged too much, if the intimacy is no longer
kept alive, then these friendships, too, will change.
When seeing a close friend after an absence, the realization may dawn on us that we have made a longer
leap in growth than he has. We notice his patterns are
much the same as before—the conversation sinks, the
old repetitive phrases sound like a broken record
and you know suddenly that your connection is brok-
en. He does not understand what you are talking about.
Your growth has taken you beyond that friendship and
it sinks inexorably into the inactive file. We may resist
it, but the recognition is inevitable. We experience the
profound sense of loss so familiar in letting go of
anything we have outgrown—our childhood, a country place, an old habit, a comfortable piece of clothing. This sense of loss may be particularly poignant
when we outgrow a friend—few of us at any one time
can have more than a handful of relationships that
are deep and true friendships.

We have thousands of acquaintances, many associations, but few real friends. Real friends are those we
freely select and choose and for this reason they play
a special part in our lives. They provide us with joy,
comfort and caring. Because they are limited to shorter
periods of time together, friendships give us a breathing spell from the intensity of our full-time primary relationships. And they can provide another context for
growth. Although there are many types of friendship,
we would like to confine ourselves here to three kinds
that are especially important in respect to the process
of shifting gears.

Just as your primary relationships, friends are not

merely for comfort and support; they are the threads keeping you connected to the world, the threads that lead you into growth. There is a special need today for what we call *feedback friends*. These are friends we respect and whose opinion we can rely on.

These are the friends you probably have shared a continuity of experiences with. You can go to them when you are troubled, perplexed, worried, or have problems that you do not yet know how to solve. They are not mentors and do not necessarily give you advice; they give you honest feedback—they can explore a problem with you and are able to see you with clarity and objectivity. A businessman who worked abroad for many years explained: "When I lived in France there was no one I could go to—and I moved out of France for that reason. I would walk through the park at night crazy to talk to someone. And I had friends there I was closer to than here but there was simply no one capable of understanding. Here in New York I can drive over to a number of people—and they are not nearly as close to me as some people in France— and they will listen to me and give me feedback. They are the people I need to go to when things get rough. It's not so much a matter of trust as getting honest feedback, and for this you have to have confidence in someone, value their insight and opinion."

When we are in crisis or need to make changes and decisions in our life, these are the kinds of friends we need the most. In our discussions with them, we gain some objectivity about our problems and selves. These friends may share with us their troubles, similar problems, and the mistakes and successes they may have made. Knowing that we are not alone in our struggles, suffering and mistakes and that others share the imperfections of man's existence can give us solace and a feeling of commonality and the inspiration to go on.

Intimate Friendship

There can be a particular quality of intimacy in friendships that offers us special opportunities for growth. In these intimate friendships we can open up facets of ourselves and gain new insights and perspectives about ourselves and others. We can stretch our minds with many friends—even old ones we know only in books—but there are few with whom we can stretch both our mental and emotional boundaries. Yet these are the ones that help us to grow in our dimensions of wholeness. They are rare—these friends with whom we have "the profound psychological and emotional relationship that," says Dr. Allan Fromme, "constitutes friendship at best."

A young woman expressed the meaning of this kind of friendship for her: "You have friends with whom you grow up and have so much in common—with whom you share your past experiences, your memories, the love for something in common like the little village where we grew up. And then you meet friends later in life with whom you can share a greater intimacy—you have so few words for friends in English, but in German they are called *Seelenverwandtschaft: Seele* is soul, and *Verwandtschaft* is relationships of kindredness. With these friends there is real exchange, we both learn so much and are able to express our closest thoughts and feelings.

"You know, it is like sometimes you think and think and get to a wall and it hurts, but if you have a good friend in discussion, he helps you. Like Plato says, he is a 'midwife,' who helps you get your thoughts out of your head and develop them. Sometimes thinking can hurt. But with these friends you make a real effort and then you break the barrier, and you go beyond. And this is a fantastic thing—you go home and lie awake because so many facets in your mind and soul have been opened. And when it is happening, I forget about everything. It's not physical at all, I can sit with a drink of water, I don't need cigarettes, wine, sex, food. It's a feeling of discovery, that something in here inside you seems to be growing, and opening and expanding. And then the next day it's like after tasting a great wine—the aftertaste of a great experience. The next day and the next day this feeling is lingering on. I am more energetic and optimistic. Going through the effort of sharing, of getting involved was worthwhile. It is an increase of power, strength, energy."

Our need for testing our inner and emotional growth is reflected in the fantastic recent growth of encounter groups and group therapy, where the conditions for intimacy are structured. In our world of mobility and telescoped time, our isolation from the full engagement and luxury of knowing friends through a lifetime becomes more acute—just at a time when authentic encounter is needed most. A deep need to disclose oneself, to find a springboard for psychological growth and solace among others in a changing world, sends people to these artificial arenas where they can strip away the banality and facade of everyday interaction and get down to basics.

The problem is that encounter groups *are* artificial. Much as these groups may help in breaking barriers and training us for intimacy, they do not provide an ongoing context for growth. We can, though, develop this ongoing context and authentic encounter with intimate friends in whom we trust, who care for us and with whom we can share disclosures of ourselves and grow. Although these intimate friendships cannot offer us the depth and the richness of mutual growth that occurs in our primary relationships with mates or partners, they can help us to expand the dimensions of our growth.

New Friends

We have already mentioned that your growth, the fact of moving into a new phase in your life, will make it necessary to change some friends. You are going to be growing and it is going to be important to find other people who are growing and who will keep you growing. Just as we must be selective, focus on what is important to us and eliminate the options that confuse and distract us, so too we must exercise this ability with friends. This is not to diminish the importance and stability of old friends with whom you have shared past experiences and with whom you may share a whole commonality of interests. But you must move in the area of friendships, too. They become a vital part of our growth, lead us into new areas, stimulate us in thinking and provide new information.

To seek out new friends requires a reorientation in your old habits. As you grow, and become more directive of your life, knowing better what you want and what gives you pleasure, there will come a time when you must say no to maintaining the social facade, to accepting and going through the same old events and dinners with people whom you love but who bore you. Sometimes our acquaintances can absorb as much time and be as distracting as the general clutter in our life —too many options, too many products, too many people. But with new direction, goals and purpose in your life it should not be too difficult to firmly say, "No, I am *not* going to go to that dinner. No, I am *not* going to spend four hours talking over something I have gone beyond."

In seeking new friends we should be aware of our customary pattern to gravitate to those who are like us, or who like us. Bathing in the warm waters of unqualified approval, or feeling comfortable in sharing commonalities is like taking aspirins—their value fades after four hours. In the spirit of exploration and experimentation and growth that characterizes shifting gears, we can seek out people who are different and through whom and with whom we can grow. "We learn new kinds of enjoyments from people who are not like us, who find their interests and values and pleasures along paths that we have never explored, and who on their part have never explored the paths most interesting to us," says L. Stringer. We have something to offer to friends who are different in some ways, and they have something to offer us. It is this mutuality of exchange in any relationship that is the essence of growth.

These kinds of friends, as well as those with whom we share our inner self, should be people who have a different outlook in some way from ours—people who have something beyond our own sphere of knowledge, relevance and feeling. They are important to enable us to shift gears, to see other possibilities, to find new ways. And they are also important after we shift gears, for then, when it is easier to risk, easier to be more sure and confident of yourself, we can be open to new ideas. It is through these friends that we continue to grow.

New Roots

Thus we have seen that relationships are essential for our growth and are an integral part of shifting gears. As we gain greater security in self and we increase our ability to focus on commitment and caring, we can find the internal consistency, or center, that enables us to feel at home in many different relationships.

Even though time speeds up, change accelerates, familiar landmarks and customs disappear, and the stability of our former roots is shattered, we can still find new roots in the present. We can weave a network of lateral roots in our inter-personal relationships that can spread over time and space and expand our connections to many others and to life. These lateral roots can provide a security that flows with time and change and that is not dependent on the familiar, static roots of the past. Our relationships can provide a security that depends on sharing our humanness and on our willingness to risk growth together. To do this we must first look for our similarities—those bonds that hold us together, regardless of the lifeways we separately follow, or the telescoping of time. We can then feel familiar in any lifeway, in any crowd, with any group, with any person. If, then, we also try to learn from our differences rather than becoming isolated and separated by them, if we cherish our shared joys and respect the pain and difficulties that mutual growth can bring in any kind of relationship, we can recognize our essential bond to other persons and ultimately to all men.

If our families change in form through mobility, separation, divorce or other circumstances, we can build non-kin families of our choosing by selecting other persons we respect to share time and experience and feelings with us, our children and friends. By being open to the unique contribution of young and old alike in meeting change we can strengthen our relatedness and ties to others.

Through caring and intimacy we nourish our closest one-to-one relationships of mutual growth. Through caring, openness, and finding the internal consistency that is our center, we can expand the dimensions of all our inter-personal relationships.

Part III

The Self Finds Security:
Integrating the Life
Strategy

CHAPTER TWELVE

Creative Maturity

Part I: Self-Management

The Challenge

If we do not rise to the challenge of our unique capacity to shape our own lives, to seek the kinds of growth that we find individually fulfilling, then we can have no security: we will live in a world of sham, in which our selves are determined by the will of others, in which we will be constantly buffeted and increasingly isolated by the changes around us. Without choice we can have no direction, without a life strategy that is our own we lose our sense of self (or never find it) and become a cipher, a nothing. As Jules Henry, the anthropologist, has commented: "For when a man is nothing, he lives only by impacts from the outer world; he is a creature external to himself, a surface of fear moved by the winds of circumstance: one circumstance colliding with another—that is the ebb and flow of thought. Or he is a cyclone of fear in which impulses from the outer world collide at random." When we live a life of sham, Jules Henry goes on to say, we do not consider reality but only try to defeat it.

The reality of the world around us, including the impact of change, is something we must meet if we are to grow—we cannot capitulate to it, we cannot abdicate the making of choices. The only way we can prevent ourselves from being overwhelmed and counteract the forces around us is to find our own center, to believe in ourselves, to ignore the conflicting voices around us and listen to our inner voices. It is only then that we can truly interact with the outside world with courage, conviction and meaning.

The consequence of letting change happen without our active involvement is abdication to the tyranny of external control, both in a societal and an individual sense. When we lose our individual autonomy and our freedom of choice, then frustration, isolation, aggression and violence are the result. If you do not manage yourself, then by default either circumstances or other people will manage you. "What modern man needs is not 'faith' in the traditional sense of that term," as philosopher Maurice Friedman has said, "but a *life-stance* [our italics]—a ground on which to stand and from which to go out to meet the ever changing realities and absurdities of a tectronic age." Our life-stance is ". . . that personal and social ground that might enable us to withstand bureaucratization and surveillance—the innumerable incursions of military, industrial, ecological, economic and political forces into our personal lives."

In order to clarify our individual life stance, to find ourselves and what we believe in and stand for, we need to know not only about the guidelines to a life strategy for change and growth mentioned in this book, but also how to integrate those guidelines and put them to work for us. And an understanding of self-management can help us to carry out this integration of the life strategy.

Taking a Stand for Yourself

Taking a stand in life, a stand for yourself, is integral to shifting gears, to growing through self-directed change. There are seven keys to creative self-management that can help you to develop a stand in life:

1. Don't ask permission	Do it
2. Don't report	Check things out with yourself, not others
3. Don't apologize unnecessarily	This is telling others you are a self-diminisher
4. Don't recriminate yourself	The missed-opportunity syndrome keeps you from moving forward
5. Don't say "I should" or "I shouldn't"	Ask "Why?" or "Why not?"
6. Don't be afraid to say *no* or *yes*	Act on what you think and feel
7. Don't put yourself completely in the hands of another	Be a self-determiner

Each of these keys is a negative because it is necessary to counteract our too frequent capitulation to cultural and social dicta that insist upon our conformity, that tells us security lies in being like other people instead of fulfilling our individual needs through continuing growth. But this negative cast doesn't mean that we must forsake others or fail to take others into account. The truth is that we can have understanding and consideration for others only to the extent that we ourselves are strong. If we are ciphers, ruled by others, then we have nothing to give others. It is only when we begin to manage our own change that we can truly give ourselves in a caring and sharing way—we give to another or to a project or situation out of our feelings of independence, self-reliance and security, not out of self-diminishment and weakness. A corollary to these keys is: be kind to yourself. Few of us can reach a compassionate kindness for others unless we can be kind to ourselves first.

These keys make it possible for us to change and

grow creatively. It is true, of course, that by saying
no, by not asking permission, we may lose old friends
—but if our friendships are based upon our weaknesses rather than our strengths, how good are they
for us? With new strength we will make new friends
who are themselves strong. If we find it necessary to
"hurt" someone else in order to determine our own
lives, what it really means is that we are no longer
willing to let them hurt us, no longer willing to let
them prevent us from realizing ourselves. Once we
stop letting others hurt us, it becomes possible out of
our new strength to give and to help them because we
care. We can then more easily accept without feeling
hurt or rejected when others say no to us.

When we have begun to take charge of our lives, to
own ourselves, there is no longer any need to ask permission of someone. If there is another person who will
be affected by what you are going to do, then you can
ask how the other feels about what you intend to do.
Ask for feedback from him or her and then utilize
this new information in your decision-making. Listening to these feelings and taking them into consideration is important, but it is not the same thing as asking
permission. To ask permission is to give someone else
veto power over your life; on the other hand, to ask for
feedback is to gather information that can be balanced
against your own needs, your own values.

Knowing your values and acting upon them means
that you have become your own person, your own
boss, your own mentor. It does not however, mean a
lack of concern about others and your responsibilities
to them or for them. We can explain to others the *why*
of our decisions and actions—or our impulsive and
thoughtless mistakes—but we should do it because we
care for others, not because we feel controlled by them.
When we explain to them we are in fact complimenting
them, treating them as people of a maturity equal to
our own. If other people do not or cannot accept our
authentic explanations of our decisions or actions be-

cause of problems of their own, they do not deserve an apology in the first place. Explanations, yes, but apologies, no. If they measure our worth only by how closely we conform to what they want us to do, they are really asking us to be worth nothing to ourselves. Such people are not themselves mature and their objections to our steps toward maturity simply are not valid.

Once you are able to accept responsibility for your actions, and can explain your reasons for these actions to other people, once you are able to examine the positive and negative aspects of yourself and by so doing begin to find your path toward change, then other people must also accept your authenticity in this regard; otherwise they show themselves to be diminishers, people whose sense of their own worth is dependent on your being less mature, less sure of your worth than they are of theirs. You can demonstrate no higher regard for other people, in the end, than by caring for them enough to tell them the truth about your needs.

Some people will undoubtedly misuse the rules for self-management we have outlined, misapplying them in the service of what currently but erroneously passes for being true to oneself—letting it all hang out, doing one's own thing without regard for others. You don't owe an explanation to others; but if you are unable and unwilling to give one, you are not moving toward mature and creative change but simply trying to escape from reality into a private fantasy in which it is no longer necessary for you to interact with the world and with the people around you. The psychologist Robert W. White notes that ". . . it is tempting to believe that we can change simply by opening a door and letting out 'true' unsullied impulses." But to misuse our keys for self-management in this way does not lead to change. To quote again from White: "Change is never so simple. What is really involved is not the releasing of a true self but the making of a new self, one that gradually transcends the limitations and pettiness of the old. This can only be done by behaving differently when interacting with other people. New strategies have to be evolved that express the new intentions and encourage others to take their reciprocal part in finer human relations."

The keys for self-management we have developed are a tool, then, a new strategy for dealing with others that allows us to express our own needs despite the cultural inhibitions against doing so. These keys express a new intention, and when they are accompanied by a compassionate explanation for our actions, they can indeed encourage others to take their reciprocal part in creative change.

But just as it is important that you don't ask permission, that you check things out with yourself rather than reporting to others for instruction, and that you don't apologize unnecessarily, it is also important not to recriminate yourself about past failures. Apologies to yourself are really the basis of the self-diminishment that leads to apologizing to others; if you spend time in self-recrimination, full of remorse over the past and the missed opportunities in your life, you are not managing yourself, but letting the past manage you. Your past holds as many potential half steps toward the future as it does missed opportunities. Mine your past for what is useful, learn from your mistakes and remember that nothing is wasted.

When you say, "I should do this," or "I shouldn't do that," you are also in many cases allowing yourself to be trapped by the past, following rules set down by parents, teachers or other mentors that may no longer have real meaning for you in our crisis culture. Many of our society's traditional mores, the *should*s and *shouldn't*s that have been handed down from one generation to another, are eminently worth preserving; but many others make sense only in terms of a kind of society that no longer exists. In order to live in the present, to move into the future and to make the most of ourselves as individuals, we have to begin to make distinctions between the *should*s and *shouldn't*s that make sense in terms of today's world and those that do not. When you find yourself saying, "I should," ask yourself, "Why?" When you find yourself saying, "I shouldn't," ask yourself, "Why not?" If you can't come up with an answer that makes sense in terms of you and your needs for growth and fulfillment, then it is obviously time to discard that rule from the past.

It may also be time to say *no*. You can say *no* to a rule from the past that no longer applies. You can also say *no* to a new development in our society that you personally find unfruitful and not in tune with your inner self. You can even say *no* to change if that is what you want. Just as there are holdovers from the past that make no sense to us as individuals, so will there be current changes that make no sense. The same woman may find herself in the position of saying *no* to her mother's dictum that abortions are sinful, and also saying *no* to the neighboring couple who are into group sex.

But as she says *no* to her mother and to her neighbors, this woman will also be defining more exactly the things she can say *yes* to. Once we have learned to say *no* we can give ourselves permission to say *yes* to the things we really want. In dealing successfully with the option glut, you will want to say *no* quite often— to extraneous diversions, false expectations, to excessive demands from others, to the people, the circumstances, the obligations that give you a sense of being trapped and frustrated. But the other side of that coin is to be able to say *yes*, fully and openly, to the people and circumstances that count for you.

The final key to creative self-management is the cardinal one: never put yourself completely into the hands of another. All of us need advice, support, encouragement and help from others—but only as a means of strengthening our own self-support. The responsible therapist does not manage his patient's life, but is there only to act as a significant and caring catalyst in the discovery of self, and in implementing positive change. In a complex existence one needs the help of others who have expertise in their own specialities. We must depend upon airline pilots and surgeons and presidents for our very existence at certain times, but the ultimate control of our life management should and can be ours as individuals. The difference between putting ourselves completely in the hands of others and retaining some personal control is the difference between the woman who says yes immediately to a major operation (which may later turn out to have been unnecessary) and the woman who, in the face of this major decision, checks one doctor's opinion with a few others, considers the risks, gets all the relevant information and *then* makes her decision, a decision she feels is right for her based on the information she has acquired. You can't sit up on the operating table and give the doctor instructions, but you can make sure beforehand that you are following the wisest possible course of action. That is the essence of self-management.

The development of self-management techniques allows you to have self-control—but control of your self in relation to the world should not be confused with holding things under control. The rigidly conforming person who fears anything new, who insists upon making his decisions according to preset patterns and who fears losing control is not managing himself. He does not have self-control, but rather is being controlled by all the external forces, edicts and expectations which he has internalized. You cannot control circumstance or other people, but you can control yourself, you can manage and direct behavior in response to circumstance and other people. Self-management leads to the finding of new directions, to a fresh sense of freedom within the limits of responsibility that true freedom entails.

The person who tries to hold things under control in a negative way, who tries to make circumstance and other people fit a preformed mold, is like the man who goes into a Chinese restaurant and always orders all his dishes from Column A. The person who practices self-management, who retains the power of decision in himself, who asks why and why not, who acts on what he really thinks and feels, has the choice of ordering not only from Column A but from Columns B and C as well—or entirely from one column if that is what he wants and finds best for himself at any given point. Or he can choose to walk out of the restaurant without ordering, too. The person who tries to hold things under control in a negative way is taking a prepackaged tour of life: this "if it's Tuesday it must be Belgium" syndrome leads him to say, "if I'm forty-five I must be home safe." But if the tour bus breaks down, or he finds that he is not home safe at forty-five, he is completely at the mercy of circumstance, as well as having missed out on much of life's varied excitement and much of his own potential. When things don't go as expected for the person who practices self-management, on the other hand, that individual has the resources to adjust his plans, to take the new circumstances into account and move forward from there. All kinds of adversities can be turned into advantage if we are willing to take our integral part in making them so.

By managing ourselves we come to know more completely what *we* want for ourselves, we come to know our priorities, our needs, our wants far more clearly, and this knowledge inevitably brings a greater sense not only of freedom but of security. The person who knows himself or herself, and manages his or her life, can tolerate a higher level of ambiguity than before, can deal more successfully with anxiety and conflict because he is sure of his own capabilities. Such people can enjoy change, can improvise confidently in unknown situations. As the psychologist Abraham Maslow suggests, such people can face tomorrow without fear because, whatever it may bring, they have the confidence of self-belief. Self-belief is eroded every time we put ourselves completely in another's hands, every time we ask permission, or report to others, or apologize unnecessarily. Self-belief is increased every time we ask ourselves, rather than others, what we should do with our lives. Self-management bolsters the meaning and the value of the self—and a fuller sense of self-worth and of self-competence is the result.

Part II: Giving Up Your Mentors

Becoming Yourself

As we become more ourselves and we learn to manage our own lives, we gradually detach ourselves from our former mentors. All of us have in the past had relationships with people whom we admired and from whom we learned about the world. These people are our counselors, our advisors, our sponsors and our guides through life. They are a part of growth—these uncles, aunts, professors, clergymen, models in our chosen profession, or friends. We need them to talk to, we need them to grow, we need them to provide us with a sense of security, a sense that we too can do it—and the hope they give us is like a self-fulfilling prophecy. If someone trusts in us, believes in us, it gives us an additional momentum toward fulfilling whatever dream we may have for ourselves.

Our parents are also mentors, but of a more complex kind. For a mentor to be truly helpful to us, he or she should be someone we have chosen. We do not learn best from imposed mentors, from schoolteachers we do not like but in whose homeroom we are stuck whether we like it or not, for instance. Some people do choose to make one or both of their parents mentors.

But others of us have more combative relationships with our parents, and some of us even look upon our parents as counter mentors, as representatives of what we do *not* want to be.

But whoever we chose as mentors, there comes a time when we are ready to give them up, break free and become ourselves. We go beyond their belief in us to a belief in ourselves. There comes a point when in order to be ourselves it may be necessary to say *no* to our mentors. Giving up your mentors means that you have learned the ropes sufficiently so that you can manage your own life. We discover that however much we admire them, we cannot fulfill ourselves any longer by following the lead of the philosophy professor at college, the high-school football coach, the older man or woman who helped us to become expert at our first adult job, or older and respected friends who have helped us guide our lives.

As with many other aspects of life, as we change and grow we move beyond our mentors, outgrowing the need for their guidance, sometimes outgrowing them as individual people. When you are ready to give them up—as mentors, not necessarily as friends, though that may follow—it means you have become an independent person, secure in self, who knows how to manage your own way of life. At the same time that we find ourselves ready to give up former mentors, we are also ready to become mentors ourselves, giving our experience and support in turn to another who looks to us for guidance. Some psychologists feel that the giving up of our mentors usually takes place in our late thirties, on the threshold of "middle-age." But just as middle-age seems to us largely a state of mind, an attitude toward life that is often affected by such false criteria as the maturity myth, we also believe that there is no special chronological point at which we do or should give up our mentors and become mentors in turn.

In fact, the crisis culture in which we live has

changed the pattern of our relationships with mentors. Fifty years ago a young man in a small town might choose the town doctor as his mentor, and eventually go on to become a doctor himself and a mentor for other young men. But in today's world, with its extraordinary mobility, with families moving constantly, it may not be possible to keep a single mentor over the years of our adolescence and early adulthood. Through force of circumstance we must look for new mentors when we move from town to city to suburb. And with so many new options open to us, we may find that we need a new mentor at fifty when we embark on a new career, even though we have already let go of previous mentors and become mentors ourselves in some areas of life. Especially when we are shifting gears we may find ourselves in the process of giving up an old mentor in order to move on and become more fully ourselves, while we are looking for a new mentor who can guide us through the early stages of the new phase of life into which we are entering. Thus the choosing and letting go of mentors becomes a continuous process, just as our own lives are a continuous process, an endless *becoming*.

It can be sad and unsettling to give up a mentor, to discover that someone we so deeply admired can no longer provide us with guidance, that our paths must diverge. But though we are giving up something that once meant a great deal, we are gaining something even more important and meaningful—ourselves. And many times, although we give up the mentor relationship with a given person, we will discover that from our new vantage point it is possible to enter into a new, different kind of relationship with that same person.

You Must Go Home Again

Thomas Wolfe's famous phrase, "You can't go home again," is true in a literal sense—you can't, of course, exactly recapture the past—but it is misleading in another sense. Many people do no want to go home again—they do not want to see their parents or do not want to involve themselves in the family situation that they found painful when they were growing up. They try to distance themselves from their parents both physically and emotionally, afraid that if they do not do so they will find themselves pressured into repeating the pattern of the previous generation that they found so disturbing when they were young.

But as we have shown before, mere distancing does not solve the problem. The man who goes to the South Seas to escape his problem inevitably takes it along with him. It is only by resolving a problem that we can be rid of it—mere distancing will not help and may indeed make things worse. If you do not confront what is disturbing in your past, if you do not resolve it, then you may more than likely begin to start acting it out again, subconsciously, in a different way. The psychological literature on family therapy is full of such case histories—the young man who doesn't want to repeat that pattern of family dynamics in which he grew up and so moves across the continent, virtually cutting off contact with his family, but suddenly wakes up one day to find that his own marriage is really nothing more than a repetition of his parents' marriage.

Thus it becomes vital to go home again, in the sense of dealing with your parents on an adult-to-adult level, once you have become your own man or woman. Once you have learned to manage your own life, once you have achieved a centered and secure self, going home can free you from the past more effectively than staying away ever can. Until you have faced that past on your own terms, out of the security of your own self, you can never be fully rid of its hold over you. Only by facing your parents and the old family situation, can you fully affirm your own individuality, fully prove to yourself that you have grown beyond that past.

We are taught that love means the acceptance of other people's defenses and myths about themselves, and that if you don't believe the myths of your family it means that you don't love them. But this is not true. Love is not "not ever having to say you're sorry"—more realistically it is being able to say you're sorry when an apology is genuinely called for but not feeling it necessary to say you're sorry when there is no reason to do so. In most families where the son or daughter has chosen a life-style vastly different from what the parents would have chosen for the child, the parents will go on trying to pressure the child into apologizing for his life until they see that he or she truly is his or her own person and truly does not feel that an apology is owed. And as long as you feel that you cannot face your parents, that you must keep them at a distance, emotionally and/or physically, it means that subconsciously you still feel you do owe them an apology for being yourself. Sensing your doubt, your parents may continue to pressure you in hopes of being told that, after all, they were right and you were wrong. But once you have truly developed the skills of self-management, and have become secure in your own choices, their pressure will no longer have any effect, and the pattern will be broken. From that point on a new relationship between you and your parents, between you and your past, inevitably begins.

Part III: A New Understanding of Loneliness

The Fear of Loneliness

We are afraid to be alone or to feel loneliness because we do not depend on ourselves. We have become so accustomed to depending on others to give us

pleasure, to fulfill our needs and to give us direction
that we are lost when alone. Fearing it, we avoid it,
throwing ourselves into random movement, into *anything* that will prevent us from being alone. Fear of
loneliness has become a national obsession. We huddle
into groups, seek twenty-four-hour solace from others,
seeking their approval—which simply means their
presence—on a nonstop basis. We chide those who do
choose to be alone at times, making a joke of Garbo
and her alleged "I vant to be alone." We think the guy
who goes to the beach alone or prefers his own company is a queer duck. Even many psychologists, while
stating that some degree of privacy is necessary to our
well-being, make a careful distinction between aloneness and loneliness. Aloneness is labeled good. Loneliness is labeled bad.

It is time to recognize that loneliness is *not* bad.
Aloneness and loneliness are two different things—and
we need both of them. We have discussed some of the
uses of aloneness both in this book and in *Open Marriage:* it gives us time for meditation, for restoring our
energies, for directed daydreaming, for exploring our
hidden potentials. Most of us can readily recognize
the benefits of this kind of self-exploration. But many
people, although they recognize these benefits, say they
always end up feeling lonely—and so reject the whole
idea of self-exploration.

We fear loneliness because we associate it with loss
and with deprivation. Someone close to us dies, we
come to the end of a long-term project, our children
grow up and leave home—and we feel a strong sense
of loneliness. We feel this not only in relation to people but to all kind of activities. Professional athletes
feel it at the end of a season, actors at the end of a run,
construction workers when they finish building a sky-
scraper. Whenever we have the sense that something
we were deeply involved in has come to an end, we
feel lonely, cut off from something that had become
a part of us. This sense of loss and nostalgia recurs

over and over in letting go of any former attachment, be it a love affair, children or an old and familiar habit.

It is the person who has little sense of self, who is insecure and who does not know his own capacities who most fears loneliness. It is in loneliness, after all, that our deficits are most glaring. And it is in loneliness that we come face to face with our essential separateness from every other human being and from the universe. And yet it is exactly because of these characteristics of loneliness that it is so necessary and important to us.

Creative Loneliness

Loneliness is necessary because it both reaffirms and emphasizes our separateness from others, from objects, from projects. That separateness is a basic fact of human existence, and if we run from it we are running from ourselves. It is only when we face that basic fact with courage that we *can* find our real bond with life, with self and with others. It is, of course, a paradox—but life is filled with paradoxes that are to be transcended. We discover ourselves most deeply in transcending self in our meeting with others. And yet we are still and always will be *individuals*. Both our glory and our despair come from the same source: our unique ability to shape our own lives, to choose, and to change our choices when the old ones no longer fulfill us.

In describing research on the nature of loneliness, Dr. Clark Moustakas writes ". . . that loneliness is a capacity or source in man for new searching, awareness and inspiration—that when the outside world ceases to have a meaning, when support and confirmation are lacking or are not adequate to assuage human suffering, when doubt and uncertainty overwhelm a person, then the individual may contemplate life from the depths of his own self and in nature. For me, this was a discovery that in a crucial and compelling crisis, in spite of comfort and sympathy from others, one can feel utterly and completely alone, that, at bottom, the experience of loneliness exists in its own right as a source of power and creativity, as a source of insight and direction, as a requirement of living no matter how much love and affirmation one receives in his work and in his relationships with others."

As with other things, it is your attitude toward loneliness that counts. You can take a negative attitude, in which case you may either run from it like the plague, or wallow in it in an orgy of self-pity. You can also take a positive attitude, recognizing it as an essential experience of each human being and using it creatively as a resource for knowing the self, discovering your center and focus in life. It is during periods of loneliness that we are most deeply in touch with the center of our human nature, that we most fully recognize the fact that we must stand alone. If we refuse to recognize that fact we can never really be secure, because we will be turning our backs on reality. It is the man who confronts reality and seeks out the best way to make use of it who has courage and is secure. It is only when we can stand alone, when we can admit our separateness, that we can make full use of our individual resources to set about finding our meaningful connections with others. When the love and the understanding with which we reach out to others is based upon a true sense of the self discovered in confrontation with our loneliness, then it is based on reality rather than on the false expectations that other people have told us we should live by.

Knowing that you alone can change yourself, that you alone can make a decision for growth, that you alone are the central point of reference in your life, can be a very lonely experience, but out of it can come a greater strength and confidence in your ability to meet life, a security that fear cannot destroy.

Part IV: Creativity

Combining the Rational and the Nonrational

Although real maturity is based on facing up to our essential aloneness, it would be a mistake to think of it as a melancholy condition. Real maturity gives us the ability to form our deepest and most meaningful relationships and, in addition, as Abraham Maslow has commented, "The most mature people are the ones that can have the most fun." By this he implies that when we are mature enough to know and accept our self the inner security that we feel makes it possible for us to best release those creative aspects of ourselves that make life exciting, meaningful *and* fun. Maslow uses the example of those who are secure enough to let themselves go at a party, speaking of the person who is "comfortable enough with his unconscious to be able to let go that much anyhow—a little crazy in this party sense; to be silly, to play along with a gag and to enjoy being nutty for a little while anyhow. . . ." This kind of openness is quite different from the response of the dignified, orderly, conscious, rational man who puts on a mask, is afraid to lose control and is not in any sense free enough of his conscious, controlling self to let himself go. The controlling man is the type of compulsive-obsessive person who is ruled by what psychologists call *secondary processes*. The secondary processes are those that are rational, logical, sensible and realistic. All of these qualities are necessary in life, but when one uses only these processes, and is ruled by them, it is usually "at the cost of giving up a portion of our deeper selves." Such people give up their imagination, their poetry, their ability to play, to fantasize, to laugh, to be spontaneous—they repress all of what Maslow calls their "healthy childlikeness."

The maturity myth unfortunately fosters the idea that to give up our childlikeness is what maturity means. And if we buy that idea, we also give up our creativity and our selves to making what is called a "good adjustment." In so doing we discard our *primary processes:* those that call upon the primitive, the archaic and the nonrational aspects of our unconscious and preconscious. But these are the qualities and resources that are essential to creativity. Using them gives us the ability, as Maslow points out, to "regress voluntarily," to be pure in a childlike sense, to bring into play our dreams, memories and fantasies, to make nonrational connections and metaphorical bridges between the familiar and the strange. Independent of "control, taboos, discipline, inhibitions, delays, planning, calculations of possibility or impossibility," they are symbolic processes, closer to raw experiences, and are the sources of our spontaneous insights, of innovation in life and attitude—they are, in fact, the sources of human inspiration.

The really mature person is able to combine both the rational, secondary processes and the nonrational, primary processes in a creative way. Maslow found that the healthy person had somehow "managed a fusion and a synthesis of both primary and secondary processes: both conscious and unconscious, both of deeper self and of conscious self." It is the unstructured, the zany, the unexpected, the surprising that we court in dipping into our primary processes—and it is by making the connection between these surprises and the practical, rational world that growth and discovery occurs.

When we let ourselves be free enough to be open to these primary processes, we can look at our problems and ourselves in new ways. Dipping into these primary processes has a utility and a purpose—it isn't just a matter of letting the unconscious well up in flights of fantasy. It is a matter of courting these instinctive creative aspects of yourself and *then* bringing your secondary rational processes to bear on your intuitions. The creative artist or scientist pokes around, experimenting, trying things on for size; he looks for connections between things, however irrational or irrelevant they may at first seem. Having let go and explored these intuitive possibilities, he then proceeds to examine them in the light of his logic, reason and common sense. But he has given himself a chance to explore and to expand the possibilities. Then and only then does he test them in the light of logic.

We can use the same technique in confronting our own problems and crises. We can use our loneliness to explore those wellsprings of creativity, and by focusing and centering and apply our intuitions to the particular situation we find ourselves in. It is in the primary process, on the fringes of consciousness and in the unconscious psyche, as Ghiselin points out, that change is not most likely to occur. The secondary processes of our conscious state are a system sustained by will and attention, and often act to inhibit change. But when we draw on our subconscious creative reservoirs, the inhibiting effect is greatly diminished, and the way to change is more easily perceived.

Actualizing Your Creativity

Unfortunately, our society makes it difficult for us to get in touch with our underlying creative resources: it trains us in various ways to wall off and suppress our primary processes. The conformity that our culture exalts and expects rules out the eccentric, the innovative and the imaginative. We have been taught to ignore our imaginative flights, to look upon them as silly and childish, and so we put the lid on, listening only to those voices that we have internalized from our past life, from our superiors and our peers.

We muffle our creative impulses, stuffing them back

into the unconscious, saying, "That won't work, how could I think of such a thing?" Because we stifle the creativity and change within ourselves we feel threatened by change in the world around us. And since the feeling of threat makes us still less willing to take risks, it becomes steadily more difficult for us to get back in touch with our primary processes. Hanging onto our defenses and our guilts, we are not free enough even to own what is particularly and uniquely ours—the individual creative impulses that exist in all of us. Our fear of making a mistake can bring us to an absolute standstill: "A person trapped by mistake-fear becomes frozen, rigid, or worse, he may shrivel or shrink through his dehumanization," comments psychologist George Brown. To think creatively we must shed our inhibitions and take the risk of making mistakes. Hopefully the preceding chapters in this book will have helped you to know yourself better and to become confident enough so that you can take the first steps toward actualizing your creativity, can allow yourself the freedom to explore and use your primary processes. Since it may be difficult to get started, some further concepts that may be of help to you follow.

Dr. Silvano Arieti, who has written extensively on creativity, has outlined six conditions for creativity. He writes that ". . . the creative man does not discard, repress, or suppress thoughts which appear irrational, inconsequential, or unrelated. He accepts them in the repertory of his consciousness." He becomes aware of "hidden structures of the good, the beautiful, and the true," and he recognizes the opportunity to externalize such structures. "He does not stick to what is, but is receptive to what may appear. He wants to make visible the invisible and audible the inaudible, and thus X-rays and the wireless are invented, and the moon is reached." Many people think of creativity as something mysterious, unfathomable, a muse to be captured rather than encouraged—but we *can* encourage creativity.

We can make the conditions for creativity possible and train ourselves to take advantage of our creativity.

The following six conditions for creativity are based on Arieti's work, and are here supplemented by some of our own interpretations.

(1) *Aloneness:* Not in withdrawal and painful solitude, but in the sense of being *with* oneself, away from the clichés and conventions of society. When you are alone it is less possible for others to overwhelm your individuality with their ideas about what you should be or do. Group situations and team efforts have their place and value, but it is obvious that a Picasso painting or a Beethoven symphony could not have been produced by a team. Without aid or help from anyone else, each one of us has his own potentials for creativity. The American ideal of togetherness and group activity may make creative aloneness more difficult to achieve, but it also makes it more necessary.

(2) *Inactivity:* Not excessive loafing, but merely a cessation of overt behavioral activity as a way of making the process of focusing and centering more fruitful. Excessive amounts of routine activities stifle mental activity and creativity. We need to give ourselves permission to be inactive in spite of the fact that our society prizes routine and hard work.

(3) *Daydreaming:* We have mentioned daydreaming of different varieties in other contexts throughout this book. It is vital to creativity and "may open to the individual new and unforeseeable paths of expansion. It is in daydream-life that the individual permits himself to diverge from the usual ways and to make little excursions into irrational worlds."

(4) *Remembrance and Inner Replaying of Past Traumatic Conflicts:* Contrary to standard belief, neurotic conflict is not a prerequisite for creativity. Whatever creative impulse exists does so in spite of neurotic conflict. When we resolve a neurotic conflict, learn to deal with it and unblock ourselves, the creative flow

can be much greater. However, once such conflicts are resolved, and are part of the past, they can be re-evoked with a sense of distance yet familiarity. Present conflicts block us, but past ones that we have success-fully dealt with can serve as a source of creativity when we play them through for ourselves in memory.

(5) *Gullibility:* This is the willingness to suspend disbelief and to accept certain underlying patterns un-til they are proved wrong by our secondary processes—to go with the creative impulse as far as it can sustain itself in the light of logic, to give it a chance. "Crea-tivity often implies the discovery of these underlying orderly arrangements, more than the inventing of new things." So we should be open and innocent and gul-lible at first, later accepting or rejecting these ideas with our secondary-process mechanisms. By being gullible and explorative, we have the opportunity to see *un-related* connections in life, objects, ideas and situations. The creative person becomes more accepting of what comes from inside and more critical of what comes in from the outside.

(6) *Alertness and Discipline:* Although they are necessary for productivity in any endeavor, these qualities take on a special meaning in creativity—the saying that creativity is ten percent inspiration and ninety percent perspiration means that for creativity to be realized it must be accompanied by the produc-tive elements of perseverance and hard work. Thus we see that while most of the conditions for creativity re-quire a suspension of control, an openness to the inner areas of the self, the last and most important is using our will to put what we have discovered into action—just as in the shifting gears process it is not enough to focus and center and make the decision. Without the commitment to action, our creativity may never emerge.

Opening ourselves up to creativity brings with it sur-prises. "The experience of surprise," Dr. Sidney Jourard writes, "is also a sign of one's readiness to grow. Amazement and wonder signify that one's concepts of self and of the world and of other people are 'loose,' ready to be reformed." It takes commitment and the ability to focus to allow ourselves the experience of surprise. The "cool" and sophisticated person has a hard time being surprised; he has everything figured out and has ". . . pledged himself never to be surprised." He has walled off his creative reservoir with a hard shell of sophistication—and it is he who is unwilling to commit himself to anything, least of all an ideal, let alone his own creativity.

"The most mature human beings living are also childlike," writes Abraham Maslow. Being childlike, as we have seen, means being open to those untapped wells of our unconscious and preconscious. If we want to change our lives, to make them a richer and fuller experience, we must use all our resources. If we want to change then we must court creativity. As Brewster Ghiselin puts it, "The first impulse toward a new order in the psychic life is . . . an impulse *away* from the clearly determined, from all that is most easily attended to and most forcefully imprints itself upon the attention." To grow we must look for the new in ourselves—and the new must be sought in unexpected places, among our hidden creative resources.

Part V: A Life Strategy for Creative Maturity

A Profile of the Mature Individual

The kind of emotional maturity we need for today's world can be boiled down to two words: *choice* and *creativity*. The ability to choose one's own direction or path and the ability to meet life creatively are the essence of self-fulfillment and individual security. We need new solutions, new paths, new ways of looking at old things and creative combinations of old and new elements to meet the changing conditions of today's world. Maturity is putting our intentionality, our will, into action, having the freedom and confidence to accept the vital forces of our inner selves and to direct them along paths of our choice. Maturity means being able to shift gears in terms of the external world, and in terms of our inner selves when either circumstance or inner desire make it necessary to do so.

Will is sometimes understood as being rigidly strong, as being "willful." But this is not the aspect of will we are talking about. Knowing your own will is not a matter of repressing the parts of you that get in the way of an immediate goal, it is not inordinate control, it is not blind forcefulness or obstinate insistence upon a single course of action. It is exercising our individuality in choosing a path toward growth and following that path to self-fulfillment. We have been told too often that maturity is the acceptance of other people's standards for us (standards which they have set down in order to protect themselves from reality)—but that is not maturity, it is not life but death, it is not self-realization but self-diminishment.

Creative maturity has a different face.

There are a number of qualities or attributes that might be included in a profile of the mature person. Such a person would be:

(1) self-aware—because he is in touch with his feelings

(2) centered—because he knows his values and priorities

(3) focused—because he is selective and able to make decisions

(4) committed—because he is involved and responsible for his actions

(5) creative—because he is innovative, flexible and open
(6) autonomous—because he thinks for himself
(7) compassionate—because he is concerned, caring and understanding
(8) competent—because he draws upon all his inner resources
(9) confident—because he knows how to shift gears
(10) secure—because he has fully accepted the challenge of growth

The creatively mature person is marked by an acceptance of self and others, by the ability to make his own standards, patterns and choices. He can meet a crisis and grow, he can look forward instead of backward. He can chart his own life. His thinking, feeling and acting are all of the same cloth because he owns his emotions. He can turn adversity to advantage because he is open to new directions, innovative and explorative. He knows that "finding himself" is an ongoing process throughout life, and for him doing is more important than having, experiencing more important than possessing. He takes responsibility for himself. He knows that happiness and security lie within himself but he knows also how to use all the creative elements of his integrated self in his personal relationships through which both he and the other can grow in a mutually enhancing way.

The Life Strategy and Creative Maturity

Shifting gears is the process by which we *choose* change; our life strategy consists of an *approach to life* that makes such choice possible, and that leads to the achievement of a creative maturity. You may have many different specific goals in your life, some of them short-term and some of them long-term, and you will have different kinds of specific plans to bring you to those goals. But above and beyond your specific goals and plans to reach them you need an overarching life strategy. Just as your particular plans and goals will differ from the next person's, because they are based on your individual capacities and needs, so will the specific nature of your life strategy differ according to your individual talents, feelings and values. But the important elements that go into your life strategy will be the same as other people's:

. . values
. . relationships
. . something to be commited to (larger than your-
    self)
. . productivity
. . the basics:
            life support activities
            contact with nature
. . creativity
. . contemplation and relaxation
. . receptivity

What kind of values are you going to live by? What kind of relationships do you want? What sort of commitment larger than yourself do you want and need? The answers to these questions will vary, and should vary, from individual to individual. But each person in developing a life strategy will want to ask himself or herself these questions and to seek answers to them. You may not always find that your job or career or goals of the moment coincide exactly with the kind of productivity that is most important to you in the long run: your truest sense of productivity may emerge, for instance, from another interest in life. Or if your profession is one that you have a very high level of commitment to, and one from which you derive a high degree of personal fulfillment—be it composing music, designing architecture or playing a professional sport—

your productivity and occupation may merge into one thing.

Returning to some of the basics of life, which Nicholas Johnson has called "life support activities," can give us a renewed sense of competency in living. Many of us have become so dependent on our society and others for everything—our transportation, our food, our clothing, communication, repairs and entertainment—that we have lost our sense of dealing with life firsthand. Instead of parceling out your life support activities to individuals, corporations and machines, begin to do some things for yourself—simplify your life, discard useless possessions, walk to work, or ride a bike, cook and repair, go camping. "Find those places where you can break through the interlocked system now and get some of those bits and pieces of your life back that you are paying other people to live for you." No matter where you live, renew your relationship and vital contact with nature periodically. Search for and nourish those personal relationships that provide a climate for growth and change. Know the values and beliefs that guide your life and feelings.

The elements of your life strategy will be the same as the next man's, but the way in which you define them and the way in which you strive to fulfill those separate elements may be utterly different. But however you define those elements—your values, your sense of creativity—your life strategy will be directed toward the lifelong goal of achieving creative maturity. And, naturally, you will want to strive to bring your specific plans and goals as completely into the service of achieving creative maturity as you can manage.

None of us can achieve creative maturity overnight. Some people with extraordinary talents or strengths may achieve it quite young—but creative maturity is not a thing, a set condition, it is a *process*. It is creative because it is ever-changing, ever-growing, as we change and grow, as the world around us takes on new aspects. Creative maturity recognizes the need to shift gears throughout life, to move on to new challenges when one goal is achieved, to create those challenges for ourselves if necessary. Creative maturity allows us to utilize all our fullness and richness as creative persons, to bring our full potential into play. There are many cases of people who do not find their particular kind of creative maturity until later in life when commitment, growth and challenge come together, sometimes with a sudden click, and they discover a new kind of self.

Albert Schweitzer wavered between church and music until he was thirty, when he found his focus and commitment in medicine and proceeded to dedicate a full and creative life to his mission at Lambaréné. Charles Darwin hated school, started out in medicine, abandoned it, and later barely managed to graduate from divinity school. It wasn't until he made his voyage with the exploratory scientific and mapping expedition on the *Beagle* that he found the focus that resulted in his great scientific theory. With commitment, passionate interest and an eye for the different that brought together all his observations in a creative synthesis, he found the focus that resulted in a great scientific theory and discovery.

The painter Dubuffet is a wonderful example of continuing growth and creativity—at seventy-one he abounds with fantasy, fantasy that he has used in creating a continually growing body of art. He has cultivated the use of his primary processes to an unusual degree, even stating that he responds only to passion and instinct. So strong has been his response to the primitive and primary instincts in our unconscious that he gave the name *art brut,* or art-in-the-raw, to his work. He tried art first at seventeen, but was discouraged by the criticisms of his friends, and it took him another twenty years to return to art—at which time he developed his true mature style.

As we begin to achieve creative maturity we inevitably surprise ourselves, drawing on parts of our nature, on hidden talents, that begin to come together in a new synthesis. Few of us will make momentous discoveries like Darwin, or become great artists like Dubuffet, and we do not need to.

Each one of us can be creative in our everyday life in many ways. Creativity is an attitude toward life. It is more a matter of improvisation and using an inspiration than of providing something labeled "creative" that is admired or socially useful. A child's invention and creativeness, Maslow reminds us, "very frequently cannot be defined in terms of product. . . . When a little boy discovers the decimal system for himself this can be a high moment of inspiration, and a high creative moment." When we see something in a new light and perspective, or discover a piece of music for the first time for ourselves, we are being creative. Each of us, if open and searching, can become creative in doing those simple things in our lives that are creative and original *to us*. We can be creative in the way we bring up our children, in our openness and response to them. We can be creative in the ordinary events of everyday life, in the way we teach, the way we communicate and listen, in innovation and discovery of a new way to do an old thing. Creativity can be expressed in the way we approach a picnic at the beach or in tending a beautiful garden, as a nurse's aide we know does. It gives her great joy but few other people will ever know about it.

Creativity is there inside us, not in the thing we produce, and with it we can discover the fullness of our own personal natures, we can grow and go on growing, we can make the most out of our lives, living up to our individual human potentials. When we can meet crisis and grow through it, when we can throw off the limiting and self-diminishing shackles of the maturity myth, we can move confidently into a creative maturity that will continue to provide excitement, growth and pleasure throughout our lives. And we may surprise ourselves more than we expect, may well discover that our potentials are far greater than we ever dreamed.

Notes and Sources

PAGE

CHAPTER 2 (*Continued*)

38   Since we have few institutionalized methods: see Chapple, Chapters 15 and 16.

38   "The phrase 'home town' . . .": Packard, p. ix.

39   Packard's statistics: Packard, pp. 6–7.

40   "two years in front of the tube": Stern, p. 2.

44   the speed of change: see Toffler.

CHAPTER 3   THE MATURITY MYTH

55   "Ripeness is all . . .": Shakespeare, *King Lear*, Act V, Scene 2, Line 9.

59   Doctors are now finding: Diamond.

59   *New York Times Magazine* article: Jacoby.

61   "The central and unchanging goal . . .": Stringer, pp. 81–82.

CHAPTER 4   SHIFTING GEARS

64   seek a niche, "join the tribe": Levinson.

76   business management techniques: Lakein, pp. 1–3. His emphasis is on effectiveness rather than efficiency.

78   confrontation between the generations: see Anthony and Benedek.

80   "may be reacting . . .": Anthony, p. 316.

87   Three types of adaptive social interaction: Edwards, pp. 132–133.

CHAPTER 5   MAKING CRISIS WORK FOR YOU

95   *utilizing* crisis for growth: see Minuchin and Barcai for a case study of therapeutically induced crisis.

98   problem solving vs. crisis resolution: Cumming and Cumming, pp. 54–55.

99   crisis directly challenges your assumptive state: in this and the following paragraphs we have drawn from the work of Caplan, Cumming and Cumming, Ittelson and Cantril.

99   developing a new assumptive state: Cumming and Cumming, Chapter 3.

103   Menninger on coping devices: Menninger, Chapter VII.

PAGE

CHAPTER 7 (*Continued*)

148 experiments in factories: Kremen.

149 "The whole self . . .": Friedman (1972a) p. 20.

149 A program for improving communication: Miller, *et al.* (1974b).

150 The Awareness Wheel: Miller, *et al.* (1974a).

151 Interpersonal Communication Program: Information on this excellent four-session training program and the book, *Alive and Aware: Improving Communication in Relationships,* can be obtained from Interpersonal Communication Programs, Inc., 2001 Riverside Ave., Minneapolis, Minn. 55404.

CHAPTER 8 DECISION-MAKING

164 Lakein: Lakein.

164 values clarification course: Simon.

167 Boy Scout Law: *Handbook for Boys,* pp. 24–39.

169 Being-values: Maslow (1971) pp. 133–135.

175 Synectics: Gordon.

175 think sideways: see De Bono for lateral thinking.

176 "I always ask my stomach . . .": Bradbury, p. 103.

CHAPTER 9 COMMITMENT MEANS ACTION

182 Risk-taking: see Klausner for studies in stress-seeking.

188 "an end in itself . . .": Friedman (1972a), p. 11.

192 Breaking out: see Biggs for personal accounts of former corporation men who changed their life styles.

195 Sanford Darling: *Life*

198–199 Recent studies on stress scores: Brody.

CHAPTER 10 CREATING YOUR OWN CHALLENGE

207 "When a much longed for goal . . .": Taylor, p. 22.

PAGE

CHAPTER 11 (*Continued*)

232   move with increasing security through changing patterns, surroundings and many different kinds of groupings.

CHAPTER 12   CREATIVE MATURITY

235   "For when a man . . .": Henry, p. 110.

236   "What modern man needs . . .": Friedman (1972b), p. 15.

239   "it is tempting to believe . . .": White, p. 387.

244   mentors: their role in adulthood discussed by Levinson.

246   "you can't go home again": Wolfe.

248   "not ever having to say you're sorry": Segal, p. 131.

248   A new understanding of loneliness: see Moustakas' (1961, 1972) excellent exploration and analysis of loneliness.

250   "that loneliness is a capacity . . .": Moustakas (1967) p. 102.

252   "The most mature people . . .": Maslow (1971) p. 92.

252   "comfortable enough with his unconscious . . .": Maslow (1971) p. 90.

252–253   secondary and primary processes: we have drawn on Maslow's (1971) positive description of these processes in his chapter on creativity.

252   "at the cost of . . .": this and the following quotes appear in Maslow (1971) pp. 86–96.

253   "manage a fusion and synthesis . . .": Maslow (1971) p. 89.

254   on the fringes of consciousness: Ghiselin, p. 22.

255   "a person trapped by mistake-fear . . .": Brown, p. 154.

255   Dr. Silvano Arieti: Arieti (1966, 1967, 1972).

255   "the creative man . . .": Arieti (1972) p. 245.

256–257   Six conditions for creativity: adapted from Arieti (1972) pp. 247–250.

257–258   "The experience of surprise . . .": Jourard (1968b) p. 14.

PAGE

CHAPTER 12 (*Continued*)

258   "The most mature human being . . .": Maslow
(1971) p. 92.

258   "The first impulse toward . . .": Ghiselin, p. 17.

262   life support activities . . .: Johnson (1971).

262   "Find those places . . .": Johnson (1973) p.
208.

263   Dubuffet: Shirey.

264   Creativity is an attitude: Maslow (1971) Chapter 4.

264   "very frequently cannot be defined . . .": Maslow (1971) p. 60.

Bibliography

Anthony, E. James. "The Reactions of Parents to Adolescents and to Their Behavior." In Anthony, E. James, and Therese Benedek, eds. *Parenthood, Its Psychology and Psychopathology*. Boston: Little Brown and Co., 1970.

Anthony, E. James, and Therese Benedek, eds., *Parenthood, Its Psychology and Psychopathology*. Boston: Little Brown and Co., 1970.

Arieti (1966), Silvano. "Creativity and Its Cultivation." In Arieti, S., ed. *Handbook of Psychiatry*. New York: Basic Books, 1966 (vol. 3).

Arieti (1967), Silvano. *The Intrapsychic Self*. New York: Basic Books, 1967.

Arieti (1972), Silvano. *The Will To Be Human*. New York: Quadrangle Books, Inc., 1972.

Baker, Russell. "Space With A Purpose." *The New York Times*, May 29, 1973.

Biggs, Don. *Breaking Out*. New York: David McKay Company, Inc., 1973.

Bradbury, Ray. "A Portrait of Genius: Ray Bradbury." An interview with Ray Bradbury in *Show*, December 1964.

Branden (1970), Nathaniel. "Romantic Love: Neurosis or Rational Ideal?" Paper delivered at the 1970 Annual Convention of the American Psychological Association, September 3, Miami, Florida.

Branden (1972), Nathaniel. *Breaking Free*. New York: Bantam Books, Inc., 1972.

Brody, Jane E. "Doctors Study Treating of Ills Brought On By Stress." *The New York Times*, June 10, 1973.

Brown, George. "The Creative Sub-self." In Otto, Herbert

A., and John Mann, eds. *Ways of Growth*. New York: The Viking Press, 1968.

Buhler (1966), Charlotte. "The Life Cycle: Structural Determinants of Goalsetting." *Journal of Humanistic Psychology*, Spring 1966 (vol. 6).

Buhler (1968), Charlotte. "Loneliness in Maturity." *Journal of Humanistic Psychology*, Fall 1968 (vol. 9).

Caplan, Gerald, ed. *Prevention of Mental Disorders in Children*. New York: Basic Books, 1961.

Chapple, Eliot D. *Culture and Biological Man*. New York: Holt, Rinehart and Winston, Inc., 1970.

Crosby, John F. *Illusion and Disillusion: The Self in Love and Marriage*. Belmont, California: Wadsworth Publishing Company, Inc., 1973.

Cumming, John, and Elaine Cumming. *Ego and Milieu*. New York: Atherton Press, 1969.

De Bono, Edward. *The Mechanism of Mind*. New York: Simon and Schuster, 1969.

Diamond, Edwin. "Can Exercise Improve Your Brain Power?" *The Reader's Digest*, May 1973.

Edwards, Carl N. "Interactive Styles and Social Adaptation." *Genetic Psychology Monographs*, 1973 (vol. 87).

Erikson (1963), Erik H. *Childhood and Society*. New York: W. W. Norton and Company, Inc., 1963.

Erikson (1968), Erik H. *Identity Youth and Crisis*. New York: W. W. Norton and Company, Inc., 1968.

Friedman (1972a), Maurice. "Dialogue and the Unique in Humanistic Psychology." *The Journal of Humanistic Psychology*, Fall 1972 (vol. 12).

Friedman (1972b), Maurice. *Touchstones of Reality*. New York: E. P. Dutton & Co., Inc., 1972.

Fromme, Allan. *The Ability to Love*. New York: Pocket Books, 1972.

Gendlin, E. T. "A Theory of Personality Change." In Worchel, P., and D. Byrne. *Personality Change*. New York: Wiley, 1964.

Gerlach, Luther P., and Virginia H. Hine. *Lifeway Leap: The Dynamics of Change in America*. Minneapolis: University of Minnesota Press, 1973.

Ghiselin, Brewster, ed. *The Creative Process*. New York: New American Library, 1952.

Gordon, William J. J. *Synectics*. New York: Collier Books, 1961.

Handbook for Boys. Boy Scouts of America. New Brunswick, New Jersey, 1945.

Henry, Jules. *Pathways to Madness*. New York: Vintage Books, 1973.

Ittelson, William H., and Hadley Cantril. *Perception. A Transactional Approach*. New York: Doubleday, 1954.

Jacoby, Susan. "What do I do for the next 20 Years?" *The New York Times Magazine*, June 17, 1973.

Johnson (1971), Nicholas. "Test Pattern for Living." *Saturday Review of Literature*, May 29, 1971.

Johnson (1973), Nicholas. "Writing Your Own Script." In Biggs, Don. *Breaking Out*. New York: David McKay Company, Inc., 1973.

Jourard (1968a), Sidney M. *Disclosing Man to Himself*. Princeton: D. Van Nostrand Company, Inc., 1968.

Jourard (1968b), Sidney M. "Growing Awareness and the Awareness of Growth." In Otto, Herbert A., and John Mann, eds., *Ways of Growth*. New York: The Viking Press, 1968.

Jung, C. G. *Modern Man in Search of a Soul*. New York: Harcourt, Brace and World, Inc. (first published in 1933), 1963.

Keniston, Kenneth. *The Uncommitted*. New York: Harcourt, Brace and World, Inc., 1965.

Klausner, Samuel Z., ed. *Why Man Takes Chances*. Garden City, New York: Anchor Books, 1968.

Kremen, Bennett. "Lordstown—Searching for a Better Way of Work." *The New York Times*, September 9, 1973.

Lakein, Alan. *How to Get Control of Your Time and Your Life*. New York: Peter H. Wyden, Inc., 1973.

Land, George T. Lock. *Grow or Die*. New York: Random House, 1973.

Levinson, Dr. Daniel J., *et al.* "The Normal Crises of the Middle Years." A Symposium presented at Hunter College, March 1, 1973, under the auspices of the New York Committee of The Menninger Foundation.

Life Magazine. "Mr. Darling Paints His Dream House." June 25, 1971.

Lindemann, Erich. "Symptomology and Management of

Acute Grief." *American Journal of Psychiatry,* 1944 (vol. 101).

Maslow (1970), Abraham H. "Psychological Data and Value Theory." In Maslow, Abraham H., ed. *New Knowledge in Human Values.* Chicago: Henry Regnery Company, 1970.

Maslow (1971), Abraham H. *The Farther Reaches of Human Nature.* New York: The Viking Press, 1971.

Masters (1966), William H., and Virginia E. Johnson. *Human Sexual Response.* Boston: Little, Brown and Company, 1966.

Masters (1970), William H., and Virginia E. Johnson. *Human Sexual Inadequacy.* Boston: Little, Brown and Company, 1970.

Mayeroff, Milton. *On Caring.* New York: Harper and Row, 1971.

Menninger, Karl. *The Vital Balance.* New York: The Viking Press, 1963.

Miller (1947a), Sherod, Elan W. Nunnally and Daniel B. Wackman with Ronald Brazman. *Alive and Aware: Improving Communication in Relationships.* Minneapolis, Minnesota: Interpersonal Communication Programs, Inc., 1974.

Miller (1974b), Sherod, Elam W. Nunnally, Daniel B. Wackman. "A Communication Training Program for Couples." To appear in *Systems Analysis of Marital and Family Therapy,* David H. Olson, ed., 1974.

Minuchin, Salvador, and Avner Barcai. "Therapeutically Induced Family Crisis." In Sagar, Clifford J., and Helen Singer Kaplan, eds. *Progress in Group and Family Therapy.* New York: Brunner/Mazel, 1972.

Moustakas (1961), Clark E. *Loneliness.* New York: Prentice-Hall, Inc., 1961.

Moustakas (1967), Clark E. "Heuristic Research." In Bugental, James F. T., ed., *Challenges of Humanistic Psychology.* New York: McGraw-Hill, 1967.

Moustakas (1972), Clark E. *Loneliness and Love.* Englewood Cliffs: Prentice-Hall, Inc., 1972.

O'Neill (1972a), Nena, and George O'Neill. *Open Marriage.* New York: M. Evans and Company, Inc., 1972; Avon Books, 1973.

O'Neill (1972b), Nena, and George O'Neill. "Open Marriage: A Synergic Model." *The Family Coordinator,* October 1972 (vol. 21).

O'Neill (1973a), Nena, and George O'Neill. "Is Your Marriage Changing More Than You Realize?" *Family Circle,* January 1973.

O'Neill (1973b), Nena, and George O'Neill. "Open Marriage: Implications for Human Service Systems." *The Family Coordinator,* October 1973 (vol. 22).

O'Neill (1974), Nena, and George O'Neill. "Marriage: A Contemporary Model." In Freedman, Alfred M., Harold I. Kaplan, and Benjamin Sadock, eds. *Comprehensive Textbook of Psychiatry.* Second Edition. Baltimore, Maryland: Williams and Wilkin, 1974.

Packard, Vance. *A Nation of Strangers.* New York: David McKay, 1972.

Perls, Frederick S. *Gestalt Therapy Verbatim.* Compiled and edited by John O. Stevens. Lafayette, California: Real People Press, 1969.

Schwartz, Barton M., and Robert H. Ewald. *Culture and Society.* New York: The Ronald Press Company, 1968.

Segal, Erich. *Love Story.* New York: Harper and Row, 1970.

Shirey, David L., "Dubuffet, at 71, Abounds With Fantasies." *The New York Times,* November 1, 1972.

Simon, Sidney B. "Star Trek." In Biggs, Don. *Breaking Out.* New York: David McKay Company, Inc., 1973.

Singer, Jerome. Quoted in *Behavior Today,* April 2, 1973 (vol. 4, No. 14).

Spradley, James P., and David W. McCurdy, eds. *Conformity and Conflict.* Boston: Little, Brown and Co., 1971.

Stern, Stanley. Quoted in *Behavior Today,* August 27, 1973 (vol. 4, No. 31).

Stevens, John O. *Awareness: Exploring, Experimenting, Experiencing.* Moab, Utah: Real People Press, 1971.

Stringer, Lorene A. *The Sense of Self.* Philadelphia: Temple University Press, 1971.

Taylor, Gordon Rattray. *Rethink.* New York: E. P. Dutton & Co., Inc., 1973.

Toffler, Alvin. *Future Shock.* New York: A Bantam Book, 1970.

Turney-High, Harry Holbert. *Man and System.* New York: Appleton-Century-Crofts, 1968.

Tyhurst, James. "The Role of Transition States—Including Disasters—In Mental Illness." *The Walter Reed Symposium on Preventive and Social Psychiatry.* Washington, D.C.: Government Printing Office, 1958.

Van Gennep, Arnold. *The Rites of Passage.* Chicago: University of Chicago Press, 1960.

White, Robert W. *The Enterprise of Living.* New York: Holt, Rinehart, and Winston, Inc., 1972.

Wolfe, Thomas. *You Can't Go Home Again.* New York: Harper and Brothers, 1940.

Work in America. A report issued by the Department of Health, Education and Welfare, 1972.

Recommended Books for Continued Reading

Browne, Harry. *How I Found Freedom in an Unfree World*. New York: The Macmillan Company, 1973.

Crosby, John F. *Illusion and Disillusion: The Self in Love and Marriage*. Belmont, California: Wadsworth Publishing Company, Inc., 1973.

Ellis, Albert, and Robert A. Harper. *A Guide to Rational Living*. North Hollywood, California: Wilshire Book Company, 1973.

Friedman, Maurice. *Touchstones of Reality*. New York: E. P. Dutton & Co., Inc., 1972.

Lakein, Alan. *How to Get Control of Your Time and Your Life*. New York: Peter H. Wyden, Inc., 1973.

Maslow, Abraham H. *Toward a Psychology of Being*. Princeton: D. Van Nostrand Company, Inc., 1968.

Maslow, Abraham H. *Eupsychian Management*. Homewood, Illinois: Richard D. Irwin, Inc. and The Dorsey Press, 1965.

Mayerhoff, Milton. *On Caring*. New York: Harper and Row, 1971.

Moustakas, Clark E. *Loneliness and Love*. Englewood Cliffs: Prentice-Hall, Inc., 1972.

Otto, Herbert A., and John Mann, eds. *Ways of Growth*. New York: The Viking Press, 1968.

Pietsch, William V. *Human Be-Ing*. New York: Lawrence Hill and Co., 1974.

Stevens, John O. *Awareness: Exploring, Experimenting, Experiencing*. Moab, Utah: Real People Press. 1971.

About the Authors

GEORGE O'NEILL and NENA O'NEILL are a husband-wife anthropology team who have done field work in Mexico, Peru, the Caribbean, and the United States. Articles on their projects have been published in anthropology journals, *The Family Coordinator,* the *Comprehensive Textbook of Psychiatry,* and other scientific publications. Since 1963, the O'Neill's primary interest has been in the area of urban anthropology and contemporary social problems. In 1967, utilizing the combined perspectives of anthropology and humanistic psychology, they focused on a study of modern marriage. This research resulted in the development of a model for contemporary marriage presented in their book, *Open Marriage: A New Life Style for Couples.* This present book is an outgrowth of their continuing research in contemporary life.

George O'Neill received his Ph.D. from Columbia University and is a professor of anthropology at the City College of New York. Nena O'Neill received her B.A. from Barnard College and is currently earning her Ph.D. in anthropology at the City University of New York.

The O'Neills have been married twenty-eight years and have two grown sons. They are now creating an institute for research and development in the area of human relations, marriage, and the family in contemporary society, called the Institute for Open Living.

The
#1
Bestseller

AVON
$1.95

Open Marriage

A
New
Life
Style
for
Couples

Nena O'Neill and George O'Neill

THE BIG BESTSELLERS
ARE AVON BOOKS

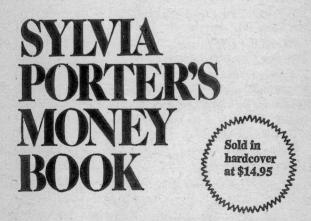

AVON ◆ THE BEST IN
BESTSELLING ENTERTAINMENT!

the Relaxation Response

by Herbert Benson, M.D.

with Miriam Z. Klipper

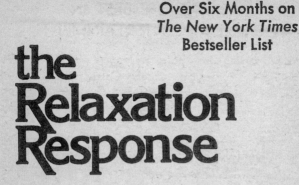

It could be the most important book of your life!

A simple meditative technique that has helped millions to cope with fatigue, anxiety and stress. Featured in *Family Circle, House and Garden, Good Housekeeping* and scores of magazines and newspapers across the country.

"In transcendental meditation you pay $125 and you get your mantra. You may do as well by reading *The Relaxation Response.*"

        Money Magazine

AVON 29439/$1.95

DYNAMIC APPROACHES TO LIVING AND LOVING
BY
LAURA ARCHERA HUXLEY

Synchronize will, imagination, and body, with the insights of the internationally famous therapist and nutritionist who shows how simple breathing techniques, muscle flexing, and changes in diet can put you in control of your life. Start to free yourself from indecision, prevent illness—and make the best of life and love right here on earth!

"Laura Huxley speaks simply at many levels. She touches us aesthetically, intellectually, practically, psychologically and spiritually."
—Ram Dass

 30924/$1.95

The life-transforming bestseller that has helped millions to achieve self-discovery and the essentials of happy living. With a Foreword by her late husband, Aldous Huxley.

"Laura Huxley offers you nothing less than a new life."
—Christopher Isherwood

HUX 10-76